Regional Comprehensive Economic Partnership

Edited by

Mahani Hamdan
Universiti Brunei Darussalam
Institute of Policy Studies,
Brunei Darussalam

Muhammad Anshari
Universiti Brunei Darussalam
Institute of Policy Studies,
Brunei Darussalam

&

Norainie Ahmad
Universiti Brunei Darussalam
Institute of Policy Studies,
Brunei Darussalam

Regional Comprehensive Economic Partnership

Editors: Mahani Hamdan, Muhammad Anshari and Norainie Ahmad

ISBN (Online): 978-981-5123-22-7

ISBN (Print): 978-981-5123-23-4

ISBN (Paperback): 978-981-5123-24-1

© 2023, Bentham Books imprint.

Published by Bentham Science Publishers Pte. Ltd. Singapore. All Rights Reserved.

First published in 2023.

need for a court order if at any point you breach any terms of this License Agreement. In no event will any delay or failure by Bentham Science Publishers in enforcing your compliance with this License Agreement constitute a waiver of any of its rights.

3. You acknowledge that you have read this License Agreement, and agree to be bound by its terms and conditions. To the extent that any other terms and conditions presented on any website of Bentham Science Publishers conflict with, or are inconsistent with, the terms and conditions set out in this License Agreement, you acknowledge that the terms and conditions set out in this License Agreement shall prevail.

Bentham Science Publishers Pte. Ltd.
80 Robinson Road #02-00
Singapore 068898
Singapore
Email: subscriptions@benthamscience.net

BENTHAM SCIENCE

CONTENTS

FOREWORD

It is remarkable how little attention the Regional Comprehensive Economic Partnership (RCEP) has garnered around the world, given the potential that this regional economic pact possesses to propel Asia into a new era of economic leadership. The 15-member countries that are signatories to the RCEP already host about 30% of the world's population and generate 30% of global GDP. Just what might transpire in regard to economic, social and environmental change in this important region should the RCEP foster the economic integration that it aspires to achieve is a deeply contextualized and nuanced question that lies at the core of Regional Comprehensive Economic Partnership (RCEP): Potentials and Challenges.

Regional Comprehensive Economic Partnership (RCEP): Potentials and Challenges is a vanguard volume that puts forth one of the most comprehensive analyses of the largest economic alliance in the world. The analysis contained in this volume benefits significantly from the diverse expertise and perspectives of the co-authors deftly assembled by esteemed co-editors, Dr. Mahani Hamdan, Dr. Muhammad Anshari, and Dr. Norainie Ahmad, all hailing from the University of Brunei Darussalam.

A foundational theme of the book centers on exploring the impact that the RCEP will have on catalyzing innovation in the region and what that might mean for national economic development and economic inclusiveness. Many of the contributing authors share a belief that connectivity and e-commerce alliances stand to yield cross-border successes that were perhaps not possible prior to the Internet age. Interconnectivity enables a region that was once solely focused on a competitive race to the bottom to create a shared foundation upon which technology and big data can be leveraged by the region's entrepreneurial SMEs to produce disruptive innovations that are commercialized through new grassroots financial models. While most of the contributing authors are optimistic about the potential of the RCEP, all have also been careful to remind the reader that inequalities in the region remain and historical animosities potentially hinder optimizing the impact of this important economic pact.

Indeed, the final two chapters explore two sub-themes that regional economic development experts are particularly concerned with: the influence of China and the need to ensure greater social inclusiveness and equality when it comes to catalyzing economic development. The manner in which China integrates its economic development strategy with the RCEP will arguably have the greatest influence on political dynamics in the region. Friend or foe; competitor or collaborator? Either way, China's economic strategy will both influence and be influenced by the RCEP. Similarly, economic growth that does not promote economic inclusiveness and stimulate enhanced social governance stands to engender the same animosities that have scuttled previous attempts at economic integration in the region. An equitable sharing of benefits will play a key role in determining whether or not the RCEP improves well-being within member nations and enhances goodwill between member nations.

All of these important questions regarding the potential of the RCEP to guide the Asia-Pacific region to a new area of harmonious, collaborative, equitable and sustainable economic development are taken up by the authors of Regional Comprehensive Economic Partnership (RCEP): Potentials and Challenges. For anyone wishing to delve into the nuances associated with the RCEP, this book is the definitive starting point.

Scott Victor Valentine, PhD
Professor of Regenerative Planning and Circular Economy
Asian and Oceanian Studies Institute
Kyushu University
Japan

PREFACE

The Regional Comprehensive Economic Partnership (RCEP) is a free-trade deal involving 10 ASEAN member states, Australia, China, Japan, New Zealand, and South Korea. It is the world's largest regional trade agreement, and it will result in the world's most populous trade area. The proposed edited book is the first on the subject of RCEP to be published. The book is multidisciplinary in nature and is intended to disseminate and discuss research and best practices on any element of RCEP. The book focuses on high-quality research projects that contribute to theory, lessons learned, best practices, and critical understanding and policy implications or formulation regarding the RCEP among member nations. Additionally, reports on the RCEP's general progress are examined in relation to the book's theme.

The book **Regional Comprehensive Economic Partnership (RCEP): Potentials and Challenges** is expected to become a significant source of information and reference for RCEP development, particularly in terms of promoting awareness, by incorporating conceptual, recent development, best practices, comparative assessment, business processes, as well as strategies and outputs from RCEP studies across multiple domains of knowledge. To assure the book's quality, each chapter was reviewed twice. Academicians and students who can use the chapters in this book as references for the latest developments in the RCEP, researchers in academia seeking a perspective on the RCEP, government organizations interested in the information about the RCEP, policymakers who need to understand the discussion about the RCEP, and members of the general public seeking information about the RCEP are likely to be readers.

The book covers a wide variety of topics, including an overview of the RCEP. The book is divided into ten chapters that cover the recent RCEP discussion on process, methods, and difficulties. Each chapter is summarized below.

Chapter 1 titled "An Overview of Regional Comprehensive Economics Partnership (RCEP)" by Mahani Hamdan, Muhammad Anshari, Norainie Ahmad, (Universiti Brunei Darussalam, Institute of Policy Studies), discusses that RCEP is a recently established Free Trade Agreement between Asia-Pacific countries with the goal of increasing trade between participating countries. RCEP established an integrated market with 15 members of the countries, which has facilitated the mobility of products and services among the participating countries. It aims to negotiate on trade in products and services, investment, intellectual property, dispute settlement, e-commerce, small and medium-sized firms, and economic cooperation. Currently, it is the world's largest free trade agreement in terms of economic impact, and it has the potential to promote trade and integration among member countries. The chapter's objectives are to evaluate the opportunities and challenges that RCEP is facing.

Chapter 2 titled "Integrating RCEP with Cross-Border E-commerce (CBE) Towards Accelerating Economic Recovery in ASEAN" by Mia Fithriyah (Indonesia Open University, Indonesia), states that connectivity is the basis of e-commerce development. E-commerce reinforces connectivity, and aims to promote a continuous stream of information, logistics, free cash flow, and so forth. A seamless connection between the virtual and physical parts of an e-commerce network could be demonstrated toward Cross-Border E-commerce (CBE). A region-wide e-commerce support environment with a Regional Comprehensive Economic Partnership (RCEP) agreement would undoubtedly support economic stabilization. Notably, this model is positively in line with the restricted conditions during the COVID-19 outbreak (Anshari *et al*., 2021a). However, businessmen should improve connectivity-derived services via technology and the internet in order to add more value to the successful implementation of

CBE. Considering today's consumers are more complex, the COVID-19 economic turbulence has resulted in a severe bankruptcy storm for business areas worldwide (Hamdan *et al.*, 2020). Hence, the potential and opportunities of CBE will be explained in detail in this study. The determinants of the successful adoption of CBE remain complex. Therefore, our framework allows us to assess the extent of concerns about CBE opportunities and the potential for accelerating economic recovery during the COVID-19 pandemic.

Chapter 3 titled "Economic Integration's Impact on Regional Comprehensive Economic Partnership" by Emil Ali (Universiti Brunei Darussalam, Institute of Policy Studies, Universiti Brunei Darussalam) and Muhammad Anshari (Universiti Brunei Darussalam, Institute of Policy Studies, Universiti Brunei Darussalam), affirms that this study examines how the Regional Comprehensive Economic Partnership (RCEP) affects the commercial and economic activities of RCEP member countries, including supply chain management (SCM), tariff reductions on trade, customs duty reductions, market expansion, and the likelihood of obtaining economies of scale in manufacturing. This chapter adopted a qualitative method approach, which involved reviewing current literature studies and interpreting them in order to make possible recommendations. The findings indicate that the Regional Comprehensive Economic Partnership will significantly impact industries in the Asia-Pacific region, such as textile and apparel supply chain integration, and that this will provide a significant opportunity for member countries to further improve their economic conditions. Additionally, improving the SCM leads to an increase in GDP, enabling many countries to achieve a favorable balance of trade and encouraging them to pursue innovation. The implementation of the RCEP agreement also has its challenges and needs to be addressed in order to make the adoption of RCEP a success.

Chapter 4 titled "The Fourth Industrial Revolution Landscape for RCEP" by Abdullah Al-Mudimigh (Dar Al Uloom University, Saudi Arabia) & Abdur Razzaq (Universitas Islam Negeri Raden Fatah Palembang, Indonesia), states that this chapter examines the Regional Comprehensive Economic Partnership (RCEP) Agreement in general, as well as how it contributes to the progression of the Fourth Industrial Revolution (4th Industrial Revolution) (4IR). It primarily focuses on the RCEP, which was signed by the Association of Southeast Asian Nations (ASEAN) countries, Australia, China, Japan, Korea, and New Zealand in order to expand and strengthen engagements with one another and their relationships to Industry 4.0, whereby the potential issues and solutions are discussed in greater depth. It also highlights the security and privacy issues and thoughts on how 4IR might help countries improve their economies over the long term. The chapter includes reflections on experiences as well as an analysis of how the information contained in the agreement affects the growth of the RCEP agreement.

Chapter 5 titled "Disruptive Innovation Reshaping Future RCEP" by Muhammad Anshari, Norainie Ahmad, & Mahani Hamdan (Universiti Brunei Darussalam, Institute of Policy Studies), discusses the relationship between the Regional Comprehensive Economic Partnership (RCEP) agreement and the advent of Disruptive Innovation. RCEP was signed in November 2020 by a total of fifteen countries, with the goal of advancing regional economic integration and exerting greater influence over the Free Trade Agreement (FTA). The main focus of this chapter is on assessing the benefits of disruptive innovation and trade under the Regional Comprehensive Economic Partnership (RCEP). We performed a literature review and applied a SWOT analysis in order to assess the strengths and weaknesses of disruptive innovation, as well as the opportunities and challenges presented by the Regional Comprehensive Economic Partnership. Disruptive innovation can be beneficial to the majority of RCEP countries, since it can raise market growth, increase profit, and increase the productivity of – and efficiency for, disruptive technologies used in manufacturing. On the other hand, the possible challenges may be detrimental to smaller emerging economies, whose employment rates may be adversely impacted, and local enterprises may be overshadowed as a result of the increased competition.

Chapter 6 titled "Is Big Data a Disruptive Innovation to RCEP?" by Ares Albirru Amsal (Faculty of Economics, Universitas Andalas, Padang-Indonesia), states that big data has a lot of potentials to increase international trade. As the largest free-trade agreement, the Regional Comprehensive Economic Partnership (RCEP) can utilize big data and related technologies to create fair and mutually beneficial trade. With the main characteristics of volume, variety, and velocity, big data provides strategic advantages for businesses that use it. The data can be processed using descriptive, diagnostics, predictive and prescriptive analytics. However, not all RCEP members have the same level of data processing capability. Their IT development also varies. Therefore, decision-makers need to resolve issues related to data utilization, especially in terms of digital literacy, security, and privacy.

Chapter 7 titled "Financial Technology Innovation - Peer-to-Peer (P2P) Lending in the RCEP Member States" by Rayna Kartika (Faculty of Economics, Universitas Andalas, Padang-Indonesia), investigates that Regional Comprehensive Economic Partnership (RCEP) aims to strengthen the economy and the free trade agreement among 10 ASEAN member states (Brunei Darussalam, Cambodia, Indonesia, Lao PDR, Malaysia, Myanmar, Philippines, Singapore, Thailand, and Vietnam) and 5 partner states (China, Japan, South Korea, Australia, and New Zealand). One of the ways to improve economic growth is to enhance the investment sector into start-ups and SMEs. Peer-to-peer lending platforms exist to ease the mechanism of funds lending and borrowing from investors to Start-ups and SMEs. Currently, the rise of P2P lending, particularly in RCEP member states, has boosted the economic growth and development of technology. The government assistance to set up the regulation regarding the mechanism of P2P lending has been carried out in order to create a clean and transparent practice of P2P lending among borrowers and lenders. Therefore, this chapter describes the introduction of RCEP member states and P2P lending, and the mechanism for adopting P2P lending platforms in RCEP member states.

Chapter 8 titled "Regional Comprehensive Economic Partnership (RCEP) and ASEAN Sustainable Development Goals" by Blessing Gweshengwe (Department of Rural and Urban Development, Great Zimbabwe University, Zimbabwe), explores that an economic partnership can play a significant role in poverty reduction in the countries involved in it. The partnership's contribution to poverty alleviation is, however, a function of its scope and the nature of participating countries and could be constrained by various factors. Considering this, the chapter addressed whether the RCEP can contribute meaningfully to achieving Sustainable Development Goal 1 within the ASEAN region. This aspect is yet to be subjected to scholarly examination. The chapter examined the potential of the RCEP to help ASEAN countries to eradicate poverty, the factors that could jeopardise this endeavour and the measures that could be taken to address these factors. The chapter found that the RCEP could indeed contribute to the realisation of Sustainable Development Goal 1 in ASEAN countries since it has the potential to contribute to poverty eradication. This is because of the partnership's capacity to, among other aspects, drive economic growth, boost real convergence and optimise the poverty eradication potential of Micro, Small and Medium Enterprises in the ASEAN region. This contribution may, however, be jeopardised with the advent of the Covid-19 pandemic, and because of political instability in some ASEAN countries. In order to mitigate the impact of both of these challenges, ASEAN countries could reinforce their social protection systems, intensify their commitment to the RCEP and address the needs of the losers in the RCEP.

Chapter 9 titled "Regional Trade Deal with China for a New Digital Economy" by Abdur Razzaq (Universitas Islam Negeri Raden Fatah Palembang, Indonesia), states that the Regional Comprehensive Economic Partnership (RCEP) will be one of the most important free trade agreements in the history of the Asia-Pacific region and the world. It will also be one of the most important agreements in the world. This is being done in an effort to improve trade ties across the Asian-Pacific region's economies. Amid the COVID-19 pandemic that has spread over the world, it has emerged as a topic that can have an influence on business. China is innovating in the way it trades by taking advantage of the digital economy to its advantage. China's economy benefits to some extent from this strategy. China's economy recovers partly due to the implementation of this digital system, becoming the world's first to do so. Throughout the outbreak of COVID-19, the country has demonstrated that it is inventive and capable of supporting its economy and speeding its development. The RCEP agreement will have a greater impact not only on China but also on the participating members.

Finally, Chapter 10 titled "Empowering The Underprivileged Community through Social Innovation and Entrepreneurship" by Fahmi Ibrahim and Dayangku Rodzi Pengiran Haji Rahman from School of Business, Universiti Teknologi Brunei (UTB), Brunei Darussalam, discusses increasing awareness of being socially responsible and addresses social problems involving various key stakeholders in the public and private sectors, as well as the corporate and businesses, and the community included. With social issues experienced globally, such as climate change, introducing diversity in society or eradicating poverty, it is imperative to use social innovation to improve or replace the way things are currently done. This paper aims to analyse the impact of social innovation of entrepreneurship to provide stable income to underprivileged and unemployed segments and youth. It discussed key elements that support the development of entrepreneurship to ensure sustainability and growth, to ensure the underprivileged segment and youth will continue to earn, thus reducing reliance on welfare assistance support. The research was conducted based on interviews and observation methods. Two significant projects investigated that employed the social innovation model, how they were applied and the implications to the society who participated in these projects. These include the process, the role of individuals and the collective action of key strategic stakeholders in managing and structuring the programs. It was concluded the importance of entrepreneurship in driving economic growth and empowering the targeted segment, such as the underprivileged, through entrepreneurship to provide employment and sustainable income. Recommendations were made in managing social issues, uncovering the importance of social inclusivity, social innovation in developing individuals and driving economic growth, involvement of all parties from the public and private sectors, as well as non-profit and non-government organization to expand the initiatives to include those who are entitled to receive the support.

After the summaries of the chapters included in the book, the book portrays and assesses RCEP's overview, potentials, challenges and future directions. The book emphasizes quality, research-based studies that contribute to theory, lessons learned and best practices, critical understanding and policy formulation on RCEP. We hope you all find them useful and interesting for research, teaching and policy studies.

Thank you,

Mahani Hamdan
Institute of Policy Studies
Universiti Brunei Darussalam
Brunei Darussalam

Muhammad Anshari
Institute of Policy Studies
Universiti Brunei Darussalam
Brunei Darussalam

Norainie Ahmad
Institute of Policy Studies
Universiti Brunei Darussalam
Brunei Darussalam

List of Contributors

Abdur Razzaq   Universitas Islam Negeri Raden Fatah Palembang, Indonesia

Abdullah Al-Mudimigh   Dar Al Uloom University, Saudi Arabia

Ares Albirru Amsal   Faculty of Economics, Universitas Andalas, Padang-Indonesia, Padang, Indonesia

Blessing Gweshengwe   Department of Rural and Urban Development, Great Zimbabwe University, Zimbabwe

Dayangku Rodzi Pengiran Haji Rahman   School of Business, Universiti Teknologi Brunei (UTB), Brunei Darussalam

Emil Ali   Universiti Brunei Darussalam, Institute of Policy Studies, Brunei, Darussalam

Fahmi Ibrahim   School of Business, Universiti Teknologi Brunei (UTB), Brunei, Darussalam

Mahani Hamdan   Universiti Brunei Darussalam, Institute of Policy Studies, Brunei, Darussalam

Mia Fithriyah   Indonesia Open University, Indonesia

Muhammad Anshari   Universiti Brunei Darussalam, Institute of Policy Studies, Brunei, Darussalam

Norainie Ahmad   Universiti Brunei Darussalam, Institute of Policy Studies, Brunei, Darussalam

Rayna Kartika   Faculty of Economics, Universitas Andalas, Padang, Indonesia

CHAPTER 1

An Overview of Regional Comprehensive Economic Partnership (RCEP)

Mahani Hamdan[1,*], Muhammad Anshari[1] and Norainie Ahmad[1]

[1] *Universiti Brunei Darussalam, Institute of Policy Studies, Brunei Darussalam*

Abstract: The Regional Comprehensive Economic Partnership (RCEP) is a recently established Free Trade Agreement between Asia-Pacific countries with the goal of increasing trade between participating countries. A total of twenty Chapters, seventeen Annexes, and fifty-four schedules of obligations are included in the agreement between its partners, with legal features correlating to the explorations of its interactions with member countries. RCEP established an integrated market with 15 member countries, which has facilitated the mobility of products and services among them. It aims to negotiate on trade in products and services, investment, intellectual property, dispute settlement, e-commerce, small and medium-sized firms, and economic cooperation. Currently, it is the world's largest free trade agreement in terms of economic impact, and it has the potential to promote trade and integration among member countries. The objectives of this chapter are to evaluate the opportunities and challenges RCEP faces. We focus primarily on secondary data gathered from scholarly journals and formal reports. RCEP has the potential to expand economic growth among the participating countries. However, one of the challenges that needs to be considered is that some countries may be in a less advantageous position, as the agreements made might affect their internal economic development. We argue that despite the numerous advantages of the Partnership, all members must be able to address the four major issues identified in this chapter if they were to benefit fully from the RCEP.

Keywords: ASEAN, Australia, China, Free Trade Agreement (FTA), Japan, New Zealand, Regional Comprehensive Economic Partnership (RCEP), South Korea.

INTRODUCTION

A Free Trade Agreement (FTA) is an agreement between two or more countries that are based on global regulation and is intended to create a free-trade zone between the cooperating countries (EduMaritime, 2021). Its primary purpose is to minimise trade restrictions between countries in order to expand business opportunities. This is accomplished through activities such as determining the

---

* **Corresponding author Mahani Hamdan:** Universiti Brunei Darussalam, Institute of Policy Studies, Brunei Darussalam; E-mail: mahani.hamdan@ubd.edu.bn

tariffs and duties that countries impose on imports and exports with the goal of reducing or eliminating trade barriers, thereby promoting international trade (The Balance, 2021). There are two economic elements of free trade agreements: trade diversion and trade creation, as well as free trade agreements for public benefits. Studies have shown that the introduction of these economic features will improve the overall national welfare of a country (International Economics Study Center, 1998).

The most recent free trade agreement (FTA) is the Regional Comprehensive Economic Partnership (RCEP), which was signed on 12th November 2020, which involves countries in the Asia-Pacific region and creates uniform regulations for e-commerce, trade, and intellectual property. The RCEP is a free trade and multilateral agreement between Australia, Brunei, Cambodia, China, Indonesia, Japan, Laos, Malaysia, Myanmar, New Zealand, the Philippines, Singapore, South Korea, Thailand, and Vietnam that includes the Asia-Pacific region (Hastuti, 2020; Swasdee *et al.*, 2020).

RCEP intends to establish a substantive and mutually beneficial economic partnership agreement that is WTO-compliant and transparent, and it will entail greater cooperation between ASEAN and its free trade agreement partners (Basu Das, 2015; Anshari, 2020). Aside from that, the trade bloc's broader economic objectives are to strengthen members' participation in regional and global production networks while simultaneously lowering the cost of trade or commerce and the shortfalls caused by multiple ASEAN-based trade agreements. Its most significant feature is that it aims to eliminate up to 90 percent of tariffs on imports between participating nations within 20 years of its implementation. In addition, it will define uniform norms for e-commerce, trade, and intellectual property rights protection (Zhou, 2020).

In this paper, we explore the advantages, potentials, and challenges of the Regional Comprehensive Economic Partnership (RCEP), in view of the long-term viability for participating member nations and the global community in general.

REGIONAL COMPREHENSIVE ECONOMIC PARTNERSHIP (RCEP)

The origins of the RCEP trade bloc can be traced back to 2006, when four countries, including Brunei, New Zealand, Chile, and Singapore, founded the Pacific Four (P4) grouping, and the United States, Australia, Malaysia, Vietnam, and Peru expressed an interest in joining them in 2008 (Cheong and Teonzon, 2013). These countries began negotiations to form the Trans-Pacific Partnership (TPP) agreement in the year 2009, which has since met with numerous challenges. ASEAN acknowledged that its relevance in East Asia could be adversely affected when the United States conducted the Trans-Pacific

Partnership (TPP) negotiations in 2009. Japan and Canada also expressed their willingness to join during the 2011 Asia-Pacific Economic Cooperation (APEC) Economic Leaders' Conference, which was hosted by the United States. In order to maintain its prominence, ASEAN has implemented a number of policies and mechanisms, including the establishment of the ASEAN Framework for Regional Comprehensive Economic Partnership (RCEP), which was formalised in 2012 and is currently in effect (Fig. **1**).

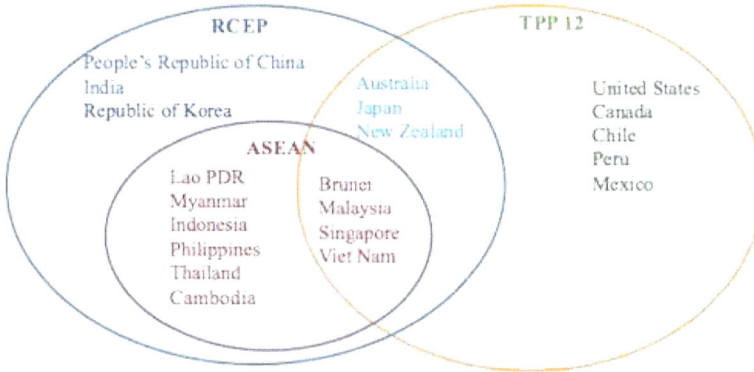

RCEP — People's Republic of China, India, Republic of Korea — Australia, Japan, New Zealand — **TPP 12** — United States, Canada, Chile, Peru, Mexico — **ASEAN** — Lao PDR, Myanmar, Indonesia, Philippines, Thailand, Cambodia — Brunei, Malaysia, Singapore, Viet Nam

Fig. (1). ASEAN, RCEP, TPP (Source: Asiafoundation, 2015.

The Trans-Pacific Partnership (TPP) is a comprehensive trade agreement that aims to strengthen economic links between 12 nations, including Peru, Canada, Mexico and Japan, by creating a new single market that is comparable to that of the European Union. This will be accomplished by removing trade barriers, such as tariffs, and promoting cross-border trade in order to stimulate economic expansion along with the RCEP. Despite the proposed agreements signed among the countries in 2016, President Trump's decision to withdraw the United States from the TPP in 2017 was one of the primary reasons for the deal's collapse, along with discrepancies between decisions makers, and rising protectionism (Lyu, 2018).

The RCEP agreement on the other hand, is a relatively new Free Trade Agreement (FTA) that was proposed in November 2012 by the ten member nations of the Association of South-East Asian Nations (ASEAN). These countries include Brunei Darussalam, Cambodia, Indonesia, Laos, Malaysia, Myanmar, the Philippines, Singapore, Thailand, and Vietnam. Another five countries, including Australia, China, Japan, New Zealand, and South Korea, also took part in the pact (Gantz, 2016). Following eight years of initial negotiations for the Regional Comprehensive Economic Partnership (RCEP), the participating nations were finally able to reach a consensus on the accord on November 15,

2020 (The Scoop, 2020). The RCEP encompasses around thirty percent of the world's economy and covers two billion two hundred million people (The Scoop, 2020). India, however, had withdrawn from the Partnership, but the country has since been given the opportunity to re-join when it is ready in the future. Due to the unique barriers and challenges that the regional grouping has encountered, the negotiations have taken longer than expected despite a scheduled end of negotiations in 2015 (Shiao, 2018). Additionally, there were countries entering free trade agreements for the first time with one another, such as China, Japan, and South Korea. Thus far, 25 rounds of RCEP discussions have taken place, with the most recent round taking place in the month of February 2019. However, there was no significant progress at the time (Mahadevan & Nugroho, 2019).

In total, the RCEP agreement contains twenty chapters, seventeen annexes, and fifty-four schedules of obligations, which include market entry, guidelines and disciplines, and economic and technical partnerships (ASEAN, 2020a). One of the main goals of the Agreement is the creation of an advanced arrangement that is up to date with respect to shifting and evolving trade certainty factors, such as electronic commerce and a developing provincial value chain. Another goal is to enhance the prospects for micro, small, and medium-sized enterprises to grow, as well as in the complexity of the market race (ASEAN, 2020b). Another goal is the comprehensiveness of their exposure and the depth of their assurances, including trade-in amenities, which contain explicit criteria on monetary, communications, and professional facilities, as well as the provisional mobility of ordinary folks (*ibid.*). Furthermore, chapters on investment, small and medium-sized firms (SMEs), economic and technical cooperation, intellectual property, government procurement, electronic commerce, legal and institutional sectors, and competition have also been established (*ibid.*).

Economic Growth

The RCEP agreement is a significant economic framework for participating nations. It is projected to contribute to the economic growth of its member countries and will become even more important following the pandemic (Anshari & Sumardi, 2020; Sugiantoro *et al.*, 2020). The agreement brought with it new opportunities and growth for the country. Member countries collaborate with the other members of the RCEP, which strengthens international commercial connections. While the information and its impact with regard to the RCEP are still in their early stages due to the agreement's negotiations having only recently concluded late last year, the outcome can be predicted by analysing the respective reviews of the RCEP guidelines, as well as disruptive technology and stipulating for its possible benefits. To increase economic improvement and exertions, participating members must collaborate with the evolving patterns of incorporation. Under the Agreement, this will be accomplished through the enhancement of modernisation, production, and income. A key component of the RCEP is the advancement of digitisation. This strategy is expected to improve competencies in innovation, trade, and SME involvement, particularly in the context of e-commerce, and integration with the aforementioned disruptive technologies.

In developing countries, tariff reductions in the distant future as a result of participation in FTAs under RCEP have the potential to stimulate numerous investments by representatives internationally to improve global value chains (Flente and Ponte, 2017, cited in Mahadevan & Nugroho, 2019). Due to this, the reduction of tariffs on tradable products handled by the RCEP has become the primary focus of discussions (Sharma, 2018). Furthermore, while looking at the combined GDP of China and the United States, it can be seen that the combined GDP of both countries accounts for around 40 percent of global GDP, indicating that they are two of the world's greatest economies. As a result, it is possible that this will have a significant impact on other economies. A remarkable amount of GDP is received by developing and rising countries, in contrast to the GDP received by developed economies (Kawasaki, 2015, as cited in Mahadevan & Nugroho, 2019). Given that tariffs account for a significant portion of GDP in many countries, such as Korea, where tariffs account for 2.77 percent (Li *et al.*, 2016), lowering supply chain impediments, rather than abolishing tariffs, will have a significant influence on welfare (Dey, 2020).

According to Kamada and Yoshida (2021), putting in place logistical arrangements that allow for local cross-border supply chains will serve to increase the international competitiveness of Japanese enterprises in the global marketplace. Specifically, Japanese firms have been constructing supply chains throughout the ASEAN area since the formation of the ASEAN Economic Community (AEC), which was announced in 2015. In recent years, they have increased their production networks, and their local output is expanding year after year, according to the company (Ahad *et al.*, 2017). As a result, it has been thought that for Japanese manufacturers, procurement, manufacturing, and sales in optimal conditions that match the features of the societies, regional economies, and countries into which they have grown are of greater importance. To facilitate the globalisation of corporate activity, effective logistics must be in operation. In supply chain networks, transportation can play a key integrative role, especially as organisations compete strategically on the basis of cost, service, and timeliness. Regarding supply chain coordination, transportation, in general, is in a great position to combine and coordinate flows throughout the supply chain (Morash & Clinton, 1997).

As a new FTA, the RCEP addresses not only traditional trade policies such as tariff barriers but also 21st-century trade initiatives such as e-commerce, competition policy, and trade facilitation, which are topics that most current FTAs in the field have never addressed (Lewis, 2013; Wilson, 2015). The RCEP is considered as China's strategic reaction to the geopolitical ramifications of Asian policies. Textiles and apparels (T&A) is an important industry in the RCEP negotiations. The impact of RCEP on the integration of textile and apparel supply chains in the Asia-Pacific region has been explored by Lu (2019). In 2015, the sixteen RCEP participants exported $405 billion in trade and investment (54 percent of the total global exports) and imported $115 billion in trade and investment (31 percent of the world share) (Lu, 2019). Many of these T&A items are manufactured in the Asia-Pacific area as part of a collaborative supply chain. As the RCEP aims to significantly reduce current trade barriers between its participants, its implementation has the potential to promote regional T&A supply chain integration further and significantly alter the current trend of T&A trade in the Asia-Pacific region.

Methodology

We focus primarily on secondary data gathered from scholarly journals and formal reports. The most recent reports, spanning the years 1990 through 2021, were chosen for consideration. The reason for selecting such time periods was that they allowed for the use of the most recent data and the most relevant information in relation to the study on free trade agreements and the RCEP. The information contained inside each data set was gathered and examined.

Discussion

Globalisation, according to Masson (2001), is a phenomenon marked by greater trade, resources, and information flow, as well as increased individual mobility across boundaries. As a result of advancements in transportation and communication technologies, global relations have seen an increase in foreign trade, as well as the spread of ideas and culture throughout the world (Hamdan & Anshari, 2020; Razzaq *et al.*, 2018). From an economic aspect, the term globalisation refers to the spread of products, services, data, technology, and the availability of financial resources (Albrow & King, 1990). It has also allowed for the removal of cross-border trade restrictions, which has made the development of global markets more viable in recent years (Kester, 1995). As a result, the expansion of trade blocs, in which trade barriers such as tariffs are decreased or eliminated among member countries, has accelerated. The European Union (EU), the United States-Mexico-Canada Agreement (USMCA), and the Association of

Southeast Asian Nations (ASEAN) are all instances of trading blocs that have gained prominence (ASEAN) (Hamdan *et al.*, 2020).

The Regional Comprehensive Economic Partnership (RCEP), which now includes 15 nations in the Asia-Pacific area, is another important example of a free trade agreement worth considering. Approximately 30 percent of the world's population (2.2 billion people) and 30 percent of global GDP ($26.2 trillion) will be represented by the 15 member countries by 2020, making it the world's largest trading bloc (Tani, 2020). The RCEP, despite its immense size and promising partnerships, is hindered by a number of potentials and challenges such as the agriculture industry, the service sector, development gaps, and human rights are among the issues that need to be addressed.

Potentials

The Regional Comprehensive Economic Partnership (RCEP) covers one-third of the world's population and, as a result, contributes to 30 percent of the world's gross domestic product. This has the potential to eliminate tariffs on 92 percent of the products that are traded among the members.

The RCEP promotes trade and investment relations between member countries by eliminating non-tariff barriers (NTBs) to goods and services trade. Because import tariffs among RCEP members were already quite low, the agreement focuses on non-tariff barriers (NTBs). Tariffs on imports have been reduced as a result of unilateral tariff reductions over the past several decades, as well as a network of established trade agreements among RCEP members, such as the ASEAN-China Free Trade Agreement, the ASEAN-Australia-New Zealand Free Trade Agreement, and the Japan-Korea Free Trade Agreement, among others.

It harmonises the laws that different countries have in place for international trade in goods, providing traders and investors with greater assurance. If the goods are produced in another member country with the same level of consumer protection, it allows importing countries to incorporate the quality requirements of that country in their own legislation (Mulyani *et al.*, 2021).

The most significant aspect of the agreement is that it harmonises origin regulations across all 15 participating countries, making it easier to incorporate RCEP members into the same supply chain. At a time when the United States-China trade war is hastening the reconfiguration of global value chains (GVCs) in and out of China, this could assist RCEP members in attracting a higher proportion of GVCs and deepening their specialisation. A number of particular service clauses are included in the RCEP, including agreements by each member not to discriminate against the investors of other members in a variety of service sectors. Finally, it facilitates the temporary movement of persons for investment and commerce objectives. A few examples of how RCEP could help are shown below.

Brunei Darussalam's timely ratification of the RCEP agreement demonstrates the country's strong commitment to assisting the region's post-pandemic recovery efforts by enhancing its economic and trade relations, expanding business possibilities, and advocating for an open, inclusive, rules-based global trading system (MOFE, 2021). While Cambodia also benefits from the substantial drop in tariffs and preferential trade treatment, as evidenced by the fact that more than 70% of intra-ASEAN commerce is managed with zero tariffs. Non-tariff trade barriers such as sanitary and phytosanitary regulations are also being addressed in Cambodia, according to the government. The Regional Comprehensive Economic Partnership (RCEP) creates long-term trade prospects that will allow Cambodia to modernise and grow its economic structure, which includes agriculture, tourism, construction, and garment manufacturing. As the largest economy in ASEAN, Indonesia will gain from expanded market access, more investment, and improved chances to engage in regional supply chains, among other things. Exports will expand as a result of these improvements, which will be critical for the country's economic progress in the long run. While RCEP will allow the Philippines to export 92 percent of its commodities, it will also affect the business process outsourcing industry. Furthermore, service professionals in the Philippines, such as seafarers, teachers, IT programmers, and engineers, may be able to gain from the demand for service employees in countries such as Japan and South Korea, according to the World Bank. Furthermore, Malaysia's commerce is dominated by RCEP members, and the agreement would enhance Malaysian enterprises' and consumers' trading prospects and partnerships. Enhanced collaboration would benefit organisations in a variety of industries, including telecommunications, banking and finance, consulting, and others. Additionally, firms in Malaysia would benefit from greater access to high-quality raw materials at reasonable pricing, according to the government. In addition, Singapore stands to benefit from the Regional Comprehensive Economic Partnership (RCEP) in terms of regional commerce and supply chains in the ASEAN area. Because of the ingredients purchased from other countries under the Regional Comprehensive Economic Partnership (RCEP), Singapore can become a more cost-effective country. The ingredients that are purchased can be seen to be originating from the country in which they are purchased, allowing them to apply their tariffs to them. Furthermore, perishable items can be cleared *via* customs in as little as six hours. Singapore can benefit from the cost reductions that are passed on to them. Thailand, which contributes to 70% of all export shipments, benefits from the Regional Comprehensive Economic Partnership (RCEP) through better integration of its economy with supply chains and wider markets in the Asia-

Pacific region. Thai exporters stand to gain in terms of trade, pricing value, and innovation, while manufacturers stand to gain in terms of lower-cost raw materials sourced from a larger range of suppliers. Additionally, the RCEP would enable Vietnamese enterprises to expand their exports, diversify their value chains, and attract greater foreign investment. Reduced import tariffs will open up new chances for items from critical sectors such as telecommunications, information and communication technology, textiles and clothing, and agriculture — all of which are seeing strong growth as a result of rising export turnovers – to enter the market.

Challenges

It is evident that the RCEP deliberations are promising, but the trade bloc will not be a simple operation, according to New Zealand's Foreign Ministry and Trade (n.d., cited in Basu Das, 2015), which said that it is hindered by economic and political challenges. It is also the first of its kind in terms of regional economic integration among predominantly poor countries, with no precedence to reflect on.

There is a significant challenge with FTA agreements when it comes to coverage issues. There are internal pressures to suppress competition in home markets even though all participating countries agree with the benefits of market access liberalisation initiatives (Chandra, 2008; Milner, 1997). Singapore and other exceptional nations like Indonesia and India are included in the RCEP, which includes countries like Indonesia and India that are anticipated to complicate market access talks in terms of goods trade (Basu Das, 2015). The RCEP has five major challenges (see Fig. **2**): agricultural, service industry, economic disparities, ICT disparities, and human capital development.

The agricultural sector, according to Kawai and Wignaraja (2009), has evolved into a protected industry in most economies, and increasing the agricultural trade range is a significant problem. Due to the fact that agriculture employs more than a third of the workforce in ASEAN member nations, protecting agricultural jobs is an important priority during trade liberalisation negotiations for the region. For example, in the situation of India, the country takes a "protective" stance on agriculture (Ramdasi, 2010). Agricultural production contributes significantly to the nation's economy in terms of employment, gross domestic product, and food security. It employs more than 40% of the workforce and generates approximately 18% of the nation's gross domestic product (GDP) (Basu Das, 2015). As the world's fifth-largest economy (according to Pleacher, 2021), India withdrew from trade negotiations at the Regional Comprehensive Economic Partnership (RCEP) summit, primarily due to concerns about imports of manufactured goods from China, as well as agricultural and dairy products from Australia and New Zealand.

Due to the low tariffs, the free trade bloc may have a negative influence on its own domestic industrial and agricultural sectors, as well as on local producers (Bureau, 2019). Several recent Indian farmer demonstrations, such as the one held in 2020-2021, are examples of this. Local farmers were concerned that large corporations would drive down crop prices as a result of the introduction of the "Three New Laws" which allow farmers to sell their goods to anyone at any price (Yeung, 2021).

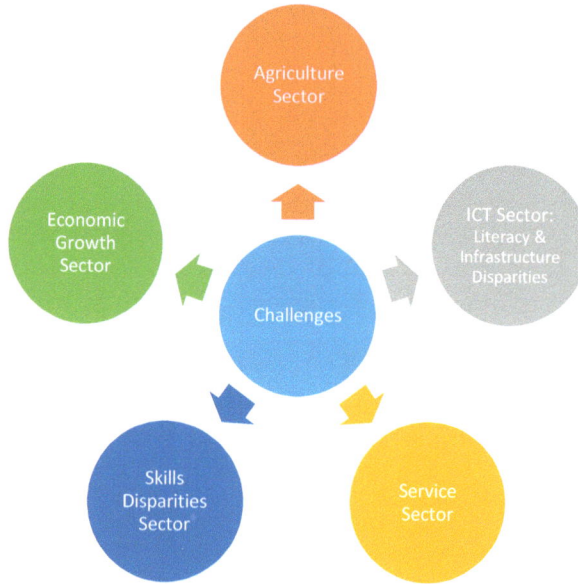

Fig. (2). RCEP Implementation Challenges (Source: Authors' Compilation, 2022).

In the RCEP, *the service sector* is responsible for a considerable amount of a country's production and employment, highlighting its importance in terms of development and job creation. When compared to the trade of goods, the multidimensional and intangible nature of the trade of services makes tracking and evaluating its cross-border movements particularly challenging (Basu Das, 2015). In accordance with the General Agreement on Trade in Services (GATS), the trade of services can be divided into four categories (World Trade Organization, n.d.): Firstly, there is the cross-border trade in services that takes place when neither producer nor consumer moves, for example, in the financial services industry. Second is international consumption, which occurs when purchasers relocate to the site of a service, such as tourism. In the third category, producers establish a long-term presence in a host country in the form of an affiliate, subsidiary, or representative office of a foreign-owned and controlled corporation that is based in the host country (*e.g.*, banks and hotel groups).

Finally, the presence of natural individuals when producers enter a host country as a result of a temporary inflow of people (*e.g.*, a foreign IT expert travelling to a site to implement its technology plan). The first two methods are similar to the traditional concept of "trade" and service flows can be estimated to a certain extent in the balance of payment statistics, but it is the last two modes that present complications (Basu Das, 2015). A number of political and economic impediments are also preventing the liberalisation of the services industry from taking place (Llanto & Oritz, 2013). In several cases, progress is impeded by liberalisation obstacles in foreign ownership investment in local firms, restrictions on land ownership, and restrictions on the movement of skilled workers throughout the country. Additionally, in cases when a settlement has been reached, local norms and regulations appear to block the real implementation of the agreement (Basu Das, 2015).

Basu Das (2015) also highlighted that the *disparity in the growth* stages of the RCEP's member countries is a key challenge for the organisation. These disparities are exhibited not only in terms of GDP per capita but also in indicators of human development such as life expectancy, literacy, public health and education spending, and poverty levels, among other things. The differences in per capita income between low-income ASEAN countries and high-income economies such as Korea, Australia, Singapore, New Zealand, and Japan are much more noteworthy when comparing low-income ASEAN countries to high-income economies such as Korea, Australia, Singapore, New Zealand, and Japan.

According to Thanh (2005), any form of economic unification could have significant *social implications* for the less-developed countries of ASEAN. A number of factors could be responsible for this, including systemic changes and the risks of becoming trapped in a low-wage labour pit where local manufacturers have little or no incentive to advance up the value chain. Consequently, reasonable economic planning and resource allocation are essential for the development of these economies. A report by Ranald (2020) asserts that the RCEP does not contain any obligations to internationally recognised labour rights and environmental standards, which the RCEP governments have supported through the United Nations and ILO. The evidence of labour and human rights issues in RCEP member countries is accumulating as a result of this. However, the RCEP does not include any rules for dealing with issues such as forced labour or child labour, and it makes no mention of climate change in its provisions.

Finally, the disparity in ICT literacy and infrastructure across participating nations may emerge to be one of the most complex challenges in ensuring efficient implementation of the RCEP. It has long been a focus of public policy to address inequalities in access to and competency in information and communication technology (ICT), particularly among socioeconomically advantaged and disadvantaged populations, and among developing and developed countries. The term "digital divide" was conceptualised to draw attention to the fact that such disparities can seriously compromise social and national cohesion by preventing people from participating fully in underdeveloped and developing countries' political or economic efficacy (OECD, 2001). As a result, given the numerous opportunities that technology makes available for all members' participation, networking, and increasing productivity of RCEP, the unequal distribution of material, cultural, and cognitive resources to take advantage of these opportunities may serve to perpetuate and even exacerbate existing social and economic disparities (OECD, 2015).

CONCLUSION

The Regional Comprehensive Economic Partnership (RCEP) agreement brings countries at various stages of development together. It harmonises country-specific regulations on goods trade, offering traders and investors greater confidence in their operations. This is possible because digitalisation has resulted in a more comprehensive information system to optimise international relations. Also included in this agreement are provisions to ensure that the agreement benefits economies at all stages of growth, businesses of various sizes, and other parties involved in the agreement. However, despite the fact that the agreement has the potential to benefit many countries, it still confronts a number of challenges. Thus, at least five major challenges must be considered in further discussions of the regional grouping: the agricultural industry, service industry liberalisation, development disparities, ICT, and human rights.

CONSENT FOR PUBLICATION

Not applicable.

CONFLICT OF INTEREST

The author declares no conflict of interest, financial or otherwise.

ACKNOWLEDGEMENTS

Declared none.

REFERENCES

Ahad, A.D., Anshari, M., Razzaq, A. (2017). Domestication of smartphones among adolescents in Brunei darussalam. *International Journal of Cyber Behavior, Psychology and Learning, 7*(4), 26-39. [http://dx.doi.org/10.4018/IJCBPL.2017100103]

Anshari, M. (2020). Workforce mapping of fourth industrial revolution: Optimization to identity. *J. Phys.*

Conf. Ser., 1477(7), 072023.
[http://dx.doi.org/10.1088/1742-6596/1477/7/072023]

Anshari, M., Sumardi, W.H. (2020). Employing big data in business organisation and business ethics. *International Journal of Business Governance and Ethics, 14*(2), 181-205.
[http://dx.doi.org/10.1504/IJBGE.2020.106349]

Albrow, M., King, E. (1990). Globalization, knowledge, and society: readings from international sociology. *Sage.*

ASEAN. (2020). *ASEAN hits historic milestone with signing of RCEP.*https://asean.org/asean-hits-historc-milestone-signing-rcep/ a

ASEAN. (2020). https://asean.org/storage/2020/11/Summary-of-the-RCEP-Agreement.pdf b

Asia foundation. (2015). TPP and RCEP: Boon or Bane for ASEAN. Retrieved From 2022 https://asiafoundation.org/2015/09/09/tpp-and-rcep-boon-or-bane-for-asean/

Basu Das, S. (2015). The Regional Comprehensive Economic Partnership: new paradigm or old wine in a new bottle? *Asian-Pacific Economic Literature., 29*(2), 68-84.
[http://dx.doi.org/10.1111/apel.12111]

Bureau, E. November 05. Rcep trade Agreement: India decides to opt out of RCEP, SAYS key concerns not addressed. (2019). Retrieved March 06, 2021, from https://economictimes.indiatimes.com/news/economy/foreign-trade/india-decides-to-opt-out-of-rcep-says-key-concerns-not-addressed/articleshow/71896848.cms

Chandra, A.C. (2008). Indonesia and the ASEAN Free Trade Agreement: Nationalists and regional integration strategy. Lexington Books.

Cheong, I., Tongzon, J. (2013). Comparing the Economic Impact of the Trans-Pacific Partnership and the Regional Comprehensive Economic Partnership. *Asian Econ. Pap., 12*(2), 144-164.
[http://dx.doi.org/10.1162/ASEP_a_00218]

Dey, D. (2020). Supply chain Management (SCM) and Recession Recovery. *Supply Chain and Logistics Management,* 1033-1052.
[http://dx.doi.org/10.4018/978-1-7998-0945-6.ch048]

https://www.edumaritime.net/icc-academy/free-trade-agreement-certificate-ftac-online

Gantz, D.A. (2016). The TPP and RCEP: Mega-Trade Agreements for the Pacific Rim. *Ariz. J. Int'l & Comp. L., 33,* 57.

Hastuti, R. (2020). https://www.cnbcindonesia.com/news/20201130110944-4-205621/world-bank-inisitor-rcep-adalah-indonesia-bukan-china

Hamdan, M., Anshari, M. (2020). Paving the Way for the Development of FinTech Initiatives in ASEAN. *Financial technology and disruptive innovation in ASEAN.* IGI Global.
[http://dx.doi.org/10.4018/978-1-5225-9183-2.ch004]

Hamdan, M., Chen, C.K., Anshari, M. (2020). Decision Aid in Budgeting Systems for Small & Medium Enterprises. *2020 International Conference on Decision Aid Sciences and Application (DASA)* IEEE.
[http://dx.doi.org/10.1109/DASA51403.2020.9317018]

International Economics Study Center. (1998) *International Trade Theory and Policy - Chapter,* 110-2A.

Kamada, K., Yoshida, K. (2021). Analysis of Rebuilding the Supply Chain in RCEP Region – From the Perspective of New-Economic Geography *Management for Sustainable and Inclusive Development in a Transforming Asia,* 273-294.
[http://dx.doi.org/10.1007/978-981-15-8195-3_16]

Kawai, M., Wignaraja, G. (2009). The Asian 'noodle bowl': Is it serious for business. *Asian Development Bank Institute (ADBI) Working Paper Series, 136.*

Lewis, M.K. (2013). The TPP and the RCEP (ASEAN + 6) as potential paths toward deeper Asian economic integration. *Asian J. WTO Int. Health Law Policy,* *8*(2), 359-378.

Li, C., Wang, J., Whalley, J. (2016). Impact of mega trade deals on China: A computational general equilibrium analysis. *Econ. Model., 57,* 13-25.
[http://dx.doi.org/10.1016/j.econmod.2016.03.027]

Llanto, G.M., Ortiz, M., Kristina, P. (2013). Regional Comprehensive Economic Partnership: reform challenges and key tasks for the Philippines (No. 2013-51). *PIDS Discussion Paper Series.*

Lu, S. (2019). Regional Comprehensive Economic Partnership (RCEP): Impact on the integration of textile and apparel supply chain in the Asia-Pacific region. *In Fashion Supply Chain Management in Asia: Concepts, Models, and Cases (pp. 21-41).* Springer, Singapore.

Lyu, H. (2018). *Why the TPP Collapsed.*https://www.chinausfocus.com/finance-economy/why-the--pp-collapsed

Mahadevan, R., Nugroho, A. (2019). Can the Regional Comprehensive Economic Partnership minimise the harm from the United States–China trade war? *World Econ., 42*(11), 3148-3167.
[http://dx.doi.org/10.1111/twec.12851]

Masson, M.P.R. (2001). Globalization facts and figures. *International Monetary Fund.*

Morash, E.A., Clinton, S.R. (1997). The Role of Transportation Capabilities in International Supply Chain Management. *Transp. J., 36*(3), 5-17.

Milner, H.V. (1997). *Interests, institutions, and information: Domestic politics and international relations.* Princeton University Press.

(2021). *Brunei Darussalam Ratifies the RCEP Agreement.* https://asean2021.bn/newslist/brunei-darussalam-ratifies-the-regional-comprehensive-economic-partnership-(rcep)-agreement

Mulyani, M.A., Yusuf, S., Siregar, P., Nurihsan, J., Razzaq, A., Anshari, M. (2021). Fourth Industrial Revolution and Educational Challenges. *2021 International Conference on Information Management and Technology (ICIMTech)* IEEE.
[http://dx.doi.org/10.1109/ICIMTech53080.2021.9535057]

OECD. (2015). Inequalities in Digital Proficiency: Bridging the Divide. Retrieved 8 Jan 2022 from https://www.oecd-ilibrary.org/docserver/9789264239555-8-en.pdf?expires=1641783353&id=id&accname=guest&checksum=ABBAC28B48AB4D4C83E6D6B9BAC8A04D

OECD. (2001). Understanding the Digital Divide. *OECD Digital Economy Papers, No. 49.* Paris: OECD Publishing.
[http://dx.doi.org/10.1787/20716826]

Ramdasi, P. (2010). An overview of India's trade strategy. *Pour le débat, (1).*

Ranald, P. (2020). *RCEP has limited TRADE gains and IGNORES labour and human rights.*https://www.internationalaffairs.org.au/australianoutlook/rcep-has-limited-trade-g-ins-and-ignores-labour-and-human-rights/

Razzaq, A., Samiha, Y.T., Anshari, M. (2018). Smartphone habits and behaviors in supporting students self-efficacy. *International Journal of Emerging Technologies in Learning (iJET), 13*(2), 94.
[http://dx.doi.org/10.3991/ijet.v13i02.7685]

Shiao, V. (2018). *RCEP fails to conclude by year-end as hoped; timeline extended to 2019.*https://www.businesstimes.com.sg/government-economy/rcep-fails-to-conclude-b--year-end-as-hoped-timeline-extended-to-2019

Sugiantoro, B., Anshari, M., Sudrajat, D. (2020). Developing Framework for Web Based e-Commerce: Secure-SDLC. *Journal of Physics: Conference Series., 1566*(1), 012020. []. IOP Publishing.].
[http://dx.doi.org/10.1088/1742-6596/1566/1/012020]

Swasdee, A., Anshari, M., Hamdan, M. (2020). Artificial Intelligence as Decision Aid in Humanitarian Response. *2020 International Conference on Decision Aid Sciences and Application (DASA).* IEEE.

[http://dx.doi.org/10.1109/DASA51403.2020.9317111]

Tani, S. (2020). *India stays away from Rcep talks in Bali.* https://asia.nikkei.com/Economy/Trade/India-stay--away-from-RCEP-talks-in-Bali

Thanh, V. T. (2005). ASEAN Economic Community: Perspective from ASEAN's Transitional Economies. Roadmap to an ASEAN Economic Community, 105.

The balance. (2021). Free Trade Agreements: Their Impact, Types, and Examples. https://www.the balance.com/free-trade-agreement-types-and-examples-3305897

The Scoop. (2020, December 16). Brunei joins world's biggest trade bloc.. *Brunei joins world's biggest trade bloc.* https://thescoop.co/2020/11/16/brunei-joins-worlds-biggest-trade-bloc/

Wilson, J.D. (2015). Mega-regional trade deals in the Asia-Pacific: Choosing between the TPP and RCEP? *J. Contemp. Asia, 45*(2), 345-353.
[http://dx.doi.org/10.1080/00472336.2014.956138]

*Basic Purpose and Concepts.*https://www.wto.org/english/tratop_e/serv_e/cbt_course_e/c1s3p1_e.htm n.d.

Yeung, J. (2021). *Farmers across India have been protesting for months.* https://edition.cnn.com/2021/02/10/asia/india-farmers-protest-explainer-intl-hnk-scli/index.html

Zhou, L. (2020). *What is RCEP and What does an Indo-Pacific free-trade deal offer China?.* https://www.scmp.com/news/china/diplomacy/article/3109436/what-rcep-and-what-does-indo-pacific-free-trade-deal-offer

CHAPTER 2

Integrating RCEP with Cross-Border E-Commerce (CBE) Towards Accelerating Economic Recovery in ASEAN

Mia Fithriyah[1,*]

[1] *Indonesia Open University, Indonesia*

Abstract: Connectivity is the basis of e-commerce development. E-commerce reinforces connectivity and aims to promote a continuous stream of information, logistics, free cash flow, and so forth. A seamless connection between the virtual and physical parts of an e-commerce network could be demonstrated in Cross-Border E-commerce (CBE). A region-wide e-commerce support environment with a Regional Comprehensive Economic Partnership (RCEP) agreement would undoubtedly support economic stabilization. Notably, this model is positively in line with the restricted conditions during the COVID-19 outbreak (Anshari *et al.*, 2021a). However, business actors should improve connectivity-derived services via technology and the internet in order to add more value to the successful implementation of CBE. Considering today's consumers are more complex, the COVID-19 economic turbulence has resulted in a severe bankruptcy storm for business areas worldwide (Hamdan *et al.*, 2020). Hence, the study aims to identify the potential and opportunities of CBE, which will be explained in detail in this study. The determinants of the successful adoption of CBE remain complex. Therefore, our framework allows us to assess the extent of concerns about CBE opportunities and the potential for accelerating economic recovery during the pandemic COVID-19. In addition, CBE requires new regulations, and Asian nations must actively take part in rule-setting in order to achieve economic benefits. CBE can also provide new opportunities for local businesses where it can reach beyond their borders.

Keywords: ASEAN, Cross Border E-commerce, Covid19, RCEP.

INTRODUCTION

COVID-19 is an unparalleled disruption to the worldwide economy. The pandemic affects manufacturing and consumption. Hence, there is a need for brand-spanking new alternate measures in reaction to the adverse effects, even though new methods and regulations substantially influence exports and imports.

* **Corresponding author Mia Fithriyah:** Indonesia Open University, Indonesia;
E-mail: mia.fithriyah@ alumni.ui.ac.id

Countries require obvious records to permit governments and buyers to preserve them in the most clear way possible, specifically in an economic recession.

Worldwide, cross-line internet business has been progressively significant in the global economy (Chen L., 2017). Various factors, for example, the use of cell phones, fast Internet, the development of online installment frameworks, advancements in customer practices, administration area advancement, and so on, have laid a solid foundation for flourishing cross-border e-commerce. Due to the COVID-19 pandemic, the economic sectors, especially in business, reported facing collapse. The potential vulnerability of the business sector to the COVID-19 shock is a significant concern for policymakers everywhere (Fithriyah *et al.*, 2022). The breakthrough that has become a concern during COVID-19 is Cross-Border E-commerce (CBE). CBE has introduced new dynamics to international trade. It typically involves fewer intermediate links between sellers and buyers but has a higher demand for services, especially information, payment, and logistics.

Economic digitalization tends to work with the global exchange as shoppers and makers can get data from a wide scope of geological areas for a minimal price inside a brief time frame. This infuses new elements into the worldwide market. With new competitors, new products, new services, and new plans, as well as changes in how development and technology are spread, prices go down, the number of products available goes up, and market competition goes up.

Worldwide income from CBE was projected to arrive at £600 billion in 2018, two times that of 2012. China is among the leaders of cross-border e-commerce. China's gross market value of cross-border e-commerce accounted for roughly one-eighth of its total exchange in 2013. Its portion was relied upon to provide an additional increment of around 20% before the end of 2017. In general, the size of the advanced economies in ASEAN is projected to increase by 5.5 occasions by 2025 (Think with Google, 2017).

Companies specialising in cross-border e-commerce have experienced a fast development in the mobile business. For example, in the case of DHgate.com, website visits from mobile devices accounted for 42% of the platform's total visits in June 2014. The number of orders sent from mobile terminals has increased over two times annually (Mulyani *et al.*, 2019). Another company, Lightinthebox.com, also saw mobile businesses as the main driving force behind its revenue growth. Over 30% of the orders in 2014 came from mobile devices (AliResearch, 2016).

The total annual revenue of the global mobile payment market was estimated to reach US$450 billion in 2015. The market is projected to expand by US$150 billion–170 billion per year. According to the projection, the size will break the mark of US$1 trillion by 2019. Mobile and PC platforms tend to interact further with each other. It has been popular for mobile businesses to adopt multi-app strategies. In the next five years, an increasing share of private consumption increment will come from global e-commerce growth. The sustained growth of online shoppers provides a solid base for e-commerce consumption. The data showed that by June 2016, the scale of online shoppers in China had reached 448 million, and the online shopping usage rate had reached 63% (CNNIC, 2016). Singapore (60%), Malaysia (52%), and Thailand (51%) are among the world's top markets with the highest online shopping penetration rate as well.

The possibility of the successful implementation of CBE was supported by the fact that the e-commerce market is progressing due to the massive adoption of advanced technology and supportive policy conditions, such as the Regional Comprehensive Economic Partnership (RCEP). The new transformation of the supply chain and trading like CBE is like bringing fresh air for economic recovery during this economic shock caused by the endless pandemic.

LITERATURE REVIEW

CROSS BORDER E-COMMERCE (CBE) BARRIERS

E-commerce is the fastest-growing area in the global economy, which shortens the distance between buyers and sellers. When online deals and transactions are conducted in different areas or countries by using information and communication technology (ICT), it is called cross-border e-commerce (CBE) (Wang, 2014; Accenture, 2012). Cross-border e-commerce (CBE) is one type of international e-commerce like cross-border e-tailing. Furthermore, CBE is a business-t--customer (B2C) process used for integrating the activities of suppliers and customers along the logistics value chain. CBE has the potential to reduce trade barriers and promote trade growth (Terzi, 2011).

In the early days of cross-border e-commerce, merchants are primarily competing in products. With the development of internet technology and supply chain optimisation, this competition is turning to service level (Analysys, 2015; Swasdee *et al.*, 2020). Those capable to provide convenient and fast service will reach a competitive advantage and consumers' loyalty. However, several barriers to implementing CBE are divided into six categories (Fig. **1**).

The flow of information and goods crosses national borders and encounters cultural differences in the middle. The typical difference is the language, which can change the sales culture and prevent consumption by foreign consumers (Youngdahl & Loomba, 2000). Besides, consumer behavior varies from country to country. More information about these foreign consumers' product preferences, delivery, and online payment options is necessary. Finally, the merchant's reputation turned out to be an important factor in making decisions with most consumers about international credibility delivery and online payment.

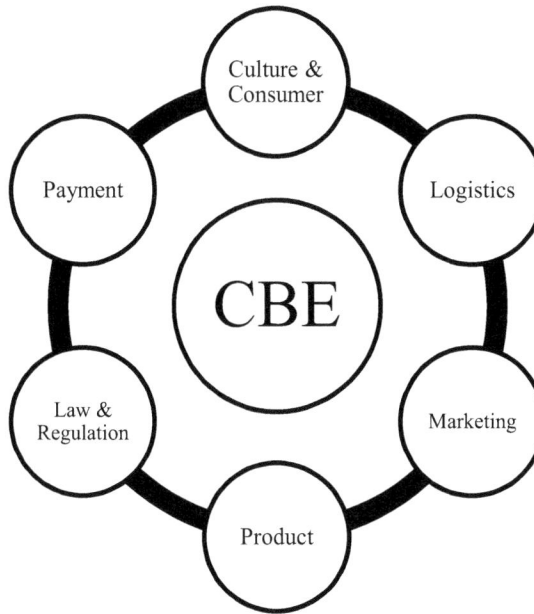

Fig. (1). Cross Border E-Commerce (CBE) Barriers.

On the other hand, e-commerce companies have a hard time finding the right information about foreign products. In market operation, for relatively unknown brands in the target market, the costs are goods advertising via multi-channel, such as improving brand awareness. In addition, companies continue to expand their presence in the global market. Overseas activities threaten domestic e-commerce companies (Liu *et al.*, 2015).

Lack of consumer confidence in cross-border sellers is often cited as one of the reasons. The most observed counterfeit products and their challenges in emerging markets are due to high standardization, popularity, and profitability; some products include computers, communications, home appliances, and so forth (Ding *et al.*, 2017).

Different laws and regulations between countries limit the ability of CBE, such as data privacy and return policy. Furthermore, when consumers purchase abroad, they must consider the total cost. High tariffs, taxation limits and VAT thresholds often reduce cross-border shopping intentions (Ding *et al.*, 2017).

E-retailers must be familiar with local payment preferences. Moreover, the unavailability to use local currency, complex conversion systems, exchange rate fluctuations and additional depreciation make cross-border shopping harder and increase consumer costs. Lastly is the lack of an effective surveillance system (Anshari *et al.*, 2021b). Fraud and non-payment result in enormous losses for e-commerce merchants, while customers worry about misuse of payment data and disclosure of personal information. On the logistic problem, the rise of e-commerce and globalization has changed consumption patterns. The logistics system should be designed to meet the needs for small, diverse, and high-frequency pickups and deliveries at different locations, in different packaging, according to different schedules and stringent customer service requirements (Hu *et al.*, 2015; Samiee, 2008; Tam *et al.*, 2003). Therefore, a need for international cooperation between all involved parties - governments, merchants, and service providers.

Integration Between RCEP and CBE

The RCEP agreement covers the ASEAN countries with the privilege that more than 90 percent of trade in goods will enjoy zero tariffs in the RCEP region, providing a favorable environment for trade and investment growth. Costs of regionally sourced raw materials for ASEAN enterprises will be significantly reduced under the trade rules of the agreement, especially the common rules of origin that only require 40 percent of regional content for goods to be considered of RCEP origin, much lower than the threshold of other free trade agreements (IGJ, 2019).

This agreement offers several opportunities to create positive impacts for ASEAN businesses to sell goods to overseas markets in the RCEP region. Asian e-commerce is growing rapidly. Hence, it has good integration between RCEP and CBE. Some institutions even report the growth of ASEAN e-commerce as one of the highest in the world in 2018. This is in line with the growth of infrastructure and the utilization of ICT (Information Communication Technology) facilities in each country. The growing number of online retail (2.8%) is still far from the total retail (offline), with more than 250 million internet users; ASEAN, which has around 850 million residents, has enormous economic development potential. The constraints of weak economic and trade supporting infrastructure and facilities in each country, through digital technology, have made the economic and trade forces that had been buried become increasingly open. Digital technology has become a hope for many community groups as an opportunity to build their economic strength. This huge economic and market potential is indeed promising (IGJ, 2019).

In the era of the digital economy and the rise of CBE, the countries that participate in international trade more efficiently achieve mutual benefit. The

RCEP signed in November 2020 will build a bridge in the Asian market with huge development potential, connect the ten ASEAN countries and China, Japan, South Korea, Australia, and New Zealand, and push the Asian economy by eliminating the trade barriers and developing themselves integrally. It is clearly described in Fig. **(2)**. (Guanhui & Zengyu, 2021).

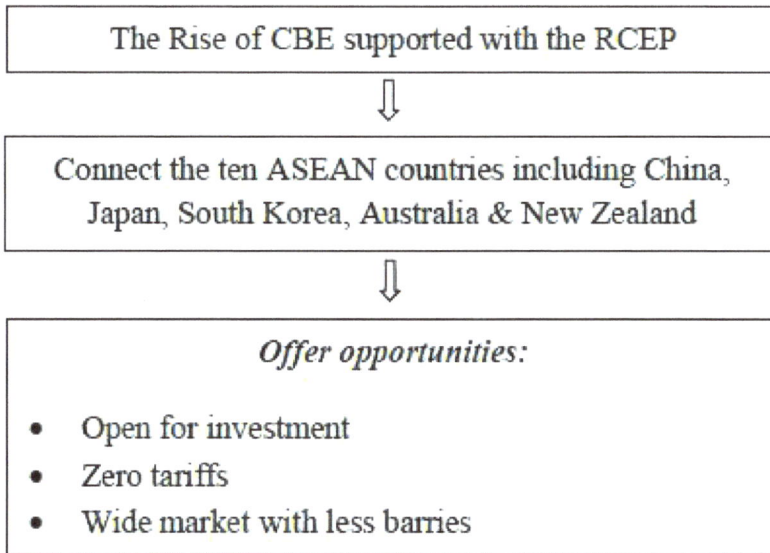

Fig. (2). The Positive Integration Between RCEP and CBE.

The Opportunities of Cross Border E-Commerce (CBE) during Covid-19

Covid-19 affects more than the trade of medical goods and essential supplies. The pandemic pushes most of the world's major economies into recession (Reuters, 2020). Advanced technology, growing demand and advantageous policies were identified as the promoting factors; meanwhile, issues about culture and consumer behavior, marketing, product, laws and regulations, payment and logistics were observed as the main barriers to its success, wherein logistics-related issues showed to be still the strongest concern to be addressed (Pitney Bowes, 2010). One of the breakthroughs that need to be a concern in terms of business and supply chain areas is the idea of the development of CBE (Ding *et al.*, 2017).

CBE is very convenient for both seller and buyer, with the usage of a mobile phone with WIFI or mobile data to access an online platform to buy or sell goods. CBE can easily access the worldwide market compared to brick-and-mortar shops (Anshari *et al.*, 2021c). Meanwhile, if divided into two aspects from the buyer and seller side, CBE could be guaranteed as the prominent model for today's daily trading, particularly during COVID-19 pandemic.

To begin with, on the buyer side, CBE is more time-saving, as the buyer has no need to queue for payment and no need to wait for change. The model can provide secure online purchase transactions with the verification and validation of credit card transactions. Moreover, the online purchasing system helps the buyer to know better about price comparison and quality of the goods from the reviews panel effortlessly (Anshari *et al.*, 2021a). More importantly, a plethora of restrictions during the outbreak could be tackled by this model, causing the buyer no need to visit or go to the shop directly. All the processes happened in the online model, and when all transactions were done, the goods would be delivered directly to the buyer's location (Fig. **3**).

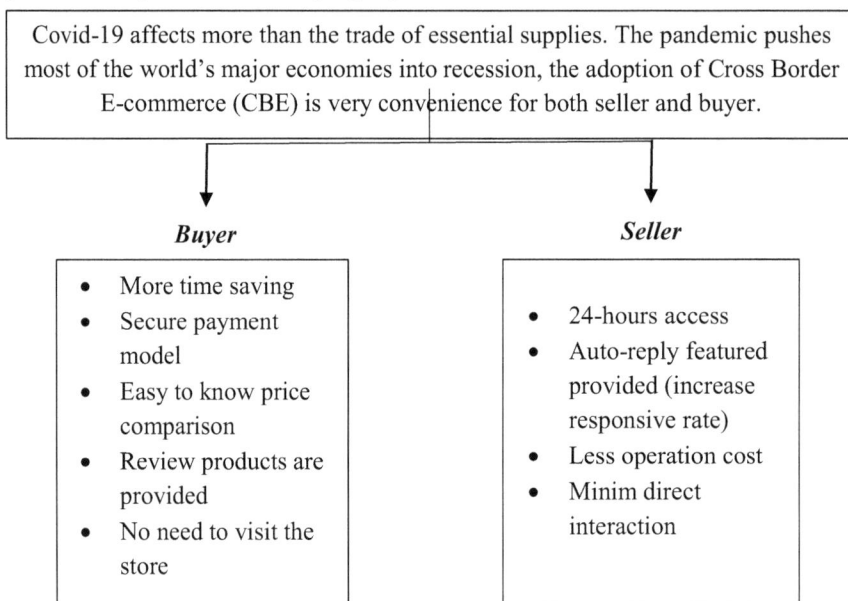

Covid-19 affects more than the trade of essential supplies. The pandemic pushes most of the world's major economies into recession, the adoption of Cross Border E-commerce (CBE) is very convenience for both seller and buyer.

Buyer

- More time saving
- Secure payment model
- Easy to know price comparison
- Review products are provided
- No need to visit the store

Seller

- 24-hours access
- Auto-reply featured provided (increase responsive rate)
- Less operation cost
- Minim direct interaction

Fig. (3). CBE opportunities for Buyer and Seller.

On the other seller side, based on Fig. **(3)**., running a physical store costs a lot of money as the owner must pay for rental fees, electrical fees, and salaries for the employees. Meanwhile, during the COVID-19 pandemic, many sellers complained about declining financial conditions (Anshari *et al.*, 2020). Hence, as the CBE model provides access and convenience for 24 hours with low operating costs, the shop is in a shape of an online store or website that only requires personnel to manage the automation and inventory management (Sugiantoro *et al.*, 2020). Also, benefit from cheap online marketing channels such as social media to spread the word of business (Anshari *et al.*, 2021a).

At the same time, CBE offers an adequate mechanism that can help domestic firms internationalize and meet the global demand for goods and services. Furthermore, CBE benefits stakeholders across the ecosystem. It allows merchants to transcend geographical boundaries to reach more markets and reduces entry barriers for small businesses (Anshari *et al.*, 2021c). CBE has also enabled many new entrepreneurs, who are able to start their own businesses easily through online market platforms or *via* social media, including segments of the population that were traditionally not participating in the formal economy, such as women. On the other hand, through CBE, consumers can easily search for, locate, and buy products that are not available in their country. Moreover, it significantly reduces distance-related trade and information costs. The components of the online infrastructure include related electronic payment systems and transmission systems, which effectively reduce the cost of international trade (Liu, 2022; Ahad & Anshari, 2017).

DISCUSSION

Different cultures and policies from different countries inevitably lead to specific consumer behavior, such as payments and goods preferences. Merchants need to consider local characteristics when designing CBE operations (Reynolds, 2001). A lack of information about the foreign market can limit business expansion. Merchants need to have the ability or the capital to develop localization strategies; cooperating with third-party service providers might be an efficient alternative. Advanced technology, growing demand and advantageous policies were identified as the promoting factors; meanwhile, issues about culture and consumer behavior, marketing, product, laws and regulations, payment and logistics were observed as the main barriers to its success, wherein logistics-related issues showed to be still the strongest concern to be addressed (Pitney Bowes, 2010). Therefore, a need for international cooperation between all involved parties - governments, merchants, and service providers as described in Fig. (**4**), are as follows (Ding *et al.*, 2017):

CBE distribution channels are risky and articulated compared to the domestic e-commerce initiative (Giuffrida *et al.*, 2020). This is due to a few factors, such as the longer distances involved, leading to longer delivery times, dependence on third-party logistics, and customs clearance challenges. Second, cross-border e-commerce entails dealing with diverse cultures, which affects logistics management (Gao & Liu, 2020). These challenges affect how CBE is managed. In the case of the huge economic gap between the ten ASEAN countries and the RCEP region, ASEAN countries like Laos, Myanmar and Cambodia should first expand the industries that can form comparative advantages over China's market, which are close to yet not homogeneous with China's market, and have trade exchanges after specializing their production respectively, to maximize the scale efficiency (Mulyani *et al.*, 2021). In addition, Brunei, a relatively developed economy, should gradually reduce its dependence on natural resources and seek sustainable and more competitive industries for mutual benefit with RCEP members.

As RCEP member countries continue to eliminate the tariff and non-tariff trade barriers and subsidies for agricultural exports, ASEAN countries will greatly support and benefit from it. It will be easy for the ASEAN to development of CBE if they can maintain the challenges excellently. The CBE adoption within the RCEP agreement related to five elements of challenges that might be prepared at the basis (Fig. **5**), such as education, internet accessibility, infrastructure capabilities (international warehouses and transshipment), digital payment system, and specific regulation (law) that supported CBE (Ding *et al.*, 2017).

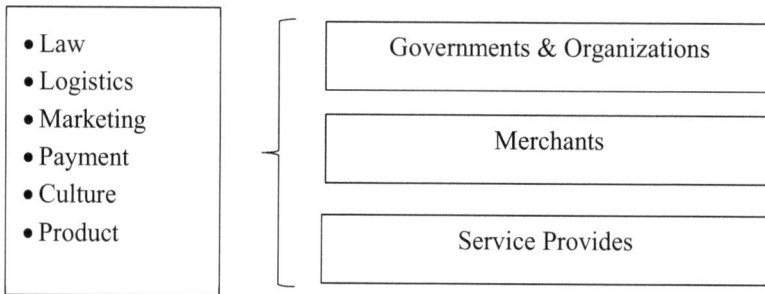

Fig. (4). A responsibility assignment for cross-border e-commerce development.

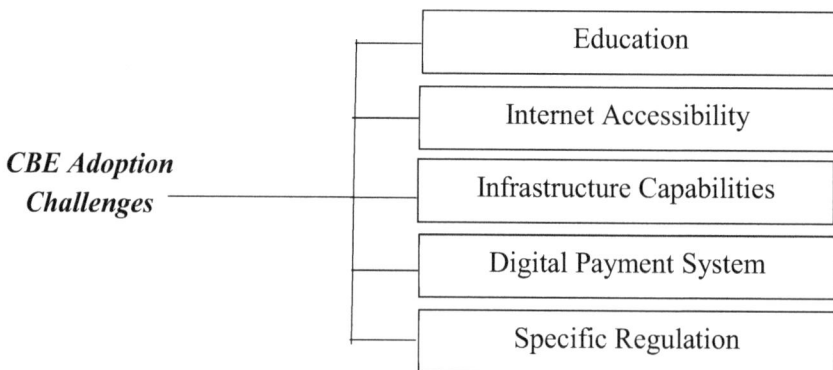

Fig. (5). Five Challenges for CBE Adoption integrating with RCEP.

The adoption of CBE with the privilege of RCEP agreement needs to also be concerned on the part of development. Developing the CBE model within this COVID-19 pandemic situation is a prominent solution. However, there are several trends of CBE development that might be a key point to consider comprising service competition, one-stop service, and Omni channel.

1. Service Challenge

The merchants/sellers should provide convenient and responsive service to reach a competitive level and buyer's loyalty (Analysys, 2015).

2. One-Stop Service

The merchants/sellers hoped to build a system that supported all at-once services, including payment processing, customer services, shipping, clearance, return processing & delivery and post-buy service (UNCTAD, 2015).

3. Omni Channel

The advanced development of multi-channel and cross-channel is where consumers can access the retailers from any platform (DHL, 2015).

On the other hand, e-business companies and platforms should offer more transparent product options and strengthen their delivery capability to help consumers save time and gain better quality products (Alas & Anshari, 2021). Moreover, related institutions should implement industry ideals and norms for material flow (Razzaq *et al.*, 2018). This would help to promote the institutionalization and standardization of the logistics industry and strengthen after-sales service, thereby enhancing the characteristics of the logistics service in e-business trade (Liu, 2022). For Asia, there are three sources of potential. First, adaptiveness – economic digitalization is a worldwide phenomenon. From the economic aspect, the information revolution is associated with the emergence of new market conditions and dynamics in the global business environment (Ahad *et al.*, 2017). This requires the Asian economy, both the public and the private sectors, to respond to those changes quickly. Second, readiness for e-commerce development needs support from technology, market, and policy (Anshari, 2020). Countries' preparation and readiness to support the digital economy will determine their business performance in e-commerce. Third, market gravitation – despite those new features of the digital economy, the development of e-commerce also depends on traditional conditions for economic development, such as market size, trade facilitation, investment freedom, and so forth (Chen, 2017).

CONCLUSION

Cross-border shopping via e-commerce is growing rapidly. Economic digitalization, mainly the improvement of cross-border e-trade, is converting the economic arena landscape. Asian nations have become concerned about this global trend. Opportunities and demanding situations come hand in hand. Fairly speaking, Asian nations are advantaged of their capability in era adoption and incremental innovation, gravitation of CBE activities. CBE could be guaranteed as the prominent model for today's daily trading, particularly during COVID-19 pandemic. Cross Border E-commerce (CBE) is very convenient for both seller and buyer, with the usage of a mobile phone with WIFI or mobile data to access an online platform to buy or sell goods. CBE can easily access the worldwide market. However, to higher hold close the possibilities for growth, CBE adoption may face several barriers in six elements: cultural & consumer, logistics, payment, law, marketing, and product (Low & Anshari, 2013). Therefore, a need for international cooperation between all involved parties, such as governments, merchants, and service providers, will improve the progress in connectivity, offerings, and regulations. Cross-Border E-commerce (CBE) requires new regulations, and Asian nations must actively participate in rule settings. In particular, the place might imagine 'soar forward' improvement in areas: Internet economic innovation and phone economy. All those measures may be greater powerful while performed withinside the local scope.

CONSENT FOR PUBLICATION

Not applicable.

CONFLICT OF INTEREST

The author declares no conflict of interest, financial or otherwise.

ACKNOWLEDGEMENTS

Declared none.

REFERENCES

Accenture. (2012). *European Cross-border E-commerce: The Challenge of Achieving Profitable Growth..* Dublin: Accenture Publications.

Ahad, A.D., Anshari, M., Razzaq, A. (2017). Domestication of smartphones among adolescents in Brunei darussalam. *International Journal of Cyber Behavior, Psychology and Learning,* 7(4), 26-39. [http://dx.doi.org/10.4018/IJCBPL.2017100103]

Ahad, A.D., Anshari, M. (2017). Smartphone habits among youth: Uses and gratification theory. *International Journal of Cyber Behavior, Psychology and Learning,* 7(1), 65-75. [http://dx.doi.org/10.4018/IJCBPL.2017010105]

Alas, Y., Anshari, M. (2021). Initiating Brunei Cross-Border Tourism (BCBT) as a Gateway to Borneo. *International Journal of Asian Business and Information Management., 12*(3), 15-25. [http://dx.doi.org/10.4018/IJABIM.20210701.oa2]

AliResearch. (2016). China Cross-border E-commerce Report. Available at http://download.dhgate.com/files/White%20Paper.pdf

Anshari, M., Almunawar, M.N., Younis, M.Z., Kisa, A. (2021). Modeling Users' Empowerment in E-Health Systems. *Sustainability (Basel), 13*(23), 12993. [http://dx.doi.org/10.3390/su132312993]

Anshari, M., Almunawar, M.N., Masri, M. (2020). Financial Technology and Disruptive Innovation in Business. *International Journal of Asian Business and Information Management, 11*(4), 29-43. [http://dx.doi.org/10.4018/IJABIM.2020100103]

Anshari, M. (2020). Workforce mapping of fourth industrial revolution: Optimization to identity. *J. Phys. Conf. Ser., 1477*(7), 072023. [http://dx.doi.org/10.1088/1742-6596/1477/7/072023]

Anshari, M., Almunawar, M.N., Razzaq, A. (2021). Developing Talents vis-à-vis Fourth Industrial Revolution. *International Journal of Asian Business and Information Management, 12*(4), 20-32. [http://dx.doi.org/10.4018/IJABIM.20211001.oa2]

Anshari, M., Almunawar, MN., Lim, S.A. (2021b). Cross-Border E-Commerce and Small Medium Enterprises (SMEs). *IGI Global: Cross-Border E-Commerce Marketing and Management.* [http://dx.doi.org/10.4018/978-1-7998-5823-2.ch012]

Anshari, M., Almunawar, M.N., Masri, M., Hrdy, M. (2021). Financial Technology with AI-Enabled and Ethical Challenges. *Society, 58*(3), 189-195. [http://dx.doi.org/10.1007/s12115-021-00592-w]

Analysys,. (2015). The research report of China's cross-border import e-commerce market. Beijing: Analysys Ltd. Publications.

Chen, L. (2017). Developing Asia in the era of cross-border e-commerce. *[Jakarta]: Economic Research Institute for ASEAN and East Asia.* https://www.econbiz.de/Record/developing-asia-in-the-era-of-cross-border-e-commerce-chen-lurong/10011871180

CNNIC. (2016). The 38th Report of China Internet Development Statistics. Available at http://www.cnnic.cn/hlwfzyj/hlwxzbg/hlwtjbg/201608/t20160803_54392.html

DHL. (2015b). *Insight on E-Commerce & Collaboration.* Brussels: DHL Publications.

Ding, F., Huo, J., Campos, J.K. (2017). The Development of Cross Border E-commerce. *Atlantis Press: Advances in Economics, Business and Management Research (AEBMR).* Volume 37 International Conference on Transformations and Innovations in Management (ICTIM-17)..

Fithriyah, M, Masri, M, Almunawar, MN, Anshari, M (2022). Financial Inclusion and Mobile Payment to Empower Small and Medium-Sized Enterprises: Post-COVID-19 Business Strategy. *IGI Global: FinTech Development for Financial Inclusiveness.* [http://dx.doi.org/10.4018/978-1-7998-8447-7.ch004]

Gao, P., Liu, Y. (2020). Endogenous inclusive development of e-commerce in rural China: A case study. *Growth Change, 51*(4), 1611-1630. [http://dx.doi.org/10.1111/grow.12436]

Giuffrida, M., Mangiaracina, R., Perego, A., Tumino, A. (2019). Cross-border B2C e-commerce to China. *Int. J. Phys. Distrib. Logist. Manag., 50*(3), 355-378. [http://dx.doi.org/10.1108/IJPDLM-08-2018-0311]

Guanhui, W., Zengyu, C. (2021). *An Empirical Study on the Trade Impact of Cross border Ecommerce on ASEAN and China under the Framework of RECP.* EDP Science.

[http://dx.doi.org/10.1051/e3sconf/202127501039]

Hamdan, M., Chen, C.K., Anshari, M. (2020). Decision Aid in Budgeting Systems for Small & Medium Enterprises. *2020 International Conference on Decision Aid Sciences and Application (DASA)* IEEE. [http://dx.doi.org/10.1109/DASA51403.2020.9317018]

Hu, Y.C., Chiu, Y.J., Hsu, C.S., Chang, Y.Y. (2015). Identifying Key Factors for Introducing GPS-Based Fleet Management Systems to the Logistics Industry. *Math. Probl. Eng., 2015*, 1-14. [http://dx.doi.org/10.1155/2015/413203]

IGJ. (2019). *E-Commerce Issues in RCEP.* Available at https://igj.or.id/wp-content/uploads/2019/02/IG--Position-Paper-E-Commerce-in-RCEP.pdf

Low, K.C.P., Anshari, M. (2013). Incorporating social customer relationship management in negotiation. *Int. J. Electron. Cust. Relatsh. Manag., 7*(3/4), 239-252. [http://dx.doi.org/10.1504/IJECRM.2013.060700]

Liu, X., Chen, D., Cai, J. (2015). The Operation of the Cross-Border e-commerce Logistics in China. *International Journal of Intelligent Information Systems, 4*(2), 15-18.

Liu, A., Osewe, M., Shi, Y., Zhen, X., Wu, Y. (2021). Cross-Border E-Commerce Development and Challenges in China: A Systematic Literature Review. *J. Theor. Appl. Electron. Commer. Res., 17*(1), 69-88. [http://dx.doi.org/10.3390/jtaer17010004]

Mulyani, M.A., Razzaq, A., Sumardi, W.H., Anshari, M. (2019). Smartphone Adoption in Mobile Learning Scenario. *2019 International Conference on Information Management and Technology (ICIMTech)* IEEE. [http://dx.doi.org/10.1109/ICIMTech.2019.8843755]

Mulyani, M.A., Yusuf, S., Siregar, P., Nurihsan, J., Razzaq, A., Anshari, M. (2021). Fourth Industrial Revolution and Educational Challenges. *2021 International Conference on Information Management and Technology (ICIMTech)* IEEE. [http://dx.doi.org/10.1109/ICIMTech53080.2021.9535057]

(2010). *Time to Get Serious About Cross-Border Ecommerce..* Stamford: Pitney Bowes Publications.

Razzaq, A., Samiha, Y.T., Anshari, M. (2018). Smartphone habits and behaviors in supporting students self-efficacy. *International Journal of Emerging Technologies in Learning (iJET), 13*(2), 94. [http://dx.doi.org/10.3991/ijet.v13i02.7685]

Reuters. (2020). RCEP Trade Pact on Track for 2020 Signing: Ministers. Online Retrieved from https://www.reuters.com

Reynolds, J. (2001). *Logistics and Fulfillment for E-Business.* (1st ed.). New York: CRC Press. [http://dx.doi.org/10.1201/9781482295566]

Samiee, S. (2008). Global marketing effectiveness *via* alliances and electronic commerce in business-to-business markets. *Ind. Mark. Manage., 37*(1), 3-8. [http://dx.doi.org/10.1016/j.indmarman.2007.09.003]

Swasdee, A., Anshari, M., Hamdan, M. (2020). Artificial Intelligence as Decision Aid in Humanitarian Response. *2020 International Conference on Decision Aid Sciences and Application (DASA)* IEEE. [http://dx.doi.org/10.1109/DASA51403.2020.9317111]

Sugiantoro, B., Anshari, M., Sudrajat, D. (2020). Developing Framework for Web Based e-Commerce: Secure-SDLC. *Journal of Physics: Conference Series., 1566*(1), 012020. [http://dx.doi.org/10.1088/1742-6596/1566/1/012020]

Tarn, J.M., Razi, M.A., Wen, H.J., Perez, A.A., Jr (2003). E-fulfillment: the strategy and operational requirements. *Logist. Inf. Manag., 16*(5), 350-362. [http://dx.doi.org/10.1108/09576050310499345]

Think with Google. (2017). *E-economy SEA Unlocking the 200 billion digital opportunity in Southeast Asia.* http://apac.thinkwithgoogle.com/research-studies/e-conomysea-unlocking-200b-digital-opportunity.html

Terzi, N. (2011). The impact of e-commerce on international trade and employment. *Procedia Soc. Behav. Sci., 24*, 745-753.
[http://dx.doi.org/10.1016/j.sbspro.2011.09.010]

(2015). *Information Economy Report 2015: Unlocking the Potential of E-commerce in Developing Countries..* New York: UNCTAD Publications.

Wang, J. (2014). Opportunities and Challenges of International e-Commerce in the Pilot Areas of China. *International Journal of Marketing Studies, 6*(6), 141-149.
[http://dx.doi.org/10.5539/ijms.v6n6p141]

Youngdahl, W.E., Loomba, A.P.S. (2000). Service-driven global supply chains. *Int. J. Serv. Ind. Manage., 11*(4), 329-347.
[http://dx.doi.org/10.1108/09564230010355368]

Economic Integration's Impact on Regional Comprehensive Economic Partnership

Emil Ali[1,*] and **Muhammad Anshari**[1]

[1] *Universiti Brunei Darussalam, Institute of Policy Studies, Brunei Darussalam*

Abstract: In this digital era, the economic sector has been transformed while gearing towards increased digitisation. In part, this has led to innovation, growth, and enhanced competitiveness, further leading to economic development. As a result, ASEAN countries have been pursuing adapting this change towards the digital era to prepare new technological advances that can create opportunities for development, including addressing possible threats. This chapter examines how the Regional Comprehensive Economic Partnership (RCEP) affects the commercial and economic activities of RCEP member countries, including supply chain management (SCM), tariff reductions on trade, customs duty reductions, market expansion, and the likelihood of obtaining economies of scale in manufacturing. We adopted a qualitative method approach, which involved reviewing current literature and interpreting them in order to make possible recommendations. The findings indicate that the Regional Comprehensive Economic Partnership will significantly impact industries in the Asia-Pacific region, such as textile and apparel supply chain integration, and that this will provide a significant opportunity for member countries to improve their economic conditions further. Additionally, improving the SCM leads to an increase in GDP, enabling many countries to achieve a favourable balance of trade and encouraging them to pursue innovation. The implementation of the RCEP agreement also has its challenges and needs to be addressed in order to make the adoption of RCEP a success.

Keyword: Asia-Pacific, Gross Domestic Product (GDP), Regional Comprehensive Economic Partnership (RCEP), Supply Chain Management (SCM).

INTRODUCTION

The Regional Comprehensive Economic Partnership (RCEP) accord has been established in order to strengthen the ties between the member countries of the Association of Southeast Asian Nations (ASEAN) and the other Asia Pacific countries. The RCEP consists of the following members: Australia, Brunei, Cam-

---

* **Corresponding author Emil Ali:** Universiti Brunei Darussalam, Institute of Policy Studies, Brunei Darussalam;
E-mail: emil.ali@ubd.edu.bn

Mahani Hamdan, Muhammad Anshari and Norainie Ahmad (Eds.)

bodia, China, Laos, Malaysia, Indonesia, Japan, Myanmar, New Zealand, the Philippines, Singapore, Thailand, the Republic of Korea, and Vietnam. India was originally part of the RCEP negotiating country but withdrew itself in 2019 because of concerns pertaining to the interest of its domestic industries and, ultimately, its national interests. One of the primary objectives of this grouping is to achieve advancement and development of high-quality business relationships among its partners in order to better their economic conditions (ASEAN, 2020).

The digitisation of the economy is currently accelerating all over the world, and it has emerged as the primary catalyst for driving the economy towards innovation, growth and enhanced competitiveness. Digital technologies such as cloud computing and social media, among others, have transformed the nature of people's everyday lives, the business environment, and a wide range of industries. Along with the billions of internet users, individuals or enterprises who are not connected to the internet are shut out of the market, making it vital for these diverse parties to adapt to technological innovation (Digital Birmingham, 2016). As a result, ASEAN countries have been proactive in adapting to this rapidly changing era of digitalisation in order to be prepared for new technological innovations, products, and services that will offer new opportunities and identify potential challenges. With the RCEP, ASEAN countries will be in a better position to adapt to digital industrialisation through the use of information, communication, and technology (ICT), as they will have international and regional regulations to facilitate this economic revolution and develop efficient strategies to further stimulate and enhance economic growth.

RCEP has notably addressed electronic commerce (e-commerce) as one of the essential components that member countries wish to develop further. This includes some cooperative commitments, such as assisting small and medium-sized enterprises (SMEs) in overcoming the challenges of using e-commerce platforms (Hamdan *et al.*, 2020), encouraging good business practices in order to gain the trust of customers, and enhancing sectors for research, training, and technical assistance, among other initiatives (Price, 2020). As a result, the RCEP has opened the door to new opportunities for e-commerce companies and start-ups, as the agreement provides a number of benefits, including tariff reductions, customs clearance, and the convenience of reaping profits from online payments made by customers. According to the co-founder of Jollybuyer, a clothing start-up based in Hangzhou, RCEP will be extremely beneficial to cross-border industries in terms of facilitating paperless trading, cashless payments, and virtual customer data protection, which includes e-signature authentication and personal information protection, all of which are in accordance with Chapter 12 of the trade agreement (Dan, 2020). RCEP has made it easier for e-businesses to grow their markets and expand their footprints throughout Southeast Asia, which is extremely advantageous for supply chain and logistics service providers (Swasdee *et al.*, 2020).

In addition, RCEP will contribute significantly to many parts of the trading process, including information exchange, reaching new markets, and increasing supply and logistics chains. This chapter will detail how the RCEP impacts global supply chain management, including how beneficial it is for the member countries, but also identifying possible problems. The next section will review the extant literature, with a focus on the current state of supply chain management in various countries. The findings from the literature review are then discussed and finally concluded by presenting the key points from the research.

LITERATURE REVIEW

RCEP represents the Regional Comprehensive Economic Partnership, a proposed agreement between the member states of the Association of Southeast Asian Nations, ASEAN, and its free trade agreement partners (FTA). It was introduced during the 19th ASEAN meeting held in November 2011, and its negotiations started during the 21st ASEAN summit in Cambodia in November 2012. Sixteen countries were involved as the member states of ASEAN and their free trade agreement partners, which include Brunei, Cambodia, Indonesia, Laos, Malaysia, Myanmar, the Philippines, Singapore, Thailand, Vietnam, China, Japan, South Korea, Australia and New Zealand. This partnership aims to create an integrated market within the 16 countries to make the products and services of its member countries easily accessible and available across the region.

The purpose of the RCEP agreement is to form a modern, comprehensive, high-quality and mutually beneficial economic partnership in order to assist in the expansion of the regional trades in goods, services, and investment as well as contribute to global economic growth and development. Moreover, RCEP negotiations also focused on intellectual property, dispute settlement, e-commerce and small and medium enterprises (ASEAN, 2020). This would create opportunities to market and open employment positions to businesses and people within the region. One of the appeals to the contemporary RCEP agreement is that it is created to be future-proof, allowing it not only to be used today but also in the future. The RCEP agreement also helps update the existing ASEAN plus one FTAs and considers the changing and emerging trade realities, including the age of electronic commerce, the difficulties in market competition and the potential of small enterprises. Another purpose of the RCEP agreement is that it is comprehensive in terms of coverage and depth of commitments. The RCEP agreement has 20 chapters in its coverage which also includes any section that has not been covered in the ASEAN plus one FTAs. The RCEP agreement has specific provisions, such as trade in goods and services, investment, legal and institutional areas, as well as market accessibility. Besides that, the RCEP agreement is also considered to be of high quality in terms of providing areas beyond the existing ASEAN plus one FTAs. It recognises the individual and the differences in the level of development as well as the economic needs of the RCEP parties. It strives to encourage healthy competition that can further enhance productivity, sustainability, responsibility and constructiveness. The RCEP agreement brings mutual benefits for each country involved as it creates a level playing field for RCEP member countries with diverse levels of development to be in sync together.

Why is RCEP Important?

RCEP helps to strengthen the relationships between the member countries in trading and investment, mostly through the reduction of non-tariff barriers on goods and services. This provides more certainty for traders and investors as it helps to harmonise the provisions imposed by countries on trade in goods. RCEP agreements align rules of origin for all members to facilitate the integration of the RCEP participants into the same production chain. Therefore, this could expand their share of global value chains (GVCs), which refers to international production sharing (Cali, 2020). RCEP is also considered important, especially because the ten members of the ASEAN countries and the five major trading partners constitute around 30 percent of the global Gross Domestic Product (GDP) as well as its population., thus making RCEP the largest free trade agreement. According to the Peterson Institute for International Economics (as cited in Iwamoto, 2021), it is estimated that RCEP's deal could make up to $500 billion of world exports in 2030. It will also be the first FTA between the Asian economic powerhouses of Japan, China and South Korea. Accordingly, as the US-China prolongs its trade disputes and COVID-19 continuously puts pressure on the company's global chain, RCEP can give a significant boost for the companies in recovering from the current economic situation through deepening of trade relations (Anshari *et al.*, 2021a).

RCEP and Supply Chain

RCEP does have an effect on supply chain management (SCM) because the agreement affects the global supply chain. This indicates that the implementation of RCEP, which is led by ASEAN, became advantageous to the supply chain management for the member countries and helped to strengthen their global supply chains by reducing tariffs on trade (Ahad *et al.*, 2017). The positive impact of RCEP on Supply Chain Management (SCM) demonstrates that it is a successful ASEAN design and implementation that focuses on a Free Trade

Agreement (FTA) while also enhancing the country's supply chain (Alas & Anshari, 2021). With this research, we may better understand how RCEP contributes to the improvement of Supply Chain Management. According to Mahadevan and Nugroho (2019), Korea has had a higher percentage of GDP growth than the other members of RCEP, due to the fact that Korea has experienced the greatest drop in tariffs among the other members of the RCEP. Tariff reductions enable economies to purchase low-cost commodities, intermediate inputs, and, most importantly, production, resulting in increased economic growth recognition (Mulyani *et al.*, 2021). For example, Singapore's initial tariffs were historically zero for virtually all commodities, making it a model for other countries. As a result, it should come as no surprise that Singapore has had virtually no impact. Increased market size and significant economies of scale in terms of production are achieved by other economies participating in the RCEP, as reflected in a reduction in tariffs. With regards to its specific function, the RCEP will assist in the organisation of advanced global supply chains that will assist Asia in becoming the world's factory (Kawai & Wignaraja, 2014, as cited in Mahadevan & Nugroho, 2019).

Apart from that, Dey (2020) asserted that if each country is able to create just two key supply chain hurdles, the GDP of that country will increase. Communication infrastructure and related services, as well as border administration and transportation, are included. When countries are able to work together on this, the global GDP could potentially expand by US$2.6 trillion (4.7 percent), and exports might potentially increase by US$ 1.6 trillion (14.5 percent). In comparison, if tariffs are completely eliminated, the world economy's GDP would grow by US$ 0.4 trillion (0.7 percent), and exports would grow by US$ 1.1 trillion (0.7 percent) (10.1 percent).

According to Mahadevan and Nugroho (2019), practically every RCEP country experiences growth in both imports and exports, indicating the existence of trade creation impacts. Regarding the influence on trade, both Singapore and China have a positive trade balance to their credit. For Singapore, this is primarily due to the fact that, even prior to the RCEP, the country had a very low tariff, to begin with. As for China, this is likely the case because they are one of the world's greatest exporters and possess a significant portion of the country. Every other RCEP country, on the other hand, has a negative trade balance, which means that their imports outweigh their exports. Due to the low tariffs within the RCEP, it is expected that imports will increase among RCEP member countries as a result of imports being diverted away from non-RCEP member nations. As a result, tariff reductions under RCEP aid in the organisation of global supply chains, and countries are able to obtain low-cost commodities.

Methodology

This study adopted the Systematic Literature Review (SLR) approach developed by Tranfield *et al.* (2003) to analyze the potential and challenges to the Regional Comprehensive Economic Partnership. The initial part of this study consisted of exploring electronic databases for pertinent data. The most recent studies, spanning the years 2011 through 2021, were chosen for consideration. Academic Source Premier was one of the databases used in the research. The reason for selecting such time periods was to ensure that the most recent data was used and that the most relevant information was available in relation to the study. As the primary purpose of this research was to investigate the impact of economic integration on RCEP, it was chosen to look for patterns, trends, similarities, and contrasts in the important domains of discussion in order to accomplish this goal.

DISCUSSION

Many researchers attempted to determine the potential economic impact of the RCEP on the economy. Many of these studies indicate that the implementation of the RCEP would strengthen the overall economic security of its members and promote economic integration in the Asia-Pacific region. However, because of variances in study design and data sources, many researchers were unable to reach a consensus on who could benefit from and who might suffer from the agreement. Despite the optimistic findings, only a few researchers have looked into RCEP's impact on the economy. The majority of recent research suggests that implementing a large free trade agreement such as RCEP will have a considerable impact on the trading practices of associated countries and regional economic integration.

The findings indicate that RCEP will result in a more streamlined supply chain in order for the RCEP to be implemented. For instance, in the textile industry, assuming that all other variables remain constant after the agreement is implemented, as much as 78.5 percent of RCEP members' textile imports determined by value will originate from within the RCEP region, up from 70.0 percent in 2015. RCEP will help to enhance the positions of Japanese, South Korean, and Chinese textile and clothing suppliers while also expanding the roles of ASEAN and China as key garment makers. The second finding indicates that, as a trading bloc, the RCEP would make it significantly more difficult for non-RCEP members to engage in the Asia-Pacific regional transportation and logistics supply chain. There are minimal options for RCEP members to engage with manufacturers from outside the region because a complete regional supply chain already exists in the Asia-Pacific region, which also includes the factor of time to market (Ahad & Anshari, 2017).

Zhang (2021) examined the influence of the RCEP on the EU-Asia Supply Chain. From one point of view, European organisations that have established intra-Asian supply chains or Asian auxiliaries can profit from a reduction in costs as a result of the blended Rule of Origin and lower taxes throughout the RCEP countries. This is especially true for European businesses that have a well-established store network in Asia, such as those in the automobile, electrical device, and material industries. According to Adidas, the Asia-Pacific region accounted for 69 percent of its suppliers in 2019. However, according to estimates from the Peterson Institute for International Economics, the EU will see a modest 0.1 percent rise in global GDP as a result of the RCEP by 2030. On the other hand, EU-produced items may face a greater risk of losing their significance in markets where intra-Asian inventory chains are well-established. As an illustration in the automobile industry, despite the fact that the EU continues to be China's largest export market, in this sector, the proportion of RCEP suppliers has been growing over time, notably among those in Southeast Asian countries. Southeast Asia's car manufacturing center has significantly increased in value terms over the course of the most recent five years by more than a factor of ten. This is mostly due to the relocation of Japanese automobile manufacturing to Thailand, which includes the production of hybrid and electric vehicles (Anshari, 2020). The cost of car manufacturing will be reduced as a result of the elimination of taxes on auto parts entering ASEAN countries and the removal of non-tax impediments to the production of automobiles through an intra-Asian manufacturing network. There is no doubt that the RCEP will aid the intra-Asian carrying effort. According to a Dynamar analysis, an additional 2.2 million will be created in intra-Asia compartment dispatching by 2030, accounting for 5.2 percent of 2019's intra-Asia holder delivering volumes, and by over 2 percent, or 3.3 million TEUs, globally by 2030.

The influence of the RCEP on the inventory network, in particular, on the Asia-Europe exchange line, could contribute to the generally diverted delivering streams eastward and westward that already exist. Those places that are well on their way to being influenced also include a significant portion of the eastward delivery infrastructure (Mulyani *et al.*, 2019). Taking the material sector as an example, research conducted in 2018 estimated that the implementation of the RCEP might reduce the EU and the United States' offers in signatory countries from 9.5 percent (in 2015) to 6.5 percent (in 2018). However, in an interview with Vogue Business, the president of the European Textile and Apparel Confederation expressed optimism that the RCEP would actually increase demand for high-quality European textiles and new materials, which would more than make up for any losses incurred as a result of the RCEP.

RCEP's Potentials

When RCEP was officially signed in late 2020 between China, Japan, South Korea, Australia, New Zealand and ASEAN-10, it was estimated to bring lots of potential benefits to its member countries. Kuo (2020) stated that this agreement is considered a big deal, which will lessen the economic obstacles among member countries that accounted for 30 percent of the world's population and production in terms of (1) countries' capital income gains, (2) demands manufacturing industries, (3) exporting commodities items and (4) increasing in investment and service trade opportunities (Wolf *et al.*, 2020). Cali (2020) mentioned that RCEP would deepen the relationship among RCEP members' countries through the reduction in non-tariff barriers on goods and services trade rather than import tariffs as it is relatively low due to the results of global unilateral tariff liberalisation trade agreement among its members such as ASEAN-China FTA, AUS-NZ FTA, China-AUS FTA and Japan-Korea FTA.

In terms of capital income gains, Kang *et al.* (2020), in their publication article, stated that RCEP members are projected to gain real income of $174 billion by 2030, which is equivalent to 0.4 percent of cumulative GDP with Cali (2020) estimating that China GDP will increase by 0.3 percent while ASEAN member countries received 0.2 percent. On the other hand, Wolf *et al.* (2020) stated that the largest estimated income gain would go to China with $85 billion, Japan with $48 billion and South Korea with $23 billion, respectively. According to Kang *et al.* (2020), the countries having such a high rise in income is due to their sheer economic size and comparative advantage in higher-end, richer value-added segments from their industrial production. In addition, Kang *et al.* (2020) stated that other significant RCEP gains would go to Indonesia, Malaysia, Thailand and Vietnam.

From the manufacturing industries' perspective, electronics, industrial machines and autos are seen to be the biggest winners from RCEP, according to Wolf *et al.* (2020), as although previously ASIA had signed with several FTA, there is no trade agreement linking China, Japan and South Korea together. By extending the coverage, it helps to enhance regional manufacturing supply chains, particularly in the technology value chain that eventually positions Japan and South Korea at the top, followed by China and ASEAN in the range of middle to lower position. Thus, the RCEP is advantageous not only to the more developed nations but also to the less developed ones among the ASEAN member countries. The agreement allows the less developed nations to hasten industrialisation within their state by enhancing their ability to participate in regional industrial chains.

According to the New Zealand Ministry of Foreign Affairs and Trade (n.d.), even though RCEP does not have a significant impact on the country's exports due to the existing FTA they signed with current RCEP member countries, the country did benefit from RCEP's additional tariff elimination on quite a number of New Zealand food products exported to Indonesia, specifically their poultry meat, fish product, dairy milk product and some of its originated fruits. This is agreed by Taunton and Sommerville (2020) as New Zealand reported having exported $36 billion of goods to fellow RCEP member countries. Moreover, Wolf *et al.* (2020) stated that the key draw of the RCEP agreement is due to China's consumer market, as the country has a trade deficit specifically in their commodities items such as consumer electronics, cosmetics, and food and beverages, which they purchase from RCEP member countries like Australia, Korea, Japan, Malaysia and New Zealand.

Last but not least, according to Wolf *et al.* (2020), RCEP has a key promise for investment and service trade liberalisation, particularly to countries like Japan, Korea, Australia and other four member countries that are using 'negative list' for service trade, or in other words, trade is not restricted unless otherwise stated. This is agreeable by the Australian Government (2020) as it will boost the country's trade in services, especially in terms of education, health, engineering, finance and professional services, as well as deliver greater investment certainty to Australian farmers as RCEP agreed to rules of origin that will eventually help suppliers' contribution to regional production chains (Anshari *et al.*, 2020).

GAPS & CHALLENGES IN RCEP

The RCEP can prove to be a beneficial bridge for all joining members in having an FTA that will strengthen the import and export of each participating country, thus boosting the economy. The establishment and implementation of RCEP was not a walk in the park; where it took several rounds of negotiations over the past eight years before the participating countries could reach a common ground. However, RCEP has several limitations that may not be beneficial for all parties involved, such as local small businesses and the labour sector in countries that have signed the RCEP agreement.

Reduction in Tariffs

The agreement involves the application of national status in the trading of Chinese goods, which means tariffs would be reduced in participating countries, with a lower cost of goods made in China. Other countries would need to keep up with the prices and profits of their local competitors. For example, producers in Vietnam would be forced to compete with China's larger and more established supply chain in order to stay afloat in the industry (Jacob, 2020).

Reduction of tariffs on Chinese goods also means that other countries have a direct rivalry with China's export of goods. For example, if China commences the export of goods to Japan, it will immediately position itself to be a huge competitor to Vietnam's export market that also sells its goods to Japan. This new competition will be a challenge to some exporters in setting prices that can be on the same level as the dominant competitor (Jacob, 2020).

RCEP can potentially provide developed countries with the upper hand over developing countries. Under the agreement, foreign companies might influence amending domestic labour laws set by the government of developing countries as the government would be restricted in regulating these policies. Adil Shariff, the appointed general secretary of the Indian National Municipal and Local Bodies Workers Federation, stated the implications of RCEP, explaining how foreign investors can alter laws, such as minimum wage to cover the increase in operational costs (Jitendra, 2017).

The reduction of tariffs also allows well-established companies to expand to other countries, which may stifle the growth of smaller or less-established domestic companies. In addition, reducing or even removing tariffs allows established companies the advantage of importing countries from countries with a lower cost of living, making it difficult for smaller, less-established companies to compete with the larger ones (Low & Anshari, 2013).

Governments that rely on revenues from tariffs will be heavily affected especially smaller economies (Anshari *et al.*, 2021b). These smaller countries may struggle to replace the income and revenue earned from the imports and exports tariffs and fees.

Global Value Chain

The General Secretary of the New Trade Union Initiative (NTUI), Gautam Mody, stated that the increase in the global value chain comes with the reduction of wages, workers layoffs, and more labour exploitation, as global value chains feed on job inconsistency and minimal social protection measures in order to reap profits for larger companies. Therefore, RCEP does not pay enough attention to the growth of technology in developing countries, subsequently affecting the employment sustainability of employment in developing countries (Jitendra, 2017).

Lack of Acknowledgements for Relative Issues

The foundation of RCEP was the already existing members of bilateral FTAs. However, with the elimination of 90 percent on tariffs, RCEP has lower coverage of trade imports and has no set regulations for participating countries in areas such as intellectual property, labour, competition policy and internet oversight. Many developing countries do not have well-established laws to protect patents and inventions, and to a certain extent, those that do have the laws do not necessarily enforce them. This can be detrimental to businesses where foreign companies may adopt and steal other businesses' ideas and get away with them easily without proper protection. Furthermore, negotiations touch upon traditional issues but less on new rules formation. An example would be excluding environmental issues (Hong, 2020).

India's Withdrawal from RCEP

Due to divided opinions within the policies laid out, India has refused to partake in this agreement and eventually withdrew from RCEP. This means RCEP's influence would be reduced, as India has an emerging economy and a strong labour force that MNCs are vying for. The absence of India in this trade agreement means that RCEP would not be able to accomplish its goal of changing the rules of the global economy and trade for members by pushing regional economic integration (Hong, 2020).

Limitations on Market Access for the Service Industry

Hong (2020) stated that RCEP is less open in market access for the services trade and industrial investments. In 2016, when RCEP negotiations were still ongoing, India had pressed for market access for the services sector. The country has raised the issue and wishes for a better and more convenient Visa movement in RCEP countries. However, most participating members were against the idea, which ultimately resulted in India's withdrawal from the agreement (The Economic Times, 2016).

Data Protection for All

Finally, all participating countries will be bound to the consensus on data privacy and security. Data flows supporting cross-border digital trade under the RCEP agreement must be carefully tailored to the evolving needs and possibilities associated with the value of cross-border data flows in order to maximise potential benefits while ensuring that sensitive data at the individual, organisational, and country level is not breached by privacy and security regulations.

CONCLUSION

In conclusion, the RCEP contributes to strengthening member countries' commercial and investment partnerships primarily through eliminating non-tariff barriers to products and services. This gives greater clarity for traders and investors by assisting in the harmonisation of national rules governing the trade of products. RCEP agreements harmonise origin regulations for all members in order to enable the integration of RCEP participants into the same supply chain. As a result, this could increase their part in global value chains (GVCs), a term that refers to the international sharing of production. RCEP is also regarded as significant, particularly because it involves ten ASEAN nations and five key economic partners.

CONSENT FOR PUBLICATION

Not applicable.

CONFLICT OF INTEREST

The author declares no conflict of interest, financial or otherwise.

ACKNOWLEDGEMENTS

Declared none.

REFERENCES

Ahad, A.D., Anshari, M. (2017). Smartphone habits among youth: Uses and gratification theory. *International Journal of Cyber Behavior, Psychology and Learning,* 7(1), 65-75. [http://dx.doi.org/10.4018/IJCBPL.2017010105]

Ahad, A.D., Anshari, M., Razzaq, A. (2017). Domestication of smartphones among adolescents in Brunei darussalam. *International Journal of Cyber Behavior, Psychology and Learning,* 7(4), 26-39. [http://dx.doi.org/10.4018/IJCBPL.2017100103]

Alas, Y., Anshari, M. (2021). Initiating Brunei Cross-Border Tourism (BCBT) as a Gateway to Borneo. *International Journal of Asian Business and Information Management,* 12(3), 15-25. [http://dx.doi.org/10.4018/IJABIM.20210701.oa2]

Anshari, M., Almunawar, M.N., Masri, M. (2020). Financial Technology and Disruptive Innovation in Business. *International Journal of Asian Business and Information Management,* 11(4), 29-43. [http://dx.doi.org/10.4018/IJABIM.2020100103]

Anshari, M., Almunawar, M.N., Younis, M.Z., Kisa, A. (2021). Modeling Users' Empowerment in E-Health Systems. *Sustainability (Basel),* 13(23), 12993. [http://dx.doi.org/10.3390/su132312993]

Anshari, M., Almunawar, M.N., Razzaq, A. (2021). Developing Talents vis-à-vis Fourth Industrial Revolution. *International Journal of Asian Business and Information Management,* 12(4), 20-32. [http://dx.doi.org/10.4018/IJABIM.20211001.oa2]

Anshari, M. (2020). Workforce mapping of fourth industrial revolution: Optimization to identity. *J. Phys. Conf. Ser.,* 1477(7), 072023. [http://dx.doi.org/10.1088/1742-6596/1477/7/072023]

ASEAN ORG. (2020). *Summary of The Regional Comprehensive Partnership Agreement.*https://asean.org/storage/2020/11/Summary-of-the-RCEP-Agreement.pdf

Australian Government. (2020). *Australia signs world's largest free trade agreement.* Austrade https://www.austrade.gov.au/News/Latest-from-Austrade/2020-Latest-from-Austrade/australia-signs-worlds-largest-free--rade-agreement#:%7E:text=RCEP%20benefits%20for%20Australian%20businesses&text=liberalised%20trade%20in%20services,of%20rules%20on%20intellectual%20property

Cali, M. (2020). *The significance of the Regional Economic Partnership Agreement.* Brookings. https://www.brookings.edu/blog/future-development/2020/11/20/the-significance-of-the-regional-economic-partnership-agreement/

Dan, Z. (2020). Global Times. RCEP's boost to e-commerce. Retrieved March 16, 2021, from https://www.globaltimes.cn/content/1207145.shtml

Dey, D. (2020). Supply chain Management (SCM) and Recession Recovery. *Supply Chain and Logistics Management,* 1033-1052.
[http://dx.doi.org/10.4018/978-1-7998-0945-6.ch048]

Digital Birmingham. (2016). *The importance of the digital economy.* Retrieved March, 2021, from http://digitalbirmingham.co.uk/blog/2016/09/07/the-importance-of-the-digital-economy/

Hamdan, M., Chen, C.K., Anshari, M. (2020). Decision Aid in Budgeting Systems for Small & Medium Enterprises. *2020 International Conference on Decision Aid Sciences and Application (DASA),* 253-257. IEEE.
[http://dx.doi.org/10.1109/DASA51403.2020.9317018]

Hong, Y. (2020). *RCEP: The benefits, the regret and the limitations. ThinkChina - Big Reads, Opinion & Columns on China.* .https://www.thinkchina.sg/rcep-benefits-regret-and-limitations

Iwamoto, K. (2021). China to gain as trade pact ripples across post-COVID world. Retrieved from https://asia.nikkei.com/Spotlight/Asia-Insight/RCEP-China-to-gain-as-trade-pact-ripples-across-post-COVID-world

Mahadevan, R., Nugroho, A. (2019). Can the Regional Comprehensive Economic Partnership minimise the harm from the United States–China trade war? *World Econ., 42*(11), 3148-3167.
[http://dx.doi.org/10.1111/twec.12851]

Jacob, S. (2020). *Vietnam in the RCEP.* https://www.lexology.com/library/detail.aspx?g=881e38bc-e811-4c6c-ac89-a6bf3fbc401f

Jitendra. (2020). RCEP will hurt local industry and allow workers' exploitation, says civil society. Down To Earth https://www.downtoearth.org.in/news/economy/rcep-will-hurt-local-industry-and-allow-workers-exploitation-says-civil-society-57814

Kang, J. W., Crivelli, P., Tayag, M. C., Ramizo, D. (2020). Regional Comprehensive Economic Partnership: Overview and Economic Impact. *Regional Comprehensive Economic Partnership: Overview and Economic Impact,* 1-8.
[http://dx.doi.org/10.22617/BRF200422-2]

Kuo, M.A. (2020). *RCEP: The Future of Trade in Asia.* The Diplomat https://thediplomat.com/2020/12/rcep-the-future-of-trade-in-asia/

Low, K.C.P., Anshari, M. (2013). Incorporating social customer relationship management in negotiation. *Int. J. Electron. Cust. Relatsh. Manag., 7*(3/4), 239-252.
[http://dx.doi.org/10.1504/IJECRM.2013.060700]

Price, T. (2020). *RCEP Asia-Pacific Trade Deal a Boost to Cross-Border eCommerce.* Retrieved March 16, 2021, from https://www.tmogroup.asia/rcep-asia-pacific-trade-deal-cross-border-ecommerce/

Mulyani, M.A., Razzaq, A., Sumardi, W.H., Anshari, M. (2019). Smartphone Adoption in Mobile Learning Scenario. *2019 International Conference on Information Management and Technology (ICIMTech), 1,* 208-211. IEEE.

[http://dx.doi.org/10.1109/ICIMTech.2019.8843755]

Mulyani, M.A., Yusuf, S., Siregar, P., Nurihsan, J., Razzaq, A., Anshari, M. (2021). Fourth Industrial Revolution and Educational Challenges. *2021 International Conference on Information Management and Technology (ICIMTech), Vol. 1*, 245-249. IEEE.
[http://dx.doi.org/10.1109/ICIMTech53080.2021.9535057]

New Zealand Ministry of Foreign Affairs and Trade. *Key outcomes.* Retrieved March 6, 2021, from https://www.mfat.govt.nz/en/trade/free-trade-agreements/free-trade-agreements-concluded-bu--not-in-force/regional-comprehensive-economic-partnership-rcep/key-outcomes

Razzaq, A., Samiha, Y.T., Anshari, M. (2018). Smartphone habits and behaviors in supporting students self-efficacy. *International Journal of Emerging Technologies in Learning (iJET), 13*(2), 94.
[http://dx.doi.org/10.3991/ijet.v13i02.7685]

Swasdee, A., Anshari, M., Hamdan, M. (2020). Artificial Intelligence as Decision Aid in Humanitarian Response. *2020 International Conference on Decision Aid Sciences and Application (DASA),* 773-777. IEEE.
[http://dx.doi.org/10.1109/DASA51403.2020.9317111]

Tranfield, D., Denyer, D., Smart, P. (2003). Towards a methodology for developing evidence informed management knowledge by means of systematic review. *Br. J. Manage., 14*(3), 207-222.
[http://dx.doi.org/10.1111/1467-8551.00375]

Wolf, A., Wang, J., Tang, Y. (2020). Who will benefit the most from the RCEP? | J.P. Morgan Private Bank *J.P.Morgan.*https://privatebank.jpmorgan.com/gl/en/insights/investing/who-will-benefit-the-most-from-RCEP

Zhang, G. (2021). *Impact of the RCEP trade agreement on the Asia-Europe supply chain.* Retrieved from https://market-insights.upply.com/en/impact-of-the-new-intra-asian-trade-agreement-on-the-asia-europe-supply-chain

CHAPTER 4

Comparative Analysis of ICT Readiness in RCEP Member Countries

Abdur Razzaq[1,*] and **Abdullah Al-Mudimigh**[2]

[1] *Universitas Islam Negeri Raden Fatah Palembang, Indonesia*

[2] *Dar Al Uloom University, Saudi Arabia*

Abstract: This chapter examines the Regional Comprehensive Economic Partnership (RCEP) Agreement in general, as well as analyse the recent status of ICT infrastructure of RCEP member countries. It primarily focuses on the RCEP, which was signed by the Association of Southeast Asian Nations (ASEAN) countries, Australia, China, Japan, Korea, and New Zealand in order to expand and strengthen engagements with one another and their relationships to Industry 4.0, whereby the potential issues and solutions are discussed in greater depth. It also highlights the security and privacy issues and thoughts on how 4IR might help countries improve their economies over the long term. The chapter includes reflections on experiences as well as an analysis of how the information contained in the agreement affects the growth of the RCEP agreement.

Keywords: Fourth Industrial Revolution (4IR), Information Communication Technology (ICT), Regional Comprehensive Economic Partnership (RCEP).

INTRODUCTION

The Regional Complete Economic Relationship (RCEP) is a mega-regional free trade agreement (FTA) that was initially proposed in November 2012, and aims to establish a comprehensive, comprehensive, high-quality, and interdependent economic partnership (ASEAN, 2012). The main goal of the RCEP is to remove many tariffs on imports, especially for goods that already get duty-free treatment under existing FTAs. However, countries may maintain tariffs on imports in industries deemed necessary. The RCEP also has rules and standards, which are general rules for products that can get preferential tariff treatment under the RCEP. RCEP offers an advantage over many current bilateral FTAs between the parties in that it allows manufacturers to source parts from participating nations while still adhering to origin rules without paying tariffs (RCEP, 2020).

[*] **Corresponding author Abdur Razzaq**: Universitas Islam Negeri Raden Fatah Palembang, Indonesia; E-mail: abdurrazzaq_uin@radenfatah.ac.id

A significant topic to discuss in the context of information and communication technology (ICT), due to its competitive advantages calibrated by the participating countries, in agreement with the international market for technologies, such as smartphones, computer systems, and so on. Examples of the aforementioned tendency may be found in countries, such as China, Japan, and South Korea, where technology-based firms, such as Huawei, Xiaomi, and Samsung, are manufacturing and exporting more than half of all mobile phones and computer products worldwide (Workman, n.d.). This would assist companies to acquire significant benefits from the agreement, as it will aid in the expansion of market access, providing them with greater opportunities to reach the global market and export their products overseas (Hamdan *et al.*, 2020).

The framework created for the Regional Comprehensive Economic Partnership (RCEP) Agreement of 2020 provides evidence of this promise of advantages for telecommunications and technology. As an example, Chapter 8 of the RCEP agreement is concerned with telecommunications services, products, and infrastructure, and contains statements that could make trades involving this section possible with a single agreement paper, if the product is manufactured for RCEP. Thus, with RCEP frameworks, transactions involving telecommunication products or services no longer necessitate several agreements for different parties under RCEP, but instead have a single reference for agreements within a product or service category. However, as of RCEP Agreement, the same degree of satisfaction cannot be achieved in electronic commerce (E-Commerce) because an agreement could not be reached on the principle of open data across several areas, as was the case with the previous agreement. This also raises the issue of IT security and privacy, which is particularly pertinent in the telecommunications industry, where sensitive data is routinely transmitted. These issues will be discussed in greater depth later in the discussion section. With the RCEP making it easier for countries under it to acquire and export products and infrastructure related to ICT and, more specifically, telecommunications, some parties are concerned about the security of data and the privacy of users.

The first half of the chapter focuses on RCEP, specifically on the importance of it as a discussion point in the context of ICT. The second half of the review paper focuses on the potentials and challenges of RCEP agreement and ICT. The next half of the review paper presents ideas on how to tackle the challenges faced by RCEP especially security and data privacy.

LITERATURE REVIEW

The chapter's primary focus will be on RCEP and ICT products or services. As small and medium-sized (SMEs) businesses are now integrating themselves with the internet technologies that have emerged as a result of technological advances in ICT. Another is the integration of enterprises with social media, which is considered an essential component of modern business operations, according to experts (Abuhashes, 2014). Businesses are rushing to implement numerous new ICT technologies in order to meet consumer demand. ICT also boosts businesses' worth by enhancing their online presence and running advertising campaigns on the internet and social media platforms. As well as increasing efficiency in the supply chain by reducing labor costs (Jafari, 2014), the integration of these technologies with businesses' information systems will allow for even greater efficiency in the future with the implementation of Industry 4.0, which will significantly reduce the cost of manufacturing and factory industry (Ericsson Consumer & Industry Lab Report 2018). It is the goal of this literature to examine how the growth of communications technology impacts the development of business (Swasdee *et al.*, 2020).

RCEP & ICT

The Annex on telecommunication services is a part of the RCEP agreement that has a lot to do with technology. RCEP seeks to protect e-business and online data privacy by developing legal regulations that are consistent with international standards of relevant organizations for their trade partners, as stated in Article 12.7 to Article 12.8 of the RCEP agreement document (ASEAN, 2020b).

RCEP trade partners would prioritize the development of an effective, relevant agency to deal with issues of ICT, as stipulated in Article 12.13 of the agreement. This will allow them to collaborate and exchange policies in the area of cyber security, as stipulated in Article 12.13. (ASEAN, 2020b). This Annex aims to develop fundamental standards for the trade in public telecommunication services that will encourage RCEP members to improve their ICT infrastructure.

This agreement makes it easier for the parties involved in the trade of services to do business together (ASEAN, 2020b). Given that the RCEP recognizes that trade is becoming increasingly digital, the agreement promotes electronic commerce among RCEP members and advises them to use electronic communication to improve trade administration (ASEAN, 2020b).

ICT development is occurring more quickly in the world today, partly because of increased competition among industries in terms of speed, cost-effectiveness and management as well as governance and production practices. For the past 40 years, many technological advances have occurred, including artificial intelligence, robots, the internet of things, autonomous cars, nanotechnology, biotechnology, materials science, energy storage, and quantum computing, to name a few (Schwab, 2017). The Internet of Things, Big Data, 5G, and Artificial

Intelligence are just a few of the technologies that are laying the groundwork for the Fourth Industrial Revolution (AKA: Industry 4.0) (Anshari *et al.*, 2022).

The Internet of Things (IoT) is a popular topic in the technology sector, policy forums, and professional communities, and has become front-page news in both the expert and general newspapers. This technology can be applied to a wide range of networked devices, systems, and sensors that take advantage of advancements in processing power, electronics downsizing, and network interconnection to give previously impossible capabilities. A vast array of conferences, studies, and news articles have been written about the potential implications of the Internet of Things revolution, ranging from new market opportunities and business models to security, privacy, and technological interoperability concerns (Karen, Scott, & Lyman, 2015).

Internet of Things (IoT) is a concept that was coined in 1999 by Kevin Ashton, a British technology pioneer, to describe a framework in which items in the physical world may be connected to the Internet through sensors. The concept of utilizing computers and networks to track and manage things has been around for decades, despite the fact that the name "Internet of Things" is a relatively recent invention. By the late 1970s, for example, systems for remotely monitoring electrical grid meters over telephone lines were already in commercial use. Modern times have widely adopted the term "Internet of Things" to characterize scenarios in which Internet connection and computing capabilities are extended to a wide range of objects, gadgets, sensors, and ordinary products (Karen, Scott, & Lyman, 2015).

With the Fourth Industrial Revolution comes the arrival of a new generation of mobile networks and technologies, referred to as the Fifth-generation mobile networks and technologies (5G) (Mulyani *et al.*, 2019). 5G can be defined as a packet-switched wireless system that provides significantly higher throughput than previous generations (4G and below) while covering a significantly larger area of coverage. It uses Code Division Multiple Access (CDMA), Band Division Multiple Access (BDMA), and millimetre wireless to provide significantly faster connection speeds and more advanced features than previous generations, resulting in higher resolutions, larger bandwidth, and improved service quality (Hossain, 2013). In general, 5G networks and technology have an impact on how rivals may access global markets more quickly to conduct research, business development, marketing, sales, and the overall supply chain of a company, among other things (Schwab, 2017).

With the advent of 5G technologies and networks, businesses will be able to better satisfy their consumers' expectations and improve their overall experience with the products and services they get. Businesses must re-evaluate their strategy in light of the 5G technological forces that are encircling the business environment. Business executives must choose between actively responding to changes in the business environment and going with the flow of 5G technologies development. This is consistent with RCEP objectives in terms of efficiency in 5G infrastructure and electronic products, as well as an indication of economic improvement for some developing countries, which will be discussed in greater detail later on how RCEP is related to those contexts and supporting the development of 5G.

Adib (2019) stated that 5G technology has the capability to help increase gross domestic product to 4% or $750 billion by 2030. Now that 5G telecommunication technology is just across the horizon and even already used in some parts of the world, it could become the innovation that has many possibilities for businesses to further expand their businesses. 5G could also create new business opportunities on the international level with increased performance, mobility, and customization (Salah Eddine *et al.*, 2017). Just like the advancement of telecommunication discussed above, businesses are predicted to make the transformations for migration and integration of their current business model to accommodate 5G technology. 5G technology, which allows for low latency, and high bandwidth communication between devices, allows businesses from different fields to take advantage of this technology to meet future demands. Essentially, new stakeholders in 5G technology, such as hardware manufacturers, internet service providers, software companies, IT services, and even consumers, will have to transform and integrate their technology to make use of, innovate, build, and integrate their technologies into the 5G ecosystem. These are some of the lists of stakeholders that could potentially evolve their business relationship throughout the development of the 5G ecosystem (Salah Eddine *et al.*, 2017).

In manufacturing, 5G will play a huge role in improving automation with low latency bandwidth. The application of 5G technology in machine-type communication used in manufacturing, factories, and agriculture will rely heavily on versatility, mobility, robustness, and reliable communication between set devices to allow low latency and almost real-time control and analysis (Brahmi *et al.*, 2015). Increased productivity is also forecasted to increase by 6% in 2035 (Saadi & Mavrakis, 2020) with the help of 5G and AI, and this can be attributed to the possibility of the highly automated factory, enhanced robotics, real-time analysis and low latency control provided by the technologies to increase safety and efficiency in manufacturing in order to reduce human casualty and risks by directly interacting with the factory line of production.

Digital Business

Telecommunication may have been playing a big part in business information as it allows businesses to communicate with business personnel to exchange information in real-time remotely through a simple phone call or video conference to email with multiple file attachments. It also allows businesses to communicate with clients and potential customers using multiple means, from simple telemarketing, social media platforms and pages, business website, video advertising, internet ad campaign, and customer service (Sugiantoro *et al.*, 2020). The use of internet and electronic commerce can be utilized to reach out to potential markets outside of their business operating region. Social media platforms also allow businesses to showcase their products with or without the option to purchase specific advertising slots, therefore becoming a cost-efficient way for businesses to reach out to their potential customers while increasing their online presence. The development of telecommunication technology in social media pushes innovation for a new business owner to run their micro or small business on the social media platform to kick-start their business; for example, Instagram has been used by a small business owner to promote as well as becoming a front for their online shop to sell products or services without relying on renting out physical spaces such as a shop. These small businesses on Instagram rely on telecommunication services to run their business pages and interact with their customers at a significantly low cost. Meanwhile, transactions can be made through preferred online payment methods. As technology in telecommunication advances and businesses try to make use of it by integrating their business with current technology, it is now being used more rapidly than ever by businesses to improve communication along the supply chain or expand their market. This shows how telecommunication technology plays a huge role in modern business. It enables businesses to take advantage of it to catch up with the continuously expanding demands of the market.

The digitization of businesses with telecommunication technology integration enables businesses to gather clientele data. The boom from Industry 3.0 that introduces digital technology to businesses brings dense data back and forth across the business' supply chain. Storing, sorting, filtering, and analyzing this data to be used by the business, allow businesses to learn from it by adjusting the efficiency of the supply chain and analyzing trends surrounding their market to help them create business decisions (Anshari *et al.*, 2021b). On the customer end of things, businesses can utilize this technology to tailor their marketing strategy to reach their target audience more effectively by observing trends through the insights calculated from big data analysis (Big Data consumer analytics and the transformation of marketing, 2016).

RCEP will, on the other hand, ensure that there is confidence in exchanging and moving data across borders, which is critical to enabling effective digital trade between countries (Sadler, 2020). Also mentioned was how many organizations rely greatly on a smooth flow of information in order to maintain track of their systems and supply chains, explore consumer preferences, and to be able to develop collaborations with international enterprises, to name a few examples. As a result of the establishment of the free-trade agreement, the decrease of regulations will cut international trade barriers while also lowering the cost of information transmission between countries. Due to this, the subject of ICT, notably telecommunications, is addressed in the agreement on a proactive basis. This is accomplished by the establishment of a proper system for regulating telecommunications services and the encouragement of firms to aid in simplifying the path of service commerce between countries, among other things. To facilitate this data and information exchange, some of the efforts being undertaken by participants in RCEP are to ensure that their public telecommunications providers provide reasonable access to submarine cable systems and that affordable mobile roaming rates are available (Sadler, 2020).

Five primary topics are concerned in order to reveal some of the most significant challenges and concerns associated with Industry 4.0. Security, privacy, interoperability, and standards are just a few of the topics covered, as are legal, regulatory, and human rights concerns, as well as growing markets and international development (Karen, Scott, & Lyman, 2015).

Analysis

Table **1.** below contains data from the E-Government Index survey conducted by the UN in 2020. This data provides complete information about the status of ICT in each country in five dimensions, namely, Telecommunication Infrastructure Index (TII), mobile cellular telephone subscriptions per 100 inhabitants, percentage of individuals using the Internet, and fixed (wired) broadband subscriptions per 100 inhabitants.

Table 1. Telecommunication Infrastructure Index 2020 (Source: UN E-Government Survey 2020).

Countries	Telecommunication Infrastructure Index (TII)	Mobile Cellular Telephone Subscriptions per 100 Inhabitants	Percentage of Individuals using the Internet	Fixed (wired) Broadband Subscriptions per 100 Inhabitants	Active Mobile Broadband Subscriptions per 100 Inhabitants
Australia	0.8825	113.58	86.55	30.69	120
Brunei	0.8209	120	94.87	11.53	120

(Table 1) cont.....

Countries	Telecommunication Infrastructure Index (TII)	Mobile Cellular Telephone Subscriptions per 100 Inhabitants	Percentage of Individuals using the Internet	Fixed (wired) Broadband Subscriptions per 100 Inhabitants	Active Mobile Broadband Subscriptions per 100 Inhabitants
Cambodia	0.5466	119.49	40	1.02	82.82
China	0.7388	115.53	54.3	28.54	93.46
Indonesia	0.5669	119.34	39.9	28.54	87.15
Japan	0.9223	120	91.28	32.62	120
Laos	0.2383	51.86	25.51	0.64	42.01
Malaysia	0.7634	120	81.2	8.55	116.7
New Zealand	0.9207	120	90.81	34.72	114.46
Philippines	0.5838	120	60.05	3.68	68.44
Singapore	0.8899	120	88.17	27.97	120
South Korea	0.9684	120	96.02	41.6	113.62
Thailand	0.7004	120	56.82	13.24	104.67
Vietnam	0.6694	120	70.35	13.6	71.89

As can be seen in the following (Fig. **1**), there is a consistent pattern across all categories, and that pattern is that developed countries have a far stronger presence than developing countries do. Laos received the lowest possible score for its readiness in the area of information and communication technology infrastructure when compared to developed countries that possess a robust infrastructure in comparison to developing countries. Therefore, this significant gap in the readiness of ICT infrastructure needs to be closed in order to transmit knowledge and transfer technology in order to achieve equality and justice in the process of bringing the RCEP agreement into realisation.

Discussion

One of the important strengths of RCEP agreement related to ICT is the inclusion of data and information issues in Chapter 12, which engages with e-commerce. The chapter discusses data-related concerns, such as the need for computing services' position in the market and the flow of information across international borders through electronic techniques (ASEAN, 2020b). Another element of the RCEP agreement is the Annex on telecommunication services, which offers the option to be flexible in choosing technology. In order to encourage greater association for reinforcing the determination of ICT foundation and assistance as well as to facilitate trade in amenities amongst participants, the Annex is being developed (ASEAN, 2020b).

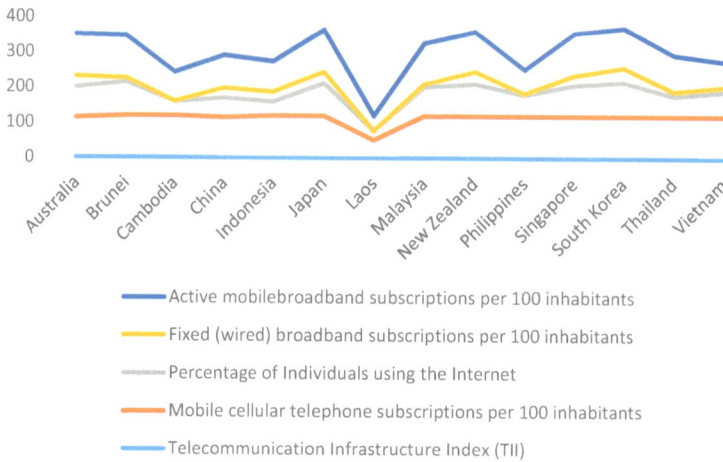

Fig. (1). Comparative ICT Adoption of RCEP Member Countries.

RCEP places a strong emphasis on trade in public telecommunication services, and the quality and distribution of telecommunication services in a nation are important in contributing to the growth of digital communication, information delivery, and internet infrastructure (Alas & Anshari, 2021). An annex on telecommunications services from the Regional Comprehensive Economic Partnership (RCEP) serves as a guideline for telecom service providers in order to ease trade between RCEP countries. E-commerce is progressively increasing in popularity around the world, and it is anticipated that by 2040, internet purchases will account for 95 percent of all transactions (99firms, n.d; Low & Anshari, 2013; Ahad & Anshari, 2017).

Smartphones are an example of information technology gadgets that can be used in e-commerce. According to ReadyCloud (2015), about half of all online customers use their smartphones to conduct their online shopping (KommandoTech, 2020). Smartphones are disruptive technologies that are slowly but steadily becoming an indispensable part of individual's everyday routine. The features of a smartphone, on the other hand, allow one to use it for both personal and professional objectives. As of last year, smartphones were owned by the vast majority of the world's population (TechJury, 2020).

Standardisation and Regulation

Regional Comprehensive Economic Partnership (RCEP) agreement will include provisions on intellectual property, telecommunications, financial services, e-commerce, and professional services, among other things, and it is projected to eliminate a range of import duties within 20 years (McDonald, 2020). Telecommunications, in particular, is defined as communication over a long distance by means of cable, telegraph, telephone, or broadcasting. Companies that use the Internet of Things to provide a suite of products and services that enhance the value of their existing networks, such as 4G and 5G, are gaining a competitive advantage (Craven, 2020). Equipment and component providers to the communications industry could play a role in rationalizing country of origin laws. When a product is developed for RCEP, it will be compatible with all 15 member countries. There have also been discussions about open data, international telecommunications collaboration, and government procurement in the recent past. In addition, the signatories committed to ensure that public telecommunications service providers provide equal and nondiscriminatory care for links to submarine cable networks, to encourage the portability of cell phone numbers, and to permit reasonable international mobile roaming costs, among other things (O'Grady, 2020).

Security Issues

It is necessary to take into consideration a number of challenges, the first of which is that the use of global requirements to restrict data storage and processing on a local level is discouraged. The data localisation for personal, non-personal, and financial facts in cross-border data transfer is another topic to consider (Anshari *et al.*, 2020). Consumer data security and digital consumer protection, which is critical to the success of e-commerce enterprises because it fosters customer loyalty, are also among the challenges to be addressed. As a result, from a security standpoint, localization can exacerbate rather than alleviate India's current crisis. In reality, just a handful of technical behemoths have access to global data, and countries such as India, which lack adequate data control, run the risk of becoming data colonizers (Agarwal, 2019).

On the other hand, the technology of 5G networks has the potential to open the door to new business prospects, goods, and services, as well as to alter the flow of some organizations. RCEP members may benefit from the advancement of 5G technology, as well as its rollout and utilization, particularly given the lower tariffs on telecommunications and electronic products that are now in effect in the country. Currently, China, South Korea, and Japan are among the nations in the Regional Comprehensive Economic Partnership (RCEP) that have 5G networks operational in some portions of their respective countries using their own technology. In contrast to developed countries such as Japan, where the previously discussed concern about network security when using Chinese 5G hardware is a major problem, other developing countries in the South East Asia region appear to have no issues with using Chinese hardware for their networks and 5G infrastructure. It is possible that this is due to the fact that Chinese products are less expensive to import and function well enough to suit the needs of emerging countries. Consequently, it is possible that developing countries are prioritizing short- and medium-term economic development while placing a lower premium on the potential long-term consequences for their country's information security (Ahad *et al.*, 2017). 5G technology, despite the possibility of a security vulnerability with Chinese-manufactured networking hardware, would still have a significant impact on businesses in developing countries under RCEP, particularly in manufacturing in factories, as it would take better advantage of current technologies, with examples such as better controlling of process automation and robotics to reduce labor costs, internet of things with machinery and devices for low latency forecasting and algorithms, and better control of process automation and robotics to improve productivity Not to mention the promise of mobile 5G technology, which might allow manufacturing and factories to be more flexible in their expansions than they are currently able to be utilizing fixed-line networks, which is currently unavailable. As a result, with RCEP, 5G technology has the potential to further boost the economic development of developing countries participating in the RCEP through lower tariffs on products, particularly in the telecommunications sector, increased manufacturing efficiency, and improved supply chains.

Potentials Improvement

The entire security and resilience of the Internet of Things are determined by how security risks are identified, analysed, and addressed. The risk of a device being hacked, the damage that a compromised device will do, as well as the time and resources required to accomplish a specific level of protection, are all aspects that are taken into consideration when establishing the overall security of a device. A variety of factors influence the outcome of this risk assessment and mitigation computation. Understanding current and potential future security concerns, as well as the projected economic and other costs of harm if the risks materialize, as well as the estimated cost of mitigating the risks, are all important considerations. In economic terms, a lack of security for Internet of Things devices results in a negative externality, which is when one party (or a group of parties) imposes a cost on another party (or groups of parties). In the classic case of pollution of the environment, the environmental damage and cleaning costs (negative externalities) resulting from a polluter's actions are borne by those who are not polluters. The major problem is that the cost of an externality imposed on others is rarely taken into account in decision-making unless an externality tax is placed on the polluter, as in the case of pollution, in order to induce them to minimize the quantity of pollution they emit (Karen, Scott, & Lyman, 2015). Externalities exist in the field of information security when a software producer does not bear the costs associated with security flaws; in this case, liability law may require the supplier to account for the externality and produce more security products; in this case, liability law may force the supplier to account for the externality and produce more security products (Bruce, 2007).

The Internet of Things (IoT) represents the next frontier in the role of ICTs in economic growth. It is being propelled forward by the declining cost of sensors and microprocessors, as well as an expanding array of affordable networking technologies, which are all being made available at a lower cost (ICT4D). The fact is that mobile wireless networks reach over 90% of the world's population, with 2/3rds of that served by 3G signals that enable secure data transfers, but a number of additional short and long-range technologies also offer a variety of data access alternatives (Karen, Scott, & Lyman, 2015). As devices and services become more accessible, Internet of Things (IoT) interventions in development (IoT4D) will become increasingly widespread. The Internet of Things (IoT) is being utilized to address some of the world's most pressing development issues in a variety of locations around the globe (Anshari, 2020). Related technologies are being leveraged to improve service delivery and development outcomes across the board, from poverty alleviation to the improvement of sustainable water and sanitation management, among other things (Anshari *et al.*, 2021a). Examples such as these and others highlight the importance of the Internet of Things as a platform for attaining the United Nations' Millennium Development Goals (MDGs) and the upcoming Sustainable Development Goals (SDGs). But there are still significant roadblocks to overcome, particularly in terms of infrastructure, technological capability, and the establishment of regulatory environments that are conducive to Internet of Things interventions (Razzaq *et al.*, 2018). An improved knowledge of the Internet of Things for Development's potential would aid in boosting its effectiveness and efficacy in addressing some of the world's most critical development concerns (Karen, Scott, & Lyman, 2015).

CONCLUSION

Even if the COVID-19 epidemic is brought to a halt, the world will continue to experience financial consequences or downturns for an extended period of time (Anshari *et al.*, 2021c). Despite the fact that Industry 4.0 revolves, the undeniable fact that the epidemic has ushered in its era has resulted in a reduction in the volume of trade entering and leaving a country. RCEP must raise its ambitions if it is to succeed in embracing digitization and Industry 4.0, which will provide them with a significant opportunity to grow its business. However, there are always other factors that must be taken into consideration, particularly in terms of security and data privacy. Security must be maintained and strengthened on a regular basis in order to prevent users' information from being illegally collected and used for illegal activities.

CONSENT FOR PUBLICATION

Not applicable.

CONFLICT OF INTEREST

The author declares no conflict of interest, financial or otherwise.

ACKNOWLEDGEMENTS

Declared none.

REFERENCES

Abuhashesh, M. (2014). Integration of Social Media in Businesses. *International Journal of Business Environment., 5*, 202-209.

Ahad, A.D., Anshari, M., Razzaq, A. (2017). Domestication of smartphones among adolescents in Brunei darussalam. *International Journal of Cyber Behavior, Psychology and Learning, 7*(4), 26-39. [http://dx.doi.org/10.4018/IJCBPL.2017100103]

Ahad, A.D., Anshari, M. (2017). Smartphone habits among youth: Uses and gratification theory. *International Journal of Cyber Behavior, Psychology and Learning, 7*(1), 65-75. [http://dx.doi.org/10.4018/IJCBPL.2017010105]

Alas, Y., Anshari, M. (2021). Initiating Brunei Cross-Border Tourism (BCBT) as a Gateway to Borneo. *International Journal of Asian Business and Information Management, 12*(3), 15-25. [http://dx.doi.org/10.4018/IJABIM.20210701.oa2]

Anshari, M., Almunawar, M.N., Masri, M. (2020). Financial Technology and Disruptive Innovation in Business. *International Journal of Asian Business and Information Management, 11*(4), 29-43. [http://dx.doi.org/10.4018/IJABIM.2020100103]

Anshari, M. (2020). Workforce mapping of fourth industrial revolution: Optimization to identity. *J. Phys. Conf. Ser., 1477*(7), 072023. IOP Publishing. [http://dx.doi.org/10.1088/1742-6596/1477/7/072023]

Anshari, M., Almunawar, M.N., Younis, M.Z., Kisa, A. (2021). Modeling Users' Empowerment in E-Health Systems. *Sustainability (Basel), 13*(23), 12993. [http://dx.doi.org/10.3390/su132312993]

Anshari, M., Almunawar, M.N., Razzaq, A. (2021). Developing Talents vis-à-vis Fourth Industrial Revolution. *International Journal of Asian Business and Information Management, 12*(4), 20-32. [http://dx.doi.org/10.4018/IJABIM.20211001.oa2]

Anshari, M., Almunawar, M.N., Masri, M., Hrdy, M. (2021). Financial Technology with AI-Enabled and Ethical Challenges. *Society, 58*(3), 189-195. [http://dx.doi.org/10.1007/s12115-021-00592-w]

Anshari, M., Syafrudin, M., Fitriyani, N.L. (2022). Fourth Industrial Revolution between Knowledge Management and Digital Humanities. *Information (Basel), 13*(6), 292. [http://dx.doi.org/10.3390/info13060292]

Agarwal, K. (2019). *Did Data and E-Commerce Issues Also Influence India's RCEP Exit?.* Retrieved from https://thewire.in/economy/india-rcep

Adib, D. (2019). *5's G Impact on Manufacturing: $740BN of Benefits in 2030.*. STL Partners, Huawei.

ASEAN. (2012). Regional comprehensive Economic Partnership (RCEP) - ASEAN: One vision one identity one community. Retrieved from https://asean.org/?static_post=rcep-regional-comprehensive-econo-ic-partnership

ASEAN. (2020a). *ASEAN hits historic milestone with signing of RCEP.*https://asean.org/asean-hits-histor-c-milestone-signing-rcep/

ASEAN. (2020b). *ASEAN hits historic milestone with signing of RCEP.* https://asean.org/storage/2020/11/Summary-of-the-RCEP-Agreement.pdf

Brahmi, N., Yilmaz, O.N., Helmersson, K.W., Ashraf, S.A., Torsner, J. (2015). Deployment strategies for ultra-reliable and low-latency communication in factory automation. *In 2015 IEEE Globecom Workshops (GC Wkshps)*. IEEE.
[http://dx.doi.org/10.1109/GLOCOMW.2015.7414016]

Bruce, S. (2007). *Information Security and Externalities*. Retrieved from https://www.schneier.com/essays/archives/2007/01/information_security_1.html

Craven, C. (2020). *How Are Telecoms Using the Internet of Things (IoT)?*. Retrieved from https://www.sdxcentral.com/5g/iot/definitions/telecom-using-iot/

*Ericsson Consumer & Industry Lab Report.*A Case Study on Automation in Mining. Retrieved from https://www.ericsson.com/en/reports-and-papers/consumerlab/reports/a-case-study-on-automation-in-mining

Hamdan, M., Chen, C.K., Anshari, M. (2020). Decision Aid in Budgeting Systems for Small & Medium Enterprises. *2020 International Conference on Decision Aid Sciences and Application (DASA)*, 253-257. IEEE.
[http://dx.doi.org/10.1109/DASA51403.2020.9317018]

Hossain, S. (2013). 5G wireless communication systems. *Am. J. Eng. Res., 2*(10), 344-353.

Jafari, S. (2014). Strategic Cost-Cutting in Information Technology: toward a Framework for Enhancing the Business Value of IT. *Iranian Journal of Management Studies., 7*, 21-39.
[http://dx.doi.org/10.22059/ijms.2014.36201]

Karen, R., Scott, E., Lyman, C. (2015). *The Internet of Things: An Overview Understanding the Issues and Challenges of A More Connected World*. Geneva, Switzerland.

KommandoTech. (2020). Smartphone Snapshot: Mobile *vs* Desktop Usage Statistics Today https://kommandotech.com/statistics/mobile-vs-desktop-usage/

Low, K.C.P., Anshari, M. (2013). Incorporating social customer relationship management in negotiation. *Int. J. Electron. Cust. Relatsh. Manag., 7*(3/4), 239-252.
[http://dx.doi.org/10.1504/IJECRM.2013.060700]

McDonald, T. (2020). *What is the Regional Comprehensive Economic Partnership (RCEP)? BBC*. Retrieved from https://www.bbc.com/news/business-54899254

Mulyani, M.A., Razzaq, A., Sumardi, W.H., Anshari, M. (2019). Smartphone Adoption in Mobile Learning Scenario. *2019 International Conference on Information Management and Technology (ICIMTech)*. IEEE.
[http://dx.doi.org/10.1109/ICIMTech.2019.8843755]

Mulyani, M.A., Yusuf, S., Siregar, P., Nurihsan, J., Razzaq, A., Anshari, M. (2021). Fourth Industrial Revolution and Educational Challenges. *2021 International Conference on Information Management and Technology (ICIMTech), 1*, 245-249. IEEE.
[http://dx.doi.org/10.1109/ICIMTech53080.2021.9535057]

O'Grady, V. (2020). *Will the RCEP deal transform Asian telecoms?*. Retrieved from https://www.developingtelecoms.com/telecom-business/10317-will-the-rcep-deal-transform-asian-telecoms.html

Razzaq, A., Samiha, Y.T., Anshari, M. (2018). Smartphone habits and behaviors in supporting students self-efficacy. *International Journal of Emerging Technologies in Learning (iJET), 13*(2), 94. [http://dx.doi.org/10.3991/ijet.v13i02.7685]

RCEP. (2020). *Duane Morris.* https://www.duanemorris.com/alerts/regional_comprehensive_economic_partnership_summary_implications_asia_pacific_rim_1220.html

Ready Cloud. (2015). *Game-Changing Mobile Ecommerce Statistics.* https://www.readycloud.com/info/rethinking-e-retailing-game-changing-mobile-ecommerce-statistics-paint-the-real-picture

Saadi, S., Mavrakis, D. (2020). 5G and AI The Foundations for the Next Societal and Business Leap.

Elayoubi, S.E., Bedo, J-S., Filippou, M., Gavras, A., Giustiniano, D. (2017). 5G innovations for new business opportunities. *Mobile World Congress.*

Sadler, D. (2020). *Regional Trade Boost for Cyber, Digital and Data.*https://subtelforum.com/regional-trad--boost-for-cyber-digital-and-data/

Schwab, K. (2017). *The fourth industrial revolution.* Currency.

Sugiantoro, B., Anshari, M., Sudrajat, D. (2020). Developing Framework for Web Based e-Commerce: Secure-SDLC. *J. Phys. Conf. Ser., 1566*(1), 012020. IOP Publishing. [http://dx.doi.org/10.1088/1742-6596/1566/1/012020]

Swasdee, A., Anshari, M., Hamdan, M. (2020). Artificial Intelligence as Decision Aid in Humanitarian Response. *2020 International Conference on Decision Aid Sciences and Application (DASA).* IEEE. 773-777. [http://dx.doi.org/10.1109/DASA51403.2020.9317111]

TechJury. (2020). 67+ Revealing Smartphone. *Stat, 2020.* https://techjury.net/blog/smartphone-usag--statistics/

Trade. (2021). The International Trade Administration. https://www.trade.gov/country-commercia--guides/brunei-ecommerce

99firms. (n.d.). *ecommerce statistics.* Retrieved from https://99firms.com/blog/ecommerce-statistics/

Workman, D. *Cellphone Exports by Country.* Retrieve http://www.worldstopexports.com/ cellphone-export--by-country/

CHAPTER 5

Disruptive Innovation Reshaping Future RCEP

Norainie Ahmad[1], **Muhammad Anshari**[1,*] and **Mahani Hamdan**[1]

[1] Universiti Brunei Darussalam, Institute of Policy Studies, Brunei Darussalam

Abstract: The arena of technological advancements continues to grow due to changing market demands, which creates inevitable competition among innovators. Thus, this leads to the emergence of disruptive innovation. This chapter examines the relationship between the Regional Comprehensive Economic Partnership (RCEP) agreement and the advent of Disruptive Innovation. RCEP was signed in November 2020 by a total of fifteen countries, with the goal of advancing regional economic integration and exerting greater influence over the Free Trade Agreement (FTA). The main focus of this chapter is on assessing the benefits of disruptive innovation and trade under the Regional Comprehensive Economic Partnership (RCEP). We performed a literature review and applied SWOT analysis in order to assess the strengths and weaknesses of disruptive innovation, as well as the opportunities and challenges presented by the Regional Comprehensive Economic Partnership. Disruptive innovation can be beneficial to the majority of RCEP countries since it can raise market growth, increase profit, and increase the productivity of – and efficiency for, disruptive technologies used in manufacturing. On the other hand, the possible challenges may be detrimental to smaller emerging economies, whose employment rates may be adversely impacted, and local enterprises may be overshadowed as a result of the increased competition.

Keywords: Disruptive Innovation, Regional Comprehensive Economic Partnership (RCEP), SWOT analysis.

INTRODUCTION

On 15th November 2020, a new Free Trade Agreement (FTA) was signed. It is known as the Regional Comprehensive Economic Partnership (RCEP) Agreement, intended to widen and deepen ASEAN's interaction with Australia, China, Japan, Korea, and New Zealand. The Regional Comprehensive Economic Partnership (RCEP) is envisaged to facilitate regional trade and investment while opening up a new market and creating new employment possibilities within and between its players. The agreement is essentially an open one that includes rules-

* **Corresponding author Muhammad Anshari:** Universiti Brunei Darussalam, Institute of Policy Studies, Brunei Darussalam; E-mail: anshari.ali@ubd.edu.bn

based multidimensional trading systems, among others (ASEAN, 2020). India was initially a member but withdrew its membership during the early stages of the discussion.

RCEP was initially announced in November 2011 during the 19th ASEAN summit, and since then, a number of intercessional and ministerial meetings, as well as more than 30 negotiations, have taken place to discuss the RCEP. Eventually, the leaders of 15 countries from the Asia-Pacific region signed the agreement in 2020. RCEP was developed to strengthen economic linkages, trade and investment activities, and to narrow the development gap between the signatory nations.

One of the objectives of the agreements includes establishing a comprehensive, high-quality, and mutually advantageous economic cooperation that will encourage trade and economic progress in this region while also benefiting all parties. RCEP is aimed at widening and deepening the present Free Trade Agreement. Indeed, RCEP has the potential to create considerable opportunities for enterprises in the Asia Pacific area, given that the 15 participating states have contributed to almost 30 percent of global GDP and more than a quarter of world exports. Its goal is to establish a framework focused on lowering trade barriers and achieving enhanced market access for businesses engaged in the trade of products and services in the region. The RCEP aims to achieve its goals by enabling and increasing the transparency of trading operations and investment contacts among its members, as well as by supporting the participation of SMEs in global and regional supply chains. It also emphasises the importance of ASEAN in the development of regional economic architecture, and it promotes economic integration as well as the strengthening of economic cooperation among the members of the RCEP.

This paper discusses the issue of whether or not RCEP can fully foster disruptive innovation that benefits society. Would the RCEP encourage enterprises and governments to share and benefit from these innovations? Are there any factors that could help enhance businesses from developed countries, which could be learned, transferred, or replicated in developing countries – and indeed, vice versa? In the absence of a more genuine perspective on the possible outcomes of disruptive innovations through RCEP, companies themselves can form a monopoly on an industry, thereby charging a much higher premium in a less competitive market and making these innovations financially inaccessible to consumers. Furthermore, in the absence of competition, innovation and technological development can get stunted because there is no pressure to continuously sustain innovation. As a result, the issue of who will genuinely benefit from the trade of disruptive innovation between economies facilitated by the RCEP remains important and requires careful analysis.

LITERATURE REVIEW

Tariffs & Free Trade Agreement

Tariffs have been prominently covered in the news headlines as they shape the current global economic and trade scenario among the 'world's developed nations. So, what are they, and where do they affect production in a country? According to Deloitte Japan (n.d.), tariffs refer to taxation applied to each imported and exported good and service in which the costs are very significant that the host countries simply cannot ignore. In other words, tariffs or customs duty is an interchangeable term that serves two main purposes: generating revenue from imported goods and services while protecting domestic production (National Geographic Society, 2019). Even though tariffs are good for the home 'country's revenue, due to the increase in multidimensional international trade in the 20th century, tariffs are seen as barriers rather than facilitators, and they are receiving greater attention in trade negotiations aiming for reduction (Britannica, n.d.). As such, the Free Trade Agreement (FTA) between member countries must be used strategically when it is set out for international trade. According to International Trade Administration (n.d.-a.), the Free Trade Agreement (FTA) reduces the barrier to import and export between two or more countries that are made through a mutual agreement that includes goods and services trading, protection for the investors, and a 'country's rights for intellectual property. Globally, 400 FTAs, including the agreement, are still undergoing the planning stage, which is enormous in terms of their economic scale, the population it covers, and the number of countries involved (Deloitte Japan, n.d.).

There are two major FTAs that are currently known to the global business: The United States-Mexico-Canada Agreement (USMCA) and the Comprehensive and Progressive Agreement for Trans-Pacific Partnership (CPTPP). The United States, Mexico, and Canada Agreement (USMCA) agreement is basically a newly updated NAFTA agreement that had been used for twenty-five years, but with improvements in the laws especially related to industrial intellectual property (IIP), the internet, investment, state-owned enterprises and currency (Swanson & Tankersley, 2020). The International Trade Administration (n.d.-b.) basically refers to the USMCA as a 21st-century trade agreement in its high standard position that results from a free market, fair trade and expansion of growth in North America economically *via* mutually beneficial trade between Canada and Mexico. It focuses on three main areas: (1) Incentives to make cars in North America, (2) Stronger labour rules in Mexico, and (3) Open Canadian markets for

American Dairy farmers that will be reviewed six years after it was signed on 1st July, 2020 and will expire 16 years later if there are disagreements between the 'pact's countries.

CPTPP is a trade agreement made among the 11 Pacific Rim nations that consist of Australia, Brunei, Canada, Chile, Japan, Malaysia, Mexico, New Zealand, Peru, Singapore and Vietnam. This agreement generates about 13 percent of the 'world's income and has been around since 2018. One of its major aims is to reduce tariffs by about 95 percent, in the trade between member nations, except for some conserved sectors. Countries were to follow regulations set by this agreement, such as food standards. However, it is not necessary for countries to have the same regulations and standards between them, as CTTPP is not a customs union, and countries may alter trade deals with one another (David, n.d.).

Disruptive Innovation

Disruptive innovation, coined by Clayton Christensen in the early 1990s, refers to a process where a product or service is initially positioned at the lower end of a market, typically offering lower prices and higher accessibility, eventually displacing established competition and incumbents as it relentlessly moves up the market. Popularised in his book "The 'Innovator's Solution" (1997), the innovations that Disruptive Innovation refers to are not technology that improves upon a product but rather innovations and/or technologies that enable a certain general product or service to be more accessible and affordable to the wider public (Anshari, 2020; Swasdee *et al.*, 2020).

Disruptive innovation can take various forms of technology – which enables the product or service to reach a wider population, innovations in Business Models – which allow the business to target non-consumers and low-end customers, and innovations in a Coherent Value Network – where the suppliers, partners, distributors and customers are each better off when a disruptive technology is successful (Anshari & Sumardi, 2020; Razzaq *et al.*, 2018). Hence, disruptive innovation affects the current market in a way that disrupts and changes the way a market or industry operates (Mulyani *et al.*, 2019; Anshari *et al.*, 2021).

In the Disruptive Innovation theory, there are three types of innovation. Market-creating innovations refer to the classic concept of disruptive innovation, where technology is transformed or adapted in a way where previously complicated products and services are made accessible and affordable (Hamdan *et al.*, 2020). Sustaining innovations is the process of continually improving current products to sustain margins and keep the market competitive; these innovations generally do not disrupt the market. Meanwhile, efficiency innovations are innovations that allow companies to do more with fewer resources, and such innovations have the potential to disrupt and eliminate competitors (Mulyani *et al.*, 2021).

Disruptive technology is defined as an innovation that dramatically affects consumers, businesses, and industries operated "(Disruptive Technology"...," 2021). Disruptive technology businesses produce new markets as it is the first of the kind in the total market. For a technology to be considered disruptive, the technology must dramatically affect how a market works to satisfy a need, completely replace predecessors, and are readily accessible to consumers. Some inventions that align with these criteria are 3D printers and Global Positioning Systems (GPS).

Patterns of disruptive innovation were described by Christensen and vary according to the dynamism of each market and industry. The first and classic pattern described by Christensen (1997), mentioned in the definitions above, refers to companies introducing their products and services in the lower end of a market in which incumbents are happy to concede, focusing instead on sustaining innovation as the disruptor does not initially affect the established companies and the market; thus the incumbents do not recognise the potential impacts these disruptors have until it is too late (Thani & Anshari, 2020). Disruptors then gradually improve the quality of their offerings, moving upmarket and displacing the incumbent market and eventually taking it over. The second and third pattern described by Christensen, as cited by Denning (2016), addressing the current market environments of today, describes disruptors introducing premium products and services and improving upon them rapidly in order to appeal to an ever-growing, interesting market, and companies introducing new technology and rapidly enhancing them swiftly, offering competitors no time to conduct any defence against it.

Following the patterns of innovation, it is posited by Christensen, as cited by Denning (2016), according to the theory of Disruptive Innovation, innovation can only be disruptive in relation to the responses of the competition and the market itself, as the Disruptive Innovation process itself is "a theory of competitive response". Thus, innovation is also considered disruptive if companies do not adapt and follow in the footsteps of the disruptor, and the companies will suffer greatly as a result.

Relating to the RCEP, government and policy regulations are important to foster disruptive technologies by supporting the introduction of innovations, and encouraging the development and sharing of knowledge and technology (Christensen *et al.*, 2000; Gui *et al.*, 2018; Pinkse *et al.*, 2014; Ruan *et al.*, 2014, as cited in Si & Chen 2020). It has also been noted that policies can affect the adoption process of said innovations, accelerate technological development and facilitate the emergence of new industries (Huesing *et al.*, 2014, as cited in Si & Chen, 2020).

An example of disruptive innovation is the existence of 3D printers, which have improved multiple markets such as the automobile, aerospace and healthcare industries. 3D printing has enhanced the process of product development in areas such as prototyping and customisation. Prototyping using 3D printing is also flexible, as modifications and improvements to certain parts of the product can be easily made while keeping it a cost-effective process. Thus, this technology allows changes in the process of prototyping from traditional manufacturing to only using 3D printing. This innovation has also dramatically affected the healthcare and automotive industry. In healthcare, this invention has aided in the customisation of hearing aid shells, dental implants and prosthetic limbs. It has also assisted surgeons in lowering errors in surgical operations as 3D printed anatomical models are able to help guide and plan the surgical procedures beforehand. While in the automotive industry, the technology has accelerated the prototyping process, which allows the test-of-concept stage to be more efficient and less costly by producing multiple automotive iterations quickly. Apart from that, it has also accelerated rapid manufacturing and assisted in car customisation, such as personalised car components. 3D printers are considered a disruptive technology because it has produced a new market that affected how industries such as healthcare operate.

Some of the strengths are that disruptive inventors benefit from their target market. As inventors with disruptive products, the target market of these items is either in a low-end market or a new market. In a new market, disruptive inventions aim to satisfy a specific target market that has been overlooked by competitors and is not satisfied within the existing market. Therefore, there is limited competition due to the unique innovation. Hence, this gives them an advantage to only focus on satisfying the needs of a single market segment that is unsatisfied by other competitors. Although disruptive inventions are likely to start off in the least profitable low-end market, with improvements of the product in quality and performance, they are able to gain 'competitors' existing consumers and subsequently will gain the mainstream market. Finally, with the growth of invention in the market, established companies may purchase the emerging business in order to eliminate competition by acquiring the business instead.

Though disruptive innovation has multiple benefits, it is still a risky business to run. One of the weaknesses of disruptive innovations is that products are too innovative for consumers to utilise. Apart from that, making consumers trust innovative products is challenging as it is the first of a kind in the market.

Moreover, there are existing products that solve the same problems as these innovations that customers already trust and are accustomed to. Hence, it is harder to convince the shift in markets. Secondly, it is challenging for a disruptive business to be sustainable in the long run. This is due to the innovations being worthless or impractical in the market, as 42 percent of start-ups are reported to fail due to this reason alone "(Why Start-ups Fail, 2019)".

Methodology

The primary goal of this paper is to examine previously published material in the areas of the Regional Comprehensive Economic Partnership (RCEP) and Disruptive Innovation in order to generate new insights that will assist in the understanding of the current state of the context in which it is being conducted. As an emerging area, research is being performed to meet the growing demand for an understanding of the RCEP point of view. As sample sources, the study uses only entire research articles from the research domain that meet the study's criteria (excluding research notes, brief communication papers, editorial notes, industrial whitepapers, and technical and non-academic documents). The next step is to conduct a content analysis of the information that has been gathered and determined to be highly relevant to the study. Following the completion of the final content analysis, the research implemented the instruments necessary to conduct a SWOT (Strength-Weakness-Opportunity-Threat) analysis.

Findings and Discussion

Disruptive innovation is a theory that surmises the process of responses toward an innovation that disrupts and changes the status quo of an industry and its incumbents. Classic patterns of disruptive innovation involve the development of an initially inferior or inaccessible technology or organisational structure into one that surpasses the predominant product or structure of the market or industry. As a result, disruptive innovation brings forth generally inaccessible and expensive technology and improves it for a wider population, which can result in a better quality of life overall. Additionally, disruptive innovations may also introduce to the industry new and efficient ways in the operations and production processes of an organisation, potentially reducing costs and, thus, price as well as allowing such products and services to reach more people. Following this, certain industries can transfer the benefits of these types of innovations into society as a whole, for example, disruptive innovations in healthcare that enable its products and services to reach people in more isolated areas around the world. Disruptive innovation also allows smaller companies and start-ups a window of opportunity to survive and compete against the predominant incumbents of a particular industry by catering to a previously neglected market segment and/or creating a new segment within the market itself and eventually consuming the wider consumer base share. As such, economically, it is also a driver of growth, increasing the competitiveness of a particular industry and possibly enabling the alleviation of an 'economy's unemployment rates.

The RCEP is important in determining the influence disruptors and their disruptive innovations have among the countries in the agreement. New ideas, products and services are usually met with initial skepticism regarding privacy and consumer safety issues. How freely an innovation can move from country to country may also be influenced by trade restrictions which can drive up prices and costs of acquiring and/or implementing such innovations. Bureaucracy can also play a part in the mobility of these innovations. Complicated processes such as differences in safety regulations and the like between economies may deter and restrict disruptive innovation. As such, lifting trade barriers between the RCEP countries and its regulations is important to determine whether disruptors and disruptive innovations can thrive.

Strengths

Disruptive innovations allow start-ups and newer, smaller companies the opportunity to grow and compete with the more dominant competitors by establishing and developing their own market segments and niche through market-creating innovations (Livingston, n.d.). These innovations would then result in the market becoming more competitive, developing the industry further and creating jobs within the economy. These market-creating innovations also enable technology to transform from previously inaccessible and/or expensive into less complicated and inexpensive technology for the general public, allowing the wider society to reap the benefits of the innovation (Denning, 2016).

Innovations can also be disruptive as they improve the efficiency of an organisation, called efficiency innovations. These innovations can be seen as roads towards market disruptions where the efficiency innovations introduced by the disruptor improve an organisation's efficiency greatly that other incumbents must adapt and follow suit in order to survive such disruptions in the market. For example, Henry 'Ford's 'Fordism' which was brought on as a result of his restructuring and streamlining of production processes in Ford motor company's factory processes using the concept of specialisation, allowed the lowering of production costs and enabled the mass production of affordable automobiles which in turn also enabled a market-creating innovation where the general public for the first time, is able to afford an automobile.

As such, disruptive innovations can greatly benefit society in general by enabling technology or a certain product or service to be more accessible and affordable to the wider population. Economically, it allows markets to be more competitive and enables smaller businesses opportunities to grow and establish themselves.

Weaknesses

According to the classic pattern of disruptive innovation posited by Christensen, cited by Denning (2016), disruptive innovation initially caters to the lower end of the market and non-consumers, with it being inferior to the predominant product or service in the market. Thus, from a business perspective, disruptive innovation will not result in big profits for businesses at the start and will take time to grow in sales and revenue. In tandem, these disruptors must also expend time, money and effort in developing and improving these disruptive innovations before the disruptors can compete against their bigger competitors upmarket. Also, due to nature as unpredictable or difficult to predict variables, these products or services also need a separate strategy to take into account and improve the disruptor's ability to adapt to unanticipated opportunities, issues, and successes. Thus, potential disruptive innovations require possible costly long-term commitment and planning focusing on an unpredictable product or service which is not guaranteed to succeed. Additionally, investors may not be willing to wait as long, desiring faster yields, placing pressure on these companies.

Economically, while efficiency innovations allow lower costs of production, certain efficiency innovations may result in fewer jobs; thus, efficiency innovations can eliminate jobs (Denning, 2016). For example, the emerging market of 3D printing allows for flexible and customised efficient production, which would require few employees to operate these systems compared to more traditional methods of production, which would result in the loss of jobs and an increase in the unemployment rate of an economy. Disruptors who manage to displace and take over as the dominant force in the industry may also develop into a monopoly, or the market developing into a monopolistic competition, depending on the competitive responses of the market, especially if the competitors opt not to adapt or implement and apply the innovations, resulting in lower competition, higher prices and a decrease in the need to innovate.

Opportunities

As the world's largest free trading bloc, which accounts for around 30 percent of global GDP and population (Sytysma, 2020), RCEP has the potential to produce a significant impact on the global economies. Furthermore, RCEP is able to reduce the regulatory barriers and allow for greater trade in intermediate input as the rules of origin from the existing trade agreements among the members are harmonised. RCEP's favourable rules of origin would also further attract foreign investments. Thus, enhancing the transparency in trade and investment as well as facilitating the ASEAN's small and medium-sized enterprises (SMEs) to global and regional supply chains. Besides that, RCEP participating members view the RCEP agreement as a Secretariat, which is referred to as a platform to discuss future trade and economic issues in Asia rather than just a static trade agreement (Sytsma, 2020). Therefore, through the platform, officials and ministers will actively engage in the RCEP agenda and lobby participating members to have a robust institutional framework to support Asian trade commitments in the future. RCEP can also be a platform to discuss and engage in 21st-century trade issues, for instance, in terms of rules regarding 3D printed goods, artificial intelligence, or blockchain technology.

According to Institut Jacques Delors (2020), the RCEP agreement focuses its main intention to remove customs duties slowly up to ninety percent of its exported goods and services thus; this is an opportunity for RCEP member countries to take advantage of each other by outsourcing (or offshoring) their products or services to produce an innovation that will disrupt their current production. For example, Singapore is always looking for new ways to exploit the Artificial Intelligence (AI) wave and turn its workforce into an AI-fueled organisation where machines can work alongside and support employees to increase productivity and provide exemplary visitor experiences; as Dr. Victor Tong, Chief Digital and Information officer in National Gallery Singapore stated that AI will have the potential to disrupt the core business processes and operation after it had increased their sales conversion by over 40 percent from the previous years (Henderson, 2019). With the help from other RCEP member countries such as Japan, China and South Korea, which are excellent in their robotic experiences, it is possible for Singapore to achieve its current goal of making progress for Smart Nation since 2014. While Tokyo has been ranked 4th, Shanghai 6th, Beijing 7th, and Seoul ranked 8th in terms of their digital innovation efforts, Singapore took the first spot in the global ranking, predicted to be a leading innovation hub over the next four years (KPMG, 2020). The country offers an advanced IT infrastructure, strong government support, and IP protection laws with a deep pool of skilled and educated talent.

RCEP will also be a facilitator of regional trade integration in the manufacturing sector, thus, it might produce exceptional effects on disruptive innovation in manufacturing industries (Institut Jacques Delors, 2020). The current state of digital manufacturing is focused on three main areas: the industrial Internet of things (IIoT), augmented reality (AR), and cloud technology; in which each of these will cause its own digital disruptions, creating a full-scale revolution (Gourley, 2020). With the combination of these three areas of technology, the connectivity of the top floor to the shop floor will be robust in every facet and in every direction, thus placing the future of manufacturing industries in a good position for earlier adopters of this incoming revolution.

Threats

Hong (2020) asserts that RCEP negotiations are mostly based on traditional issues only and have less emphasis on important issues concerning the establishment of a high-level regional free trade zone such as state-owned enterprises, labour standards, environmental protection and intellectual property protections. For instance, in participating member countries such as China and Myanmar, criticisms have largely centred on issues concerning labour rights treatment and human rights abuse. However, RCEP does not have the provisions to deal with such issues in which there has been a demand from the unions (Ranald, 2020). In addition, the negotiating text was only released after the agreement was signed on the 15th November 2020, thus not providing adequate opportunity for a public debate on the implications of the RCEP. The government is no longer able to disregard issues on labor standards which are rising in the RCEP countries. As the liberalisation commitment is increasing for further integration of the global value chains in the region, it may witness a decline in the labour-intensive sector with a negative employment consequence in some developing countries ("Trade union express concern over RCEP", 2020)

Moreover, RCEP has a ruling that could force small nations to give away one of the resources of the country, which is their data, to larger, more established countries such as China and South Korea. This can be detrimental to local businesses in small countries, including SMEs, as products that are being sold online will compete with those sold offline. E-commerce moguls such as Alibaba in China will overtake domestic retail stores and their products (Jitendra, 2017). This means that if disruptive innovation were to be traded amongst participating nations, these new technologies could use the data given to make foreign e-commerce companies more appealing to the market of the countries, which may outperform and overtake local businesses. At the same time, as more disruptive technologies such as AI and 3D Printing are adopted, there is a possibility of job elimination, which could increase national unemployment rates.

Furthermore, there is a risk of geopolitical takeover from this agreement. Geopolitics can be defined as the power that transcends geographical barriers and is usually associated with major powers' international relations and geostrategic issues (Reuber, 2009). One of the major reasons for India's withdrawal from RCEP was their concern that the agreement was becoming beyond just economic and instead would eventually lean towards a geopolitical strategy. They are wary of China making use of the agreement to take over greater market access in India to further increase their influence in Asia (Hong, 2020). This concern could be applicable to other developing countries as well, especially if their data is vulnerable to other bigger nations and runs the risk of geopolitical takeover for the greater benefit of richer countries.

CONCLUSION

RCEP was established to strengthen the regional economic integration of the participating ASEAN countries with the other five countries by reducing tariffs to gain greater market access. This will increase the number of markets in member countries, as well as create employment opportunities, and encourage development, subsequently boosting the economy. Disruptive innovations introduce new ways in the operations and productions of many different organisations that could reduce costs and provide customers more access to these products and services. The success in the trading of disruptive technology, such as 3D Printing and AI, is determined by the regulations and policies set by RCEP.

This agreement has its fair share of benefits that includes market and labor growth, which allows opportunities such as turning the manufacturing process of an organisation into an AI-fueled system that can improve productivity level and efficiency in manufacturing. This is supported by one of the strengths of Disruptive Innovation, which is its ability to disrupt an existing process by making it faster and more efficient, allowing for mass production and lower cost of operation. This can majorly change the way technology works in a country, thus benefiting the population.

However, with the gaps in RCEP, come threats and weaknesses that may be detrimental to those who are in a disadvantaged position – especially small economies with weak laws, underdeveloped and underinvested industries, and poor labour protection practices. Local businesses and the labour sector of a country, specifically that of smaller nations, run the risk of job elimination and losses and being overshadowed by these disruptive innovations. The rise in demand for these disruptors and emphasis on the global value chain can lead to employee layoffs and enable large corporations to take over smaller domestic businesses, further increasing the country's unemployment rates.

Through the analysis and readings, it can be seen that Disruptive Innovation trading would be advantageous within the RCEP member countries and can allow RCEP to reach their goal of breaking barriers of economic and trading. In order to overcome threats that come with this trade, member countries must make certain that these technologies can be accessible and inexpensive so that consumers can benefit from this trade in general, especially if the innovation involves improvement in healthcare and education. Generally, it also depends on the level of acceptance of consumers towards these Disruptive Technologies and to adapt to the new changes that come along with them. It is also crucial that RCEP member countries reach a consensus where all parties can reach a win-win situation and not be taken advantage of by stronger, advanced, and bigger economies.

CONSENT FOR PUBLICATION

Not applicable.

CONFLICT OF INTEREST

The author declares no conflict of interest, financial or otherwise.

ACKNOWLEDGEMENTS

Declared none.

REFERENCES

Anshari, M. (2020). Workforce mapping of fourth industrial revolution: Optimization to identity. *Journal of Physics: Conference Series, 1477*(7), 072023. []. IOP Publishing.].
[http://dx.doi.org/10.1088/1742-6596/1477/7/072023]

Anshari, M., Sumardi, W.H. (2020). Employing big data in business organisation and business ethics. *International Journal of Business Governance and Ethics, 14*(2), 181-205.
[http://dx.doi.org/10.1504/IJBGE.2020.106349]

Anshari, M., Arine, M.A., Nurhidayah, N., Aziyah, H., Salleh, M.H.A. (2021). Factors influencing individual in adopting eWallet. *J. Financ. Serv. Mark., 26*(1), 10-23.
[http://dx.doi.org/10.1057/s41264-020-00079-5]

Britannica. (n.d.). Tariff - Tariff reduction and the growth of international trade. Encyclopedia Britannica. Retrieved March 15, 2021 https://www.britannica.com/topic/tariff/Tariff-reduction-and-the-grow-h-of-international-trade

David, D. (n.d.). UK wants to join the club - but what is the CPTPP? BBC. https://www.bbc.com/news/explainers-55858490

Japan, D. (n.d). Advantages of Free Trade Agreements (FTAs). Retrieved March 15, 2021, from https://www2.deloitte.com/jp/en/pages/strategy/articles/cbs/trade-compass02.html

Denning, S. (2016). Christensen updates disruption theory. *Strategy & Leadership.* Retrieved from https://www.emerald.com/insight/content/doi/10.1108/SL-01-2016-0005/full/html10.1108/SL-01-2016-0005

Technology, D. (2021). *Definition and How To Use It.* Retrieved from https://www.indeed.com/career-advice/career-development/disruptive-technology

Gourley, L. (2020). *Digital Disruption in the Manufacturing Industry.* PTC https://www.ptc.com/en/blogs/iiot/digital-disruption-in-manufacturing-industry

Hamdan, M., Chen, C.K., Anshari, M. (2020). Decision Aid in Budgeting Systems for Small & Medium Enterprises. *2020 International Conference on Decision Aid Sciences and Application (DASA),* 253-257. IEEE.
[http://dx.doi.org/10.1109/DASA51403.2020.9317018]

Henderson, J. (2019). *ASEAN CIOs outline the most disruptive technologies of 2019.* CIO.

https://www.cio.com/article/3405591/asean-cios-outline-the-most-disruptive-technologies-of-2019.html

Hong, Y. (2020). *RCEP: The benefits, the regret and the limitations.*https://www.thinkchina.sg/rcep-benefit--regret-and-limitations

Institut Jacques Delors. (2020). *RCEP: the geopolitical impact from a new wave of economic integration.*https://institutdelors.eu/en/publications/rcep-the-geopolitical-impact-from-a-new-wave-of-economic-integration/

KPMG. (2020). *Technology Innovation Hubs.* https://home.kpmg/content/dam/kpmg/il/Publications/PDF/2020/03/tech-innovation-hubs_2020.pdf

Livingston, J. (n.d.). How Disruptive Innovation Benefits The Marketplace. Innovation Enterprise Channels. Retrieved from: https://channels.theinnovationenterprise.com/articles/how-disruptive-innovation-benefits-th-
-
marketplace#:~:text=It%20can%20benefit%20both%20competition,and%20protected%20as%20intellectual%20property

Mulyani, M.A., Razzaq, A., Sumardi, W.H., Anshari, M. (2019). Smartphone Adoption in Mobile Learning Scenario. *2019 International Conference on Information Management and Technology (ICIMTech), Vol. 1*, 208-211. IEEE.
[http://dx.doi.org/10.1109/ICIMTech.2019.8843755]

Mulyani, M.A., Yusuf, S., Siregar, P., Nurihsan, J., Razzaq, A., Anshari, M. (2021). Fourth Industrial Revolution and Educational Challenges. *2021 International Conference on Information Management and Technology (ICIMTech), Vol. 1*, 245-249.IEEE..
[http://dx.doi.org/10.1109/ICIMTech53080.2021.9535057]

National Geographic Society. (2019). Tariffs. https://www.nationalgeographic.org/encyclopedia/tariffs/

Ranald, P. (2020). *RCEP has limited trade gains and ignores labour and human rights.*https://www.internationalaffairs.org.au/australianoutlook/rcep-has-limited-trde-gains-and-ignores-labour-and-human-rights/

Razzaq, A., Samiha, Y.T., Anshari, M. (2018). Smartphone habits and behaviors in supporting students self-efficacy. *International Journal of Emerging Technologies in Learning (iJET), 13*(2), 94.
[http://dx.doi.org/10.3991/ijet.v13i02.7685]

Reuber, P. (2009). https://www.sciencedirect.com/topics/earth-and-planetary-sciences/geopolitics

Si, S., Chen, H. (2020). A literature review of disruptive innovation: What it is, how it works and where it goes. *Journal of Engineering and Technology Management, 56*, 101568.
[http://dx.doi.org/10.1016/j.jengtecman.2020.101568]

Sytsma, T. (2020). *RCEP forms the world's largest trading bloc.*https://www.rand.org/blog/2020/12/rcep-forms-the-worlds-largest-trading-bloc-what-does.html

Swasdee, A., Anshari, M., Hamdan, M. (2020). Artificial Intelligence as Decision Aid in Humanitarian Response. *2020 International Conference on Decision Aid Sciences and Application (DASA),* 773-777. IEEE.
[http://dx.doi.org/10.1109/DASA51403.2020.9317111]

Swanson, A., Tankersley, J. (2020). *What is the USMCA? Here's What's in the New NAFTA.*https://www.nytimes.com/2020/01/29/business/economy/usmca-deal.html

Thani, F.A., Anshari, M. (2020). Maximizing Smartcard for Public Usage. *Int. J. Asian Bus. Inf. Manage., 11*(2), 121-132. [IJABIM].
[http://dx.doi.org/10.4018/IJABIM.2020040108]

https://economictimes.indiatimes.com/news/economy/foreign-trade/india-presses-for-greater-market--ccess-in-services-
at-rcep/articleshow/51122538.cms?utm_source=contentofinterest&utm_medium=text&utm_campaign=cppst

Trade unions express concern over RCEP. Industrial. Retrieved from http://www.industriall-union.org/ trade-unions-express-concern-over-rcep

What is RCEP? (n.d.). Retrieved from https://www.business-standard.com/about/what-is-rcep

Why Startups Fail. (2019). Top 20 Reasons 1 CB Insights. (2019). Retrieved from https://www.cbinsights.com/research/startup-failure-reasons-top/

CHAPTER 6

Is Big Data a Disruptive Innovation to RCEP?

Ares Albirru Amsal[1,*]

[1] *Faculty of Economics, Universitas Andalas, Padang, Indonesia*

Abstract: Big data does not only revolve around how much storage is needed for data, but rather its capability of assisting in many areas, such as economics, healthcare, educational institutions and others. Big data has a lot of potential to increase international trade. As the most significant free-trade agreement, the Regional Comprehensive Economic Partnership (RCEP) can utilise big data and related technologies to create fair and mutually beneficial trade. With the main characteristics of volume, variety, and velocity, big data provides strategic advantages for businesses that use it. The data can be processed using descriptive, diagnostics, predictive and prescriptive analytics. However, not all RCEP members have the same level of data processing capability. Therefore, this study examines how RCEP members utilise big data by extracting data from secondary sources. The results showed that each of the RCEP members' IT development also varies, and so does the use of big data. Therefore, decision-makers need to resolve issues related to data utilisation, especially in terms of digital literacy, security, and privacy.

Keywords: ASEAN, Big Data, Regional Comprehensive Economic Partnership (RCEP).

INTRODUCTION

Big data is evidence of technological progress inseparable from today's business. Big data brings new possibilities and opportunities to advance business more effectively and efficiently, including international trade. The cross-border exchange of goods and services cannot stand alone from the exchange of data and information. The data becomes a reference and impetus for making better decisions to conduct international trade. The establishment of the Regional Comprehensive Economic Partnership (RCEP) is a giant leap for Southeast Asian regional trade. As the most significant free trade agreement to date, RCEP will be a gigantic-free trade with 15 members from 10 members of ASEAN, China, Japan, Korea, Australia and New Zealand. Of course, the role of data from 15 countries will be centered on creating modern collaborations and producing mutu-

---

[*] **Corresponding author Ares Albirru Amsal:** Faculty of Economics, Universitas Andalas, Padang, Indonesia; E-mail: aresalbirruamsal@eb.unand.ac.id

Mahani Hamdan, Muhammad Anshari and Norainie Ahmad (Eds.)

al benefits. Practical and competitive trading requires high-quality data to identify potential markets that drive economic growth. In addition, the presence of data can encourage investment policies and regulations to comply with market needs. Therefore, data collection that focuses on creating economic activity could be a priority for the policymaker.

THE DEFINITION OF BIG DATA

Big data can be defined as data with three main characteristics: volume, variety, and velocity. Doug Laney first suggested the characters in 2001 (Kitchin & McArdle, 2016), which could be formed in structured, semi-structured, and unstructured data. The data is beneficial in machine learning applications, statistical modelling or other analytical methods. Usually, big data improve company operations, customer service, and digital marketing performance, which is expected to increase company revenue and profits (Anshari & Lim, 2017).

Businesses that use big data possess a competitive advantage because they can plan and access information faster than competitors (Sugiantoro *et al.*, 2020; Anshari *et al.*, 2019a). For example, an extensive data-driven marketing program can be employed to increase competitive advantage and conversion rates. Big data derived from historical data and real-time data can be analysed to enable faster business adaptation to changing market preferences. In addition, big data is now also commonly adopted in various fields. In financial services, big data is used by banks to minimise the risk of bad loans; in the transportation sector, big data is used to improve the supply chain by avoiding congestion or the closest route. The government has also begun to adopt big data for various purposes, such as building smart cities, disaster management, and crime prevention (Anshari *et al.*, 2019b; Zulkarnain *et al.*, 2017).

Volume, the first character, can be defined as a large quantity of data that requires advanced analytical methods to produce helpful information (Anshari & Almunawar, 2019). The data is usually stored not only on ordinary computer devices but also stored on a server or cloud. However, big data does not always mean large amounts of data, but it is integrated into the data source, such as streaming data and data logs.

Variety is the diversity of data sources taken not only from traditional sources. Data can be retrieved from social media, mobile phones, and health devices. Based on the type, variations of structured data can be in the form of financial reports and transactions. On the other hand, unstructured data can be text, documents, and multimedia taken from social media. Semi-structured data could be generated from activity log data on websites, sensors, or internet of things devices. Various types of these data can be collected and processed in one application system. The application integrates different types of data through data processing (Anshari *et al.*, 2015; Zulkarnain & Anshari, 2016).

Furthermore, velocity means the speed of data growth and the availability in almost real-time. This fast-growing data also requires a fast processing system. Besides processing in daily, weekly, or monthly cycles, big data can be processed in near-real time to make decisions on the spot (Anshari & Almunawar, 2018). Machine learning applications or artificial intelligence greatly influence big data processing speed, where patterns and insightful information can be generated with automated processes.

As research and big data applications develop, several other Vs have been added to complement the previous 3 *Vs*. However, two popular additional v's are veracity and value. Veracity is data quality determined from credible sources. Data sources must be trusted. Data taken from various random sources can result in poor quality, so it would take a long time to be processed or cleaned (Anshari *et al.*, 2016a; Arifin *et al.*, 2017). Bad data causes analysis errors that reduce the effectiveness of the data. Furthermore, value means the capacity of the data to provide meaningful input to support stakeholder decision-making. Here, the user must confirm the benefits that provide value-added for organisations.

Big data is not stored in ordinary data warehouses based on relational databases. Relational databases can only accommodate structured data. Big data is stored in data lakes built using Hadoop, cloud services, NoSQL or other platforms. The big data repository can interact with other platforms, including conventional databases (Anshari *et al.*, 2016b; Mulyani *et al.*, 2019). Big data processing requires a powerful engine because it processes unstructured data. Popular engines in big data processing are Hadoop and Spark.

(Big) Data Analytics

Data analysis is mainly divided into four categories: descriptive analytics, diagnostic analytics, predictive analytics, and prescriptive analytics. Each of these analyses has its benefits and objectives. The descriptive analysis uses data for statistics to describe events in the past. It helps businesses to understand past performance through visualisations such as graphics, charts, reports, and dashboards. The presentation format of the data is intended to be easy to understand (Anshari *et al.*, 2021b). This analysis is a fundamental analysis to prepare for further analysis. The basic form of descriptive analysis uses simple mathematics and statistics such as mean, median, and modus (Razzaq *et al.*, 2018).

The descriptive analysis uses two main methods, namely data aggregation and data mining, to obtain historical data. Data is collected and arranged to get a data set which will then be processed. The results will describe patterns and trends presented in an easy-to-understand form (Anshari & Alas, 2015).

In business, descriptive analysis is used to view daily, weekly, or monthly operations. A company report containing available inventory, sales, and revenue is an example of a descriptive analysis of a company. The data used can easily be collected because it comes from internal companies. In terms of big data, social media analysis is included in this category. The number of followers, likes, and shares could determine the products' level of popularity. The number of user comments on these social media platforms can also be used in this analysis. However, the descriptive analysis does not reveal the predictions from the historical data. Further analysis is needed to gain future insight in order to reveal the pattern of data.

Since descriptive analysis relies on data from the past, it is not difficult to obtain. Data analysis can also be easily carried out because it does not require high-level statistical skills. However, these data only provide surface information. Some other examples related to descriptive analysis are financial reports, marketing reports, social media engagement, and simple survey results.

Diagnostic analysis reveals why something happened. This analysis focuses on 'why' or what reasons have resulted in the current state of the situation. Therefore, this analysis still focuses on historical data. Understanding why a trend occurs will make the business run more efficiently. This analysis prevents companies from making wrong decisions over and over again.

In general, many factors cause a trend or event to occur. The diagnostic analysis provides an overall rationale for a comprehensive decision. It can also reveal what factors are the main drivers of events. This analysis still uses some descriptive analysis methods because it is still limited to historical data. However, diagnostic analysis digs deeper and sees the relationship between existing data.

Companies also need to use historical data outside of company data to make the analysis more comprehensive. An example of diagnostic analysis is understanding the downward trend in shopping for specific reasons. These reasons could be the company's internal factors (product changes) or external (the emergence of new competitors).

The third type of data analysis is predictive analytics. This analysis takes the data to a different level of analysis to predict the future. Often, machine learning models are used to predict future events. Analysing past data can provide insight into possible futures, which help in making anticipatory plans, avoiding risks, or setting goals.

The predictive analysis combines statistical-probability modelling techniques, data mining, and machine learning. The probability of an event occurring in the future is determined by the algorithm used. Deep learning can also be utilised in data analytics. This branch of machine learning imitates human thinking patterns called human neural networks. In its application, the interpretation of satellite images based on incident patterns could represent economic development progress in a particular area.

An example of predictive analysis is inventory forecasting to predict future inventory demand. For example, in E-commerce, companies can predict consumer preferences based on past purchase patterns. The prediction can also determine whether the customer will make a transaction or leave the store based on customer activity on the website.

Prescriptive analytics is at a higher level because it predicts the future and recommends anticipatory steps. This analysis offers a variety of activities that can be taken as well as a prediction of the output of these activities. This analysis is the final level of the type of analysis that helps in planning and predicting the results so that the best action can be resolved to solve the problem.

The complexity of prescriptive analysis requires specialists in statistics and data analysis. Therefore, this analysis is not used in daily operations. Machine learning is still used in this analysis but is more advanced. The data that has been collected will be stored in machine learning variables that combine internal and external data on the activities of a business. Data such as inventory reports and trend movements on social media can be used in this analysis. This analysis can anticipate what, when, why, and what results will occur from several action options. The recommendations given can be considered based on the opportunities and risks. This means prescriptive analysis offers several future solution options. The weakness of this system is that it needs skilled resources for analysis. It also requires enormous amounts of data to produce action and prediction models. However, this weakness is equal to its benefits which can parse crucial decision-making errors in the future (Anshari, 2020).

The example of descriptive analysis most often encountered in everyday life is GPS technology which can recommend travel route options. These options can plan the delivery time and estimate the product arrivals in the supply chain. This technology analyses based on real-time location data of road density taken from the user's mobile phone. Furthermore, the data is translated into traffic density information. The system then gives the driver the choice of the fastest route and several other options. Each route is equipped with distance travelled, travel time, and estimated arrival (Anshari & Sumardi, 2020).

Big Data for International Trade

RCEP members can utilise big data in various fields. According to the World Bank Group, there are several types of use of big data in international trade. These benefits are related to understanding economic activity, encouraging investment, optimising logistics and supply chain management, as well as increasing the competitiveness of cities and marginalised groups (World Bank Group, 2017).

Economic growth is one of the determinants of balanced and mutually beneficial trade activities. Each country produces its own data to measure its productivity. The data varies from taxes, contracts, and trade contracts. In addition, other fundamental data will also be utilised as a reference in the final calculation results. The complexity of the data must be presented in statistical models that provide insight into the economic trends of a country.

Correspondingly, the increasing complexity of economic connectivity between countries will become very difficult for decision-making. Moreover, tracking economic growth in low-middle-income countries is not easy because there are data limitations. Analysing these data using traditional tools will be very challenging. This is undoubtedly an opportunity to innovate big data solutions as an alternative for governments, businesses, and individuals who have difficulty accessing economic information in RCEP member countries.

For example, policymakers can use supporting evidence such as mobile phone use, facility images, and transaction records to determine how market and company conditions affect productivity. This information can be used as a basis for making decisions for economic intervention. Companies can also leverage data on price inequality from different markets of similar goods to understand competition in those markets. From an individual perspective, for example, big data can provide information related to commodity price data in the market before they bring it to the market.

Economic improvement can also be made through investments based on big data analysis. Investment is a significant component of economic growth to transfer technology and develop infrastructure and human resources. Providing an attractive business climate for investors is a priority for policymakers of RCEP members. Therefore, they must ensure the availability of efficient, transparent, and fair regulations to support investment in priority sectors of the economy.

The availability of regulations that support the current investment climate is getting better. Based on the Business Report by World Bank Group, it was revealed that the arrangement for the formation of a business entity had been accelerated from days to 20 days in the 2003 to 2015 period (World Bank Group, 2017). However, even though the progress was good, economic barrier factors remained, including for RCEP members. Policymakers must obtain relevant information to reduce investment disincentive factors. Accurate information also allows investors to understand the investment flow and the supporting or hindering factors. Investors also need data that enables them to see risk accurately. Big data can facilitate both parties to gain insight into the investment climate of a particular region. For policymakers, this information can increase the effectiveness of the regulations that have been made. Meanwhile, for investors, this information reduces investment errors in non-potential markets.

In international trade, logistics and supply chain flows affect the speed of the flow of goods and commodities between countries. The flow is influenced by infrastructure, which is the lack of road facilities. These obstacles caused the flow of goods to slow down, resulting in a decline in trade performance. In addition, there are also illegal levies during the trip, which make transportation costs swell. Policymakers must ensure the availability of adequate transportation facilities to support the supply chain by gathering information on how goods and services change. Each supply chain can generate big data, especially transactions supported by digital technology. With the spread of e-commerce among RCEP members, such as the Alibaba group in China and the GoTo group in Indonesia, the traditional retail revolution is becoming a reality.

In this era, big supply chain analytics is vital to master. Big supply chain analysis uses data and big data analysis methods for its trading activities. The data used is not only from internal companies but also external data. This method implements high-level computation of the data. As a result, the data analysis is able to provide input regarding front-line operations, strategic choices, and appropriate supply chain models. The use of big data in the supply chain cannot be represented from the aspects of planning, sourcing, production, warehousing, transportation, point-of-sales, and consumers (McKinsey) (Alicke, 2016). In the planning aspect, big data plays a role in minimising risk and product forecasting. In addition, the accuracy and optimisation of previously executed plans can also be assessed. In the aspect of sourcing, big data plays a role in identifying costs, calculating benefits from planning posts, making digital contracts, and balancing supply and demand. Big data can be utilised at the production level for production scheduling, just-in-time applications, quality control, and lot sizing. Warehousing locations close to consumer centres are big data applications in warehousing. In addition, stock relocation and workload optimisation also drive data-driven efficiency.

In transportation, big data helps schedule efficient deliveries to consumers and helps monitor delivery progress in real-time. Prevention of stock-outs, optimisation of shelf space and scheduling of sales employees can be big data applications in the point-of-sales sector. Big data makes it easier for companies to provide credit ratings and determine the appropriate payment terms for consumers. Big data can also detect product returns and provide preventive feedback. In e-commerce, consumer analysis can be carried out to provide relevant product recommendations based on previous purchase history. Through the application, decision-makers can encourage the formation of efficient trade. Moreover, if it is joined with the use of the Internet of Things on a national scale to monitor and provide recommendations for optimising logistics, it can create efficient and inclusive international trade.

To increase equal trade, every RCEP country must increase the competitiveness of cities and poor communities. Urbanisation occurs on an exponential scale. Urban residents will become the majority population in 2055, which is 66 percent. In developing countries, the urban population in 2018 was 31 percent and is projected to continue to increase to 41 percent by 2030. This growth has a significant impact on the competitiveness of the urban economy. On the other hand, increasing the competitiveness of entrepreneurs and businesses in RCEP countries still requires attention. The impact of urban growth still leaves a debt for the government to even out the development of human capital for the poor. Barriers to the progress of the poor are thought to be the result of a lack of financial inclusion. Their limited access to conventional financial services results in a lack of capital to build a business.

The government must anticipate the undirected development of the city due to massive urbanisation. The government can use big data to detect the distribution of poverty and develop empowerment programs. Big data can also be used to build entrepreneurial catalyst resources or business incubators to help communities thrive. Financial inclusion can also gain benefits from big data. Financial services can use big data to reach segments that were previously undetected. Access to electronic bills or telephone bills can bridge the creation of credit scoring for the marginalised, where using conventional credit scoring methods cannot be done. Fintech companies have started using mobile-phone data to detect behaviour and convert it into credit scores. In addition to this data, data from customers' social media can also be used to assess the digital reputation of fund borrowers. In the insurance industry, reliable patient track record data is used to offer insurance services. This data, connected to the internet, can also be used as a control that someone routinely conducts health checks. For example, customer data with a history of serious illness can be integrated into an insurance policy. Insurance can pay for health benefits if the patient takes regular treatment. Data on health facilities in the customer's city can also be considered to provide relevant benefits and insurance costs.

THE DEVELOPMENT OF BIG DATA IN RCEP MEMBERS

Big Data in Singapore

Singapore currently has the highest level of digital literacy among RCEP member countries. This is not surprising because Singapore hosts data from big companies like Facebook and Alibaba. The data analytics industry is also a crucial part of Singapore's economy, with a contribution of US$730 million per year. Connectivity in the city-state is also highly ranked in the world, ahead of Hong Kong, Iceland, and South Korea. This results from investing in infrastructure with the Smart Nation project that drives innovation and technology development activities. The adoption of big data in Singaporean companies is also high. In the health sector, hospitals have used real-time tracking of patient temperatures. In the financial sector, data analysis has been used for recruitment, increasing employee productivity and reducing attrition rates (EDB Singapore, 2018).

Big Data in Malaysia

Malaysia holds great potential in the big data market. The Malaysia Digital Economy Corporation (MDEC) projects that big data analytics will grow from 1.1 billion USD in 2021 to 1.9 billion USD in 2025 (Goh, 2021). The services sector is predicted to contribute 64% of spending, followed by banking and communications with one-third of the total spending. This progress cannot be separated from Covid-19, which drives the demand for big data analytics as well as its supporting facilities such as cloud services. This accelerates digital transformation and strengthens business sustainability. Companies that have invested in BDA will continue to increase their activities as Malaysia is the centre of their regional and global business operations. The increase in big data can be strengthened by the birth of start-ups. Big data is at the centre of the digital economy as it has resulted in significant growth in AI, IoT and automation technologies in Malaysia (DNA, 2021).

Big Data in the Philippines

The Philippines has established the Philippines Statical System (PSS) for national policy development and planning (Ordinario, 2018). Based on the 2018-2023

Philippine Statistical Development Program (PSDP), PSS will be strengthened for government administrative activities using big data. The government has strengthened the data ecosystem by strengthening data administration and exploring big data as a source of official statistics. For this reason, the government has intensively conducted statistical training for staff to use the latest software in the field of data processing. In addition to government employees, the training will bring academics, the private sector, and the representation of big data users. This training, in the future, will improve computing in the field of big data management. Through these activities, the Philippine government is expected to be able to handle the challenges of SDGs, big data, citizen-generated data, and the integration of the Philippines into membership in ASEAN (Philippine Statistics Authority, n.d.).

Big Data in Australia

The Australian government has included open data as a driving force for the creation of a smart city. A lot of data has been released to the public to support the creation of efficiency in the city's strategic planning. Urban big data contributes to the creation of better value for stakeholders. The data can encourage an increase in urban life. The use of this data must collaborate with other techniques in order to maximise its potential. Traditionally, big data has been stored offline and analysed in batches. However, the increasing speed of real-time data growth has created new opportunities for rapid decision-making. In the public sector, big data is still not widely used, even though the government is quite aware of the benefits of this data. Big data technology has the potential to apply data analysis applications to aspects of predictive, real-time, and natural language analysis (Watson & Ryan, 2020).

Big Data in Korea

The 'Korean New Deal' is a post-pandemic stimulus project launched by the Korean government as well as a sign of Korea's national ambition for big data. Korea has also established a Presidential Committee on the Fourth Industrial Revolution, or PCFIR, to accelerate the industrial revolution. Accompanying the project, 'Korea Data 119' has also been launched to support the success of the PCFIR agenda. The vision of PC FIR is to drive the digital economy through the safe disclosure, distribution and use of public data. The use of big data and AI will be applied to all sectors, from consumption, finance, logistics, and health. Korea also pays attention to privacy, which regulates the use of data for handling the pandemic. Data from public facilities such as CCTV, public transportation, credit cards, and telecommunications will be used to detect Covid-19 infections. Currently, there are three challenges in using big data in Korea. First is the insufficient utilisation of data by the private sector. Second is the decentralisation of data collection by various government agencies. Third, big data applications are still at an early stage. To address these challenges, the Korean government took the initiative to create a private-sector-friendly ecosystem and promote a comprehensive data policy (Salmon, 2021).

Big Data in New Zealand

New Zealand has updated the Government Data Strategy and Roadmap 2021, which was first compiled in 2018 (Data Lead, 2021). The Roadmap is designed to create an inclusive and integrated data system that supports the investment climate. Data inclusion means that everyone has access to decision-making information. There are four fundamental components of a government data system, namely data, capability, leadership, and infrastructure. Recently, New Zealand has built a data centre with the hope of boosting the economy by 1.4 billion USD (Sharon, 2022). This is the second data centre located in Auckland, the country's capital city. The construction of the data centre is expected to experience significant growth in the next few periods. However, privacy-related issues are considered a major issue along with the market's growth. In the health sector, big data applications have been tried to be applied to the elderly population (Kotlarsky & Oshri, 2020). Motion sensor technology in the elderly was created to detect the behaviour of the elderly in their homes. This is useful for monitoring health and taking quick steps if an emergency situation occurs.

Big Data in Brunei Darussalam

Brunei Darussalam's readiness has been studied by Sait & Ali (2022). The study assessed the readiness of technology implementation using social, technological, environmental, and policy (STEP) aspects. The social aspect is the capacity of the community in deep knowledge, expertise, and literacy, which is related to the digital world. The technological aspect represents the availability of supporting devices, such as smartphones and internet connections (Ahad *et al.*, 2017; Anshari *et al.*, 2021a). The drive to adopt digital technology is a reflection of environmental factors. Finally, the policy involved takes the form of a regulation issued by the government regarding digital security and society. Based on this research, Brunei meets three of the four categories, namely social, technological, and environmental aspects.

Big Data in China

Big Data has great potential to revolutionise the Chinese economy. China, as the world's largest consumer market, produces a large number of export goods. Big Data can provide insight for economic actors. The amount of data currently produced by China occupies the number two position in the world. The data comes from Chinese IT-based companies, such as Tencent Holdings. The use of Big Data is not only by the IT sector. Big Data is the trigger for significant growth in the automotive industry. Through big data analysis, Chinese automotive companies have succeeded in providing the best offers to potential customers. The automotive industry also collaborates with each other to design new car designs to reduce costs. China's largest computer company 'Lenovo' is also participating in promoting the use of big data and AI in the automotive manufacturing industry. This development will certainly be a big capital for China to make greater exports to RCEP member countries (Mordor Intelligence, 2021).

Big Data in Indonesia

The Indonesian government, since 2020, has been trying to issue policies to promote digital transformation and drive decision-based data (Rahman, 2020). Indonesian research institutes have drawn up a national strategy to develop artificial intelligence that will be utilised for the public and private sectors. This strategy is expected to sustain economic growth and reduce inequality by using AI in the health sector, bureaucratic reform, education and research, food security, and building smart cities. Currently, Indonesia still suffers from a lack of 4G access for 15 percent of villages and sub-districts. In addition, the challenges of HR and organisational culture are still a record for the implementation of big data in Indonesia.

Big Data in Japan

Japan has started processing regulations aimed at driving the flow of 'industrial big data' generated from the sale of goods and services. The regulation also aims to prevent misuse of the information that companies exchange. Industrial big data will be collected from sites in automotive manufacturing, robotics, healthcare, and other industries. In addition, data from US-based IT companies such as Google, Apple, Facebook, Amazon, and IT companies from China will be included in the processing of industrial big data. The data will be exchanged to encourage the acceleration of innovation in the Japanese industry (NIKKEI, 2021). In addition, the Japanese ministry of economy, trade and industry has also promoted the use of IoT, blockchain, sharing economy, AI and other technologies with the support of regulatory reform (METI, 2021).

Big Data in Thailand

Thailand has placed big data as one of the main national developments. Together with the national big data policy, Thailand formed a steering committee for the implementation of big data, data centres, and cloud computing policies

(Pornwasin, 2018). The team covers three aspects, namely legislation, IS government architecture and integration, and the development of human data sources. The targets of using big data in Thailand's policy are to improve the quality of life of citizens, conduct smart operations, provide citizen-centered services, share resources for national development, and help save the national budget. The big data industry in Thailand is expected to continue to grow. The main users of big data are financial and banking services, communication media, transportation, manufacturing, and construction. Big data will be the key to economic growth, as well as help reduce financial inequality and grow from middle-income countries to high-income countries. There are four factors driving Thailand's digital economy; security, infrastructure, government, manpower and applications. The government will focus on providing infrastructure so that fast internet can be felt throughout the country (Fang, 2018).

Big Data in Lao PDR

Not much information is found regarding big data in Laos. This ASEAN country does not have a coastline and is still trying to apply big data to its government. The progress of big data studies can be felt in universities with the holding of the 3rd International Conference on Big Data Applications and Services (BIGDAS-L) in 2018 in Vientiane (The Laotian Times, 2016). The topic of big data has been widely taught in universities, especially in engineering faculties. Based on the global digital overview report for 2020, mobile phone users from Laos are 79%, with internet penetration only reaching 43% of the population. Laos' population is increasing by 1.5% annually, with mobile phone growth below that of 1.3% between 2019-2020. Internet penetration growth was faster at 6.5%, and social media users increased by 12% (43% of the population). The progress of the Internet and mobile phone penetration is expected to encourage big data applications for the Lao government and people (Yap, 2020).

Big Data in Vietnam

Vietnam has experienced rapid digital progress. Technological skills are sufficient for government employees, entrepreneurs, and citizens. This is also the impact of Covid-19, which drives social and economic transformation digitally. Currently, citizens can register and pay electricity bills using a smartphone. E-commerce has helped increase agricultural sales 174 times. In 2021, Vietnam's technological development was evidenced by the addition of 5,600 digital companies in the country (Dharmaraj, 2021, 2022).

Big Data in Cambodia

The agricultural sector is the main target for big data implementation in Cambodia. In 2019, the agricultural sector only contributed 20.7% to the gross domestic product, a drastic decrease from 28.8% in 2014. To overcome this, the government has set a target for modernising the agricultural sector by 2030. The plan integrates cutting-edge technologies, such as IoT and big data, through smart farming. Cambodia's Ministry of Agriculture, Forestry and Fisheries (MAFF) has released the Agricultural Big Data Platform (ABDP), which enables production monitoring and the use of tracking systems. With more and more buyers and sellers connecting to the internet, there is potential to model price fluctuations that can improve farmers' livelihoods (Lim, 2020).

Big Data in Myanmar

Big data technology has been closely linked to the provision of open data in Myanmar. Open data is data that can be used and shared free of charge by anyone, to anyone, for any purpose. The use of open data aims to support the HR sector. The data has been used for making road images, as well as mapping the impact of disasters. The data helps bridge social issues between policymakers and the public. The challenges of using this data are the limited use of the internet in rural and conflict areas, lack of data literacy, and language barriers (Nuam & Chaudhary, 2018).

Big Data Challenges in RCEP Members

For big data to be meaningful and advantageous, data analyst talent and skills are required. These talents are expected to shape human resource needs, which require capabilities in big data utilisation as well as in the crafting of policies relevant to trade among the RCEP countries. However, based on digital skills index data, there are still RCEP members who are below the world median. The digital skill index shows the results of a survey on population skills using digital skills, such as computers, basic coding, and digital reading.

Table **1** shows the digital skills index of 14 out of 15 RCEP members. The data was taken from 2017 to 2019. The data does not include Myanmar due to the unavailability of data at the World Bank. Overall, the majority of members show a downward trend in digital skills. Only 4 out of 14 countries experienced an increase, namely Malaysia, Brunei, Lao RDR, and Cambodia. At the same time, China has the same data for the three years. With the world median at 4.2, there are member countries that are below the Lao PDR, Vietnam and Cambodia. These results should certainly be of concern to the government and policymakers in order to be able to provide human resources who are data literate. The digital skill gap between member countries must also be a concern. Countries with high data proficiency will have a better competitive advantage in RCEP.

Table 1. Digital skills among the population.

Country	2017	2018	2019
Singapore	5.76	5.66	5.58
Malaysia +	5.35	5.39	5.37
Philippines	4.54	5.14	5.06
Australia	5.23	5.15	5.02
Republic of Korea	5.04	4.98	4.99
New Zealand	5.39	5.2	4.93
Brunei +	4.54	4.66	4.86
China	4.66	4.66	4.66
Indonesia	4.77	4.73	4.51
Japan	4.48	4.59	4.43
Thailand	4.38	4.37	4.26
Lao PDR +	4.05	3.91	4.14
Vietnam	3.97	3.67	3.77
Cambodia +	3.46	3.61	3.57
Myanmar	-	-	-

Source: (World Bank, 2020), World median: 4.2.

The digital skill index more or less describes big data literacy in a country. The skills to learn from big data are becoming increasingly important for governments, businesses and individuals alike. Understanding the opportunities that big data brings makes trading even more profitable. Not only skills in taking data, processing and interpreting data are the key to balanced and fair trade.

Literacy is defined as the ability to learn or read. Data literacy reflects the ability to read data, learn, and make plans based on that data (Christozov & Toleva-Stoimenova, 2015). The use of IT represents this skill, sometimes also called computer literacy.

Maintaining trade growth and performance while maintaining positive information has become difficult. This is a challenge for big data users in the field of international trade because a lot of business and country data is stored. In the daily cycle, a lot of sensitive data is processed by businesses that are members of RCEP. If the wrong party owns this information, the consequences can be dire. Traditional security approaches cannot completely secure the data. Cyber-attacks often occur in companies, requiring a special team to counteract them. The more data is collected, the more expensive and difficult it is to maintain. There have been many cases of the leaking of sensitive data to the public, which has harmed many parties. This incident shows how important data security is.

With regard to privacy, the government, social media, and companies must be very careful about whom the data is handed over. Big IT organisations like Google and Facebook (Meta) may own where the users live and their activities. The possibility of sensitive information mining overshadows user privacy. In a business context, a lack of control over IT can lead to IT fraud or business rivals taking data illegally. As a result, the company can suffer huge losses because the data leak contains financial reports, personal information, or new product information.

Privacy policies vary from country to country. Some RCEP countries give governments full access to user data, and others do not. The alignment of perspectives is a challenge for RCEP members in order to limit the rights of a country to access sensitive data. The method in the form of terms and agreement in use has been applied. However, users who surf the internet still leave a digital footprint. Therefore, if necessary, the company needs to use an anonymous account, so the trace is not tracked. Privacy-related policy interventions must be implemented jointly to ensure that company privacy is respected and ethical practices are implemented. Privacy in the global era can be a central issue for decision-makers.

CONCLUSION

Big data is certainly an asset that is valuable to these countries. Each of the RCEP members used big data in many ways, as it has many functions. As big data contains important information, thus the RCEP members must also provide security to prevent data leakage. This study also highlights the importance of digital skills as they must be possessed and continue to enhance to utilise big data successfully. The knowledge of using big data can be vast and applied to many settings, but issues such as literacy, skilling, and privacy must also be considered.

CONSENT FOR PUBLICATION

Not applicable.

CONFLICT OF INTEREST

The author declares no conflict of interest, financial or otherwise.

ACKNOWLEDGEMENTS

Declared none.

REFERENCES

Ahad, A.D., Anshari, M., Razzaq, A. (2017). Domestication of smartphones among adolescents in Brunei darussalam. *International Journal of Cyber Behavior, Psychology and Learning, 7*(4), 26-39.
[http://dx.doi.org/10.4018/IJCBPL.2017100103]

Alicke, K. (2016). *Big data and the supply chain: The big-supply-chain analytics landscape (Part 1) | McKinsey.* Operations. https://www.mckinsey.com/business-functions/operations/our-insights/big-data-and-the-supply-chain-the-big-supply-chain-analytics-landscape-part-1

Anshari, M. (2020). Workforce mapping of fourth industrial revolution: Optimization to identity. *J. Phys. Conf. Ser., 1477*(7), 072023.
[http://dx.doi.org/10.1088/1742-6596/1477/7/072023]

Anshari, M., Sumardi, W.H. (2020). Employing big data in business organisation and business ethics. *International Journal of Business Governance and Ethics, 14*(2), 181-205.
[http://dx.doi.org/10.1504/IJBGE.2020.106349]

Anshari, M., Arine, M.A., Nurhidayah, N., Aziyah, H., Salleh, M.H.A. (2021). Factors influencing individual in adopting eWallet. *J. Financ. Serv. Mark., 26*(1), 10-23.
[http://dx.doi.org/10.1057/s41264-020-00079-5]

Anshari, M., Almunawar, M.N., Razzaq, A. (2021). Developing Talents vis-à-vis Fourth Industrial Revolution. *International Journal of Asian Business and Information Management, 12*(4), 20-32.
[http://dx.doi.org/10.4018/IJABIM.20211001.oa2]

Anshari, M., Nurmaini, S., Lim, S.A., Caesarendra, W. (2019). Big Data and Big Challenge for Knowledge Management. *2019 International Conference on Electrical Engineering and Computer Science (ICECOS)* IEEE.
[http://dx.doi.org/10.1109/ICECOS47637.2019.8984508]

Anshari, M., Almunawar, M.N., Lim, S.A., Al-Mudimigh, A. (2019). Customer relationship management and big data enabled: Personalization & customization of services. *Applied Computing and Informatics, 15*(2), 94-101.
[http://dx.doi.org/10.1016/j.aci.2018.05.004]

Anshari, M., Almunawar, M.N. (2019). Big Data in Healthcare for Personalization & Customization of Healthcare Services. *2019 International Conference on Information Management and Technology (ICIMTech)* IEEE.

Anshari, M., Almunawar, M.N. (2018). Social customer relationship management, election and political campaign. *Int. J. Electron. Cust. Relatsh. Manag., 11*(4), 332-346.
[http://dx.doi.org/10.1504/IJECRM.2018.096239]

Anshari, M., Lim, S.A. (2017). E-government with big data enabled through smartphone for public services: Possibilities and challenges. *Int. J. Public Adm., 40*(13), 1143-1158.
[http://dx.doi.org/10.1080/01900692.2016.1242619]

Anshari, M., Alas, Y., Guan, L.S. (2016). Developing online learning resources: Big data, social networks, and cloud computing to support pervasive knowledge. *Educ. Inf. Technol., 21*(6), 1663-1677.
[http://dx.doi.org/10.1007/s10639-015-9407-3]

Anshari, M., Alas, Y., Sabtu, N. P. H., Hamid, M. S. A. (2016). Online Learning: trends, issues and challenges in the Big Data Era. *Journal of e-Learning and Knowledge Society, 12*, 1.

Anshari, M., Alas, Y., Sabtu, N.I., Yunus, N. (2016). A survey study of smartphones behavior in Brunei: A proposal of modelling big data strategies. *International Journal of Cyber Behavior, Psychology and*

Learning, *6*(1), 60-72.
[http://dx.doi.org/10.4018/IJCBPL.2016010104]

Anshari, M., Alas, Y., Yunus, N., Sabtu, N.I., Hamid, M.H. (2015). Social customer relationship management and student empowerment in online learning systems. *International Journal of Electronic Customer Relationship Management,* *9*(2/3), 104-121.
[http://dx.doi.org/10.1504/IJECRM.2015.071711]

Anshari, M., Alas, Y. (2015). Smartphones habits, necessities, and big data challenges. *Journal of High Technology Management Research,* *26*(2), 177-185.
[http://dx.doi.org/10.1016/j.hitech.2015.09.005]

Arifin, F., Hariadi, M., Anshari, M. (2017). Extracting Value and Data Analytic from Social Networks: Big Data Approach. *Adv. Sci. Lett.,* *23*(6), 5286-5288.
[http://dx.doi.org/10.1166/asl.2017.7360]

Christozov, D., Toleva-Stoimenova, S. (2015). Big Data Literacy. *Adv. Knowl. Acquis. Transf. Manage.,* 156-171.
[http://dx.doi.org/10.4018/978-1-4666-8122-4.ch009]

Data Lead. . (2021). *Government Data Strategy and Roadmap 2021 - data.govt.nz.* Docs. data.govt.nzhttps://www.data.govt.nz/docs/data-strategy-and-roadmap-for-new-zealand-2021/

Dharmaraj, S.. (2021). *Vietnam Added 5,600 New Digital Technology Firms in 2021 – OpenGov Asia.*https://opengovasia.com/vietnam-added-5600-new-digital-technology-firms-in-2021/

Dharmaraj, S.. (2022). *Surge in Digital Transformation of Services Across Vietnam – OpenGov Asia.* .https://opengovasia.com/surge-in-digital-transformation-of-services-across-vietnam/

DNA. . (2021). *Malaysia's Big Data Analytics market to grow to US$1.9bil in 2025: MDEC | Digital News Asia.*https://www.digitalnewsasia.com/business/malaysias-big-data-market-grow-us19bil-2025-idc

Singapore, E.D.B. (2018). *Singapore's big ambitions for big data in 2019.* https://www.edb.gov.sg/en/business-insights/insights/singapore-s-big-ambitions-for-big-data-in-2019.html

Fang, Y. (2018). How Is Thailand Using Big Data? - Thai News. Tech. https://www.thailand-busines-news.com/tech/70563-how-is-thailand-using-big-data.html

Goh, J. (2021). MDEC's commissioned study shows Malaysia's big data analytics market expected to grow to US$1.9b by 2025 • MDBC. 2021. https://www.mdbc.com.my/mdecs-commissioned-study-shows-malay-ias-big-data-analytics-market-expected-to-grow-to-us1-9b-by-2025/

Kitchin, R., McArdle, G. (2016). What makes Big Data, Big Data? Exploring the ontological characteristics of 26 datasets. *Big Data Soc.,* *3*, 1.
[http://dx.doi.org/10.1177/2053951716631130]

Kotlarsky, J., Oshri, I. (2020). Using big data analytics and AI to help NZ prepare for an ageing population - The University of Auckland. Business School, Business and Economy. https://www.auckland.ac.nz/en/news/2020/06/23/using-big-da-a-analytics-and-ai-to-help-nz-prepare-for-an-ageing.html

Lim, G. (2020). *How Cambodia can revive agriculture with big data | ASEAN Today. Cambodia.* .https://www.aseantoday.com/2020/09/how-cambodia-can-revive-agriculture-with-big-data/

METI. (2021). Information Economy / METI Ministry of Economy, Trade and Industry. Information Economy. https://www.meti.go.jp/english/policy/mono_info_service/information_economy/index.html

Mordor Intelligence. (2021). Big Data Technology in China Market | 2022 - 27 | Industry Share, Size, Growth - Mordor Intelligence. Industry Reports. https://www.mordorintelligence.com/industry-reports/investmen--opportunities-of-big-data-technology-in-china

Mulyani, M.A., Razzaq, A., Sumardi, W.H., Anshari, M. (2019). Smartphone Adoption in Mobile Learning Scenario. *2019 International Conference on Information Management and Technology (ICIMTech).* IEEE.

[http://dx.doi.org/10.1109/ICIMTech.2019.8843755]

NIKKEI. (2021). *Japan to set rules to promote "industrial big data" utilization - Nikkei Asia. Business Trends.*https://asia.nikkei.com/Business/Business-trends/Japan-to-set-rules-to-promote-industrial-big-data-utilization

Nuam, C. D., Chaudhary, S. (2018). Open Data & Big Data: *their relevance and impact on Myanmar's humanitarian/development sectors.*

Ordinario, C. (2018). *Philippines meets 'Big Data' challenges through PSDP 2018-2023. The Broader Look.* .https://businessmirror.com.ph/2018/11/01/phl-meets-big-data-challenges-through-psdp-2018-to-2023/

Philippine Statistics Authority (n.d). *Bigdata - Objectives and Expected Outcomes | Philippine Statistics Authority.* Retrieved January 28, 2022, from https://psa.gov.ph/content/bigdata-objectives-and-expec-ed-outcomes

Pornwasin, A. (2018). Big data making giant leaps . Tech. https://www.nationthailand.com/tech/30354999

Rahman, D.F. (2020). *Indonesia works on use of big data for better decision-making process - Business - The Jakarta Post. Business.* .https://www.thejakartapost.com/news/2020/10/15/indonesia-works-on-use-o--big-data-for-better-decision-making-process.html

Razzaq, A., Samiha, Y.T., Anshari, M. (2018). Smartphone habits and behaviors in supporting students self-efficacy. *International Journal of Emerging Technologies in Learning (iJET), 13*(2), 94. [http://dx.doi.org/10.3991/ijet.v13i02.7685]

Sait, M.A., Ali, M.A. (2022). Assessing Brunei Darussalam Public and Private Sector Readiness Towards Big Data Application. *International Journal of Asian Business and Information Management, 13*(2), 1-22. [http://dx.doi.org/10.4018/IJABIM.20220701.oa7]

Salmon, A. (2021). *Korea aims for the sky in masterplan for big data - Asia Times. South Korea.*https://asiatimes.com/2021/03/korea-aims-for-the-sky-in-masterplan-for-big-data/

Sharon, A. (2022). https://opengovasia.com/massive-new-data-centres-to-boost-nz-economy/

Sugiantoro, B., Anshari, M., Sudrajat, D. (2020). Developing Framework for Web Based e-Commerce: Secure-SDLC. *J. Phys. Conf. Ser., 1566*(1), 012020. [http://dx.doi.org/10.1088/1742-6596/1566/1/012020]

The Laotian Times. (2016). *Conference Boosts Big Data Use - Laotian Times. Business, Tech.* .https://laotiantimes.com/2016/12/23/conference-boosts-big-data-use/

Watson, R.B., Ryan, P.J. (2020). Big Data Analytics in Australian Local Government. *Smart Cities, 3*(3), 657-675. [http://dx.doi.org/10.3390/smartcities3030034]

World Bank. (2020). *GCI 4.0: Digital skills among population - TCdata360. TCdata360.* https://tcdata360.worldbank.org/indicators/hb0649ed2?country=BRA&indicator=41400&viz=line_chart&years=2017,2019

World Bank Group. (2017). *Harnessing the Power of Big Data for Trade and Competitiveness Policy.* https://openknowledge.worldbank.org/handle/10986/26266

Yap, J. (2020). https://laotiantimes.com/2020/07/09/digital-2020-report-on-laos-released-internet-mobile-and-social-media/

Zulkarnain, N., Anshari, M. (2016). Big data: Concept, applications, & challenges. *2016 International Conference on Information Management and Technology (ICIMTech)* IEEE. [http://dx.doi.org/10.1109/ICIMTech.2016.7930350]

Zulkarnain, N., Anshari, M., Almunawar, M.N. (2017). Big data and mobile learning in generating pervasive knowledge. *2017 International Conference on Information Management and Technology (ICIMTech)* IEEE. [http://dx.doi.org/10.1109/ICIMTech.2017.8273533]

CHAPTER 7

Financial Technology Innovation - Peer-to-Peer (P2P) Lending in the RCEP Member States

Rayna Kartika[1,*]

¹ Faculty of Economics, Universitas Andalas, Padang, Indonesia

Abstract: Regional Comprehensive Economic Partnership (RCEP) aims to strengthen the economy and the free trade agreement among 10 ASEAN member states (Brunei Darussalam, Cambodia, Indonesia, Lao PDR, Malaysia, Myanmar, Philippines, Singapore, Thailand, and Vietnam) and five partner states (China, Japan, South Korea, Australia, and New Zealand). One of the ways to improve economic growth is to enhance the investment sector into start-ups and SMEs. Peer-to-peer lending platforms exist to ease the mechanism of funds lending and borrowing from investors to start-ups and SMEs. Currently, the rise of P2P lending, particularly in RCEP member states, has boosted the economic growth and development of technology. The government assistance in setting up the regulation regarding the mechanism of P2P lending has been carried out in order to create a clean and transparent practice of P2P lending among borrowers and lenders. Therefore, this chapter describes the introduction of RCEP member states and P2P lending and the mechanism for adopting P2P lending platforms in RCEP member states. P2P is indeed a platform that RCEP members can practice. However, the risks must be considered and addressed in order to prevent threats to their economic growth.

Keywords: Borrowers, Economic Growth, Lenders, Peer-to-peer Lending, RCEP.

OVERVIEW OF THE RCEP MEMBER STATES AND PEER-TO-PEER LENDING

Regional Comprehensive Economic Partnership (RCEP) is a free trade agreement involving 10 ASEAN member countries (Brunei Darussalam, Cambodia, Indonesia, Lao PDR, Malaysia, Myanmar, Philippines, Singapore, Thailand, and Vietnam) with five partner countries (China, Japan, South Korea, Australia, and New Zealand). The world's largest free-trade block was launched in 2012 with the aim of deepening economic ties among the 16 Asia-Pacific Countries (Fig. **1**). In 2015, it was originally planned to be completed but repeatedly missed deadlines; in 2016, six rounds' talks were held, and in 2017, the First RCEP Summit was

---

* **Corresponding author Rayna Kartika:** Faculty of Economics, Universitas Andalas, Padang, Indonesia;
E-mail: raynakartika@eb.unand.ac.id

Mahani Hamdan, Muhammad Anshari and Norainie Ahmad (Eds.)

held in the capital city of the Philippines, Manila. In 2018, the second RCEP Summit was held in Singapore, and in 2019, the talks accelerated when the 15 RCEP participating countries completed text-based negotiations and all market access issues in Bangkok, Thailand, with the aim of signing the free trade Mega Pact. That year, to be precise, on November 15, 2020, the RCEP agreement was agreed upon and signed by all ASEAN members and five partner countries at the 37th ASEAN Summit, which was held virtually with Vietnam as the host House.

The ASEAN General said the rapid ratification process by the signatory countries is a clear reflection of members' firm commitment to a fair and open multilateral trading system for the benefit of the peoples of the region and the world. The implementation of the RCEP Agreement, which started on January 1, 2022, will provide a tremendous boost to the post-COVID-19 economic recovery efforts.

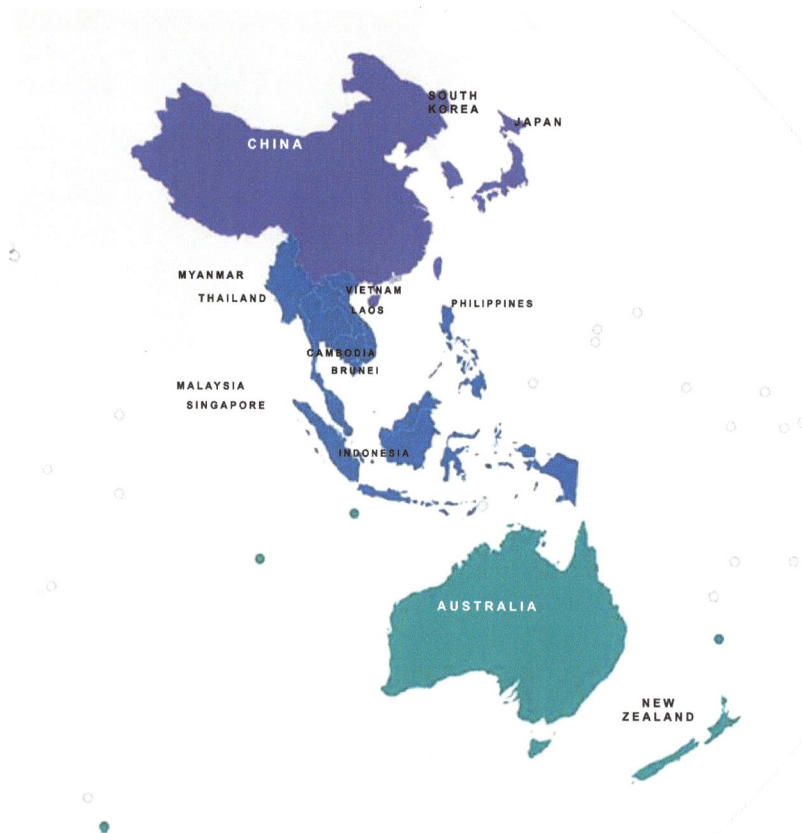

Fig. (1). Regional Comprehensive Economic Partnership Member States.

Southeast Asia is a very strategic area in terms of trade, natural resources, and also human resources. These factors are extremely attractive for other countries to cooperate and invest in because they have good prospects for the future. Countries in the Southeast Asian region also have a positive response by opening up and constantly innovating. The ASEAN Free Trade Area (AFTA) is a way to develop local production throughout ASEAN countries. Investment in the form of shares is still the attraction of the ASEAN region. The performance of the stock market tends to show a positive stretch. As a form of ASEAN's response to the dynamics in the global region, RCEP is believed to provide economic potential and market integrity of 3.2 billion people (45% of the population) and economic regions with a Gross Domestic Product (GDP) of USD 20 Trillion (28% of world GDP).

The Regional Comprehensive Economic Partnership will open a market network that will become an opportunity for countries in the world. Therefore, all countries must be able to enter the market, specially manufactured products that will provide added value to the intellectual property because the participating countries are also struggling entirely to agree on several provisions and respond to various dynamics of changes in the world economy in implementing the RCEP agreement, which is targeted to be ratified in the first quarter of 2021 due to global shocks caused by the trade war and the Covid-19 pandemic.

According to the Indonesian Minister of Economy, the implementation of the RCEP agreement will create many benefits for Indonesia, including certainty and uniformity of trade rules, a more conducive investment climate, increased business opportunities for goods and services as well as strengthening investment and integration into the Regional Value Chain (RVC). In a comprehensive and modern agreement, RCEP not only regulates market access but also contains several important features, such as the creation of a conducive electronic trading system (e-commerce) ecosystem and increasing the capacity of MSME actors, especially in terms of promotion and digital access to enter the regional supply chain.

RCEP requires its member countries to adapt to technology, and the financial sector is no exception. Now, anyone can send money only online, known as Peer-to-peer (P2P) Lending. The current growth is increasingly rapid, and it is easily accessible to people who still find it difficult to get loan funds. P2P Lending will facilitate access to loans that will help funds for education and health with their respective standards ranging from loan creditworthiness, and interest rates to security.

P2P Lending services are proliferating due to the ease of access provided to prospective borrowers, where prospective borrowers no longer need to bother queuing at banks or other financial services to get loan funds (Ahad *et al.*, 2017;

Anshari *et al.*, 2020; Arifin *et al.*, 2017). Not only that, but users are also not too bothered with administrative problems, such as supporting letters and so on. To borrow online on the P2P Lending platform, users only need an I.D. card (Hamdan *et al.*, 2020; Thani & Anshari, 2020).

In the midst of the increasing popularity of P2P lending in the world, several ASEAN countries have participated in the alternative financing arena (Anshari *et al.*, 2021c; Mulyani *et al.*, 2019; Swasdee *et al.*, 2020). Four countries with quite developed P2P lending are Indonesia, Malaysia, Singapore, and Thailand. The largest P2P lending market share in ASEAN is currently controlled by Singapore. P2P Lending creates an online platform that provides facilities for fund owners to provide loans directly to debtors with higher returns, while fund borrowers can apply for credit directly to fund owners with more accessible terms and a faster process compared to conventional financial institutions (Mulyani *et al.*, 2021; Anshari, 2020; Zulkarnain *et al.*, 2017). RCEP requires the State to run its economy by maximising investment in all fields, either directly or indirectly.

This investment in P2P Lending promises a fairly high return per year, and we can imagine if the cooperation of every country in RCEP can make the most of it. However, investing must be in accordance with the profile and risk appetite and how to manage it. The earliest step in the P2P Lending process is to understand the risks.

The way P2P Lending works is as follows:

a) Membership registration. Users (Lenders and Borrowers) register online *via* a computer or smartphone.

b) Borrowers apply for loans.

c) The P2P Lending platform analyses and selects a suitable borrower to apply for a loan, including determining the risk of the borrower.

d) The selected borrower will be placed by the P2P Lending platform in the online P2P lending marketplace, along with comprehensive information about the profile and risks of the borrower.

e) P2P Lending investors analyse and select borrowers listed in the P2P Lending marketplace provided by the platform.

f) P2P Lending investors make funding to selected borrowers through the P2P Lending platform.

g) Borrowers return loans according to the loan repayment schedule to the P2P

Lending platform.

h) P2P Lending investors receive loan repayments from borrowers through the platform.

The Economy of the RCEP Member States and Its Nature of P2P Lending Platforms.

Brunei Darussalam

Brunei Darussalam's economy is centered on the oil and gas sector and trade. Brunei Darussalam's GDP is considered to be one of the highest in the world. The Brunei Darussalam economy uses the Brunei Dollar currency pegged with the Singapore Dollar, thus sharing the same value with the latter. Brunei Darussalam's economic resources lie in the natural, tourism and industrial sectors. Economic resources in the field of natural products include geographical conditions in the form of lowlands and hills, abundant oil and gas, as well as coconut, rubber and oil palm plantations. Economic resources in the tourism sector are in the form of cultural tourism, the floating market community and the palace of the Sultanate of Brunei. In the industrial sector, the source of the economy comes from the oil and gas industry as well as onshore and offshore mining. Brunei Darussalam's economy is mainly built by workers in the service sector (77.2%) and a small part in the industrial sector (21.4%) and plantations (1.4%). Local communities develop Brunei Darussalam's economy through social development and economic development supported by the government.

The government encourages the people of Brunei Darussalam to become entrepreneurs by establishing an economic association or organisation. Local people work in the field of production and promotion of local handicrafts, assisted by the government through the form of exposure and exhibitions. Brunei Darussalam's economic development is managed by the Brunei Economic Development Council (BEDC). It also develops the economy through micro-enterprises for youth working in the private sector. The International Monetary Fund determined that Brunei's per capita gross domestic product is one of the highest in the world.

To stimulate developments in Brunei 'Darussalam's FinTech sector, The Monetary Authority of Brunei Darussalam (AMBD) launched the FinTech Regulatory Sandbox, promoting responsible experimentation by FinTech start-ups in collaboration with AMBD as its regulator. AMBD also has put forward precise regulatory requirements for P2P lending providers to protect investors, ensure the proper functioning of P2P platforms, promote fairness and transparency, manage any conflict of interest and ensure the treatment of users both in terms of users getting capital or providing capital *via* the platform. By increasing the number of entrepreneurs in this country, P2P lending platforms exist to finance individual and local enterprises. It is suggested that Brunei Darussalam foster an inclusive and attractive FinTech ecosystem by:

a. Providing an attractive and favourable regulatory environment for FinTech

b. Establishing a vibrant capital ecosystem through dedicated funds for FinTech

c. Building a strong talent pool to create and nurture FinTech talent

d. Connecting Brunei Darussalam to global FinTech markets

e. Establishing Brunei 'Darussalam's 1st and 'Asia's most attractive Islamic FinTech Hub.

Cambodia

The Cambodian economy has shown a very rapid growth rate in the last decade; although per capita income has shown an increase, this figure is still far below that of neighbouring countries in the Southeast Asian region. Agriculture is the primary sector of the economy in Cambodia. Cambodia's economy is also supported by tourism activities and the textile industry. The economic slowdown occurred in Cambodia during the 1997 Asian financial crisis. The economic slowdown was accelerated by the unstable political situation in Cambodia due to various conflicts in society in Cambodia.

Micro, Small and Medium Enterprises (MSMEs) account for 99% of the total business in Cambodia, with most businesses being micro-enterprises with less than ten employees. While P2P lending or other alternative financing is not an entirely new concept in Southeast Asia, Cambodia still has a void to fill for such service; only 66% of 'SME's face challenges in access to working capital.

One of the potential platforms in P2P lending is Rai Capital which is a pioneer in the P2P lending marketplace designed for micro-entrepreneurs and individuals to promote financial inclusion. This also eases local financing options for local businesses and small and medium-sized enterprises, providing them with smoother access to credit and investment. Being licensed and regulated by the Securities and Exchange Commission of Cambodia (SECC), Rai Capital noted that it is a joint venture with Singapore-based Goldbell Financial Services Pte Ltd.

Indonesia

Indonesia is a country that has high economic potential, the potential that has begun to be noticed internationally. Indonesia - Southeast Asia's largest economy - has a number of characteristics that put the country in a great position to experience rapid economic development. In addition, in recent years, there has been strong support from the central government to curb Indonesia's dependence on (raw) commodity exports while increasing the role of the manufacturing industry in the economy. Infrastructure development is also the primary goal of the government, and it needs to have a multiplier effect on the economy. Meanwhile, the Indonesian Financial Services Authority (OJK) announced that it was in the stage of drafting a policy.

In Indonesia, Fintech can be divided into Fintech 2.0, namely the development of Fintech by the financial services industry, including banking, capital markets, and the non-bank financial industry (Anshari & Alas, 2015; Anshari *et al.*, 2021a). Meanwhile, Fintech 3.0 is a Fintech developed by start-up companies. Before 2016, Indonesia did not yet have a law regulating Fintech activities, so it was feared that it could harm the public due to potential problems. For this reason, in early 2016, OJK regulated P2P Lending in OJK regulation number 77. The Financial Services Authority has also established a Fintech Lending Directorate to build a licensing system in this sector. For example, Amartha P2P Lending is one of the platforms that has obtained OJK permission. Lenders can provide loans starting from IDR 3 million (222 USD) to women entrepreneurs in rural areas, anytime, anywhere, and make a profit.

Moreover, Indonesia is a country with a remarkably high development of the fintech industry (after China) because Fintech originated to facilitate more loans to small and medium enterprises (SMEs) across the archipelago. Although Indonesia has several challenges, such as geography and infrastructure development, regulators have faced additional problems such as moral hazard, platform viability, and borrower eligibility.

Based on the OJK report, the accumulated amount of FinTech loans in Indonesia in December 2019 reached 54.72 trillion rupiah and increased by 166.51%. In September 2019, the number of lender accounts reached 558,766 entities, an increase of 169.28% from 2017. This growth occurred because users of Indonesian P2P lending applications appreciated the speed of requests approved as an alternative to traditional funding (Anshari *et al.*, 2021b; Hamdan & Anshari, 2020). However, there are six core problems in P2P lending, namely information asymmetry, determination of borrower credit scores, moral hazard, investment decisions, platform feasibility and immature regulations and policies for the protection of personal data. For this reason, each stakeholder (OJK, SWI, Ministry of Communication and Technology, and Fintech Association) is expected to immediately agree to the FinTech lending industry code of ethics (Anshari & Sumardi, 2020; Razzaq *et al.*, 2018; Zulkarnain & Anshari, 2016). P2P lending practices in Indonesia are regulated in the law on Fintech Lending Operators under the Financial Services Authority Regulation (POJK) 77/POJK.01/2016. Based on these rules, registered and licensed FinTech practices must meet several criteria, such as regulations in supervision, interest and fines, compliance with regulations, billing processes, joining an association, loan conditions, customer complaint services available, and restrictions on access to personal data.

Lao PDR

Laos' economy is largely dependent on the Mekong River. The largest source of Laos' economy is agriculture and plantation products. The lowlands on the banks of the Mekong River are used as agricultural areas. The Mekong River is used to drive turbines in hydroelectric power plants, which are used as an economical source by selling electrical energy to Vietnam and Thailand. Lao PDR began to implement economic openness in the early 21st century. Single or joint foreign capital has been permitted in Laos foreign direct investment by revising the law on foreign direct investment. Foreign companies are also given investment facilities in the form of tax-free for the first five years of business activities and are allowed to send the profits earned for use outside the Lao territory. The Lao government established a trade information centre on import and export activities called the Lao Trade Center in 2012. Laos' economy continued to experience improvement from 2001 to 2012. Laos boosted its economy by establishing several special economic zones. In addition, the Lao economy is improving along with the establishment of international trade and regional cooperation.

The BOL-GIZ-OECD-ADBI conference on the role of Financial Education and Consumer Protection in supporting Financial Inclusion aimed at discussing how financial education and financial consumer protection frameworks can support financial inclusion strategies in the Lao PDR and other CLMV countries (Cambodia, Lao PDR, Myanmar, and Viet Nam). The use of P2P lending in the Lao PDR is still not significant because the products of Fintech are associated with the financial literacy of society.

Malaysia

Malaysia's economy is the third-largest in Southeast Asia and the twenty-ninth in the world by GDP. Inflation of only 0.4% and a poverty rate of 3.5% made

Malaysia one of the countries whose economy developed rapidly after the 1998 economic crisis that rocked Asia. Malaysia is rich in rubber and oil production; Malaysia is also known as a business-friendly country with abundant agricultural products. The authorities also support the rapid progress of P2P lending in ASEAN. In 2015, the Malaysian Government finally issued a regulation regarding P2P Lending known as the CMSB (Capital Markets and Services Bill). Malaysia provides broad opportunities for individual investors to participate in P2P lending, with a maximum investment of RM 50,000 per year.

Myanmar

Myanmar's economy is one of the lowest in East Asia and the Asia-Pacific regions. At the beginning of 2014, the per capita income of Myanmar's population was only US$1,105. Myanmar's economic resources are indirectly dependent on the Mekong River, while Myanmar's economy is more dependent on the existence of the Nu Salween River. The source of electrical energy for economic activities and the livelihood of the Myanmar population depends on hydroelectric power. Economic development in Myanmar is hampered due to delays in the construction of road infrastructure and inadequate electricity supply. Myanmar's economic growth depends on the countries that are members of the Greater Mekong Subregion.

A rising number of start-ups as well as small and medium enterprises (SMEs) are emerging in Myanmar as business opportunities arise. However, many companies fail to achieve their full potential and contribute substantially to the economy because capital assistance is lacking in the country. Most businesses have resorted to P2P lending for funds since the demand is enormous and the market is massive. One of the goals of P2P lending is to serve unbanked customers who are unable to access formal financial services such as credit, savings, and deposits. In Myanmar, there is no development in P2P lending market platforms compared to other neighboring countries, as P2P lending could alter not only the technical factors but also the psychological factors such as behaviours of the lenders and borrowers.

The Philippines

The Philippines' economy is the fourth largest economy in Southeast Asia and the thirty-sixth in the world by gross domestic product. The Philippines has a mixed economic system, with the primary industries being food processing, textiles, electronics and automotive. Industrial centres are generally located in the Metro Manila and Metro Cebu areas. Agriculture still plays a significant role in economic development in the Philippines. The United States and Japan have become the Philippines' main export partners. In addition, the Philippines also cooperates with China, Singapore, Hong Kong, South Korea and Germany in export activities. Most of the exports are in the form of electronic components and semiconductors. In addition, natural products such as natural gas, coconut oil and fruits are the mainstay of the export sector of natural products. The Philippines is a member of several international economic forums, such as the Association of Southeast Asian Nations (ASEAN), the World Trade Organization (WTO) and the Asia Pacific Economic Cooperation (APEC).

The P2P lending in the Philippines may be unfamiliar to many Filipinos, but it can be a good option for those who have a bit of money to invest or those who need a loan without going to different banks. An investor or a lender just needs PHP 5,000 to start in a P2P lending platform in the Philippines. There are some advantages to investing in P2P lending platforms in the Philippines:

a. Higher rates of return

b. Option to build or diversify portfolio

c. Additional passive income stream

d. Affordable investment option

e. A fast and convenient way to get a loan

f. No hard credit checks

g. No collateral required

However, there are some risks to investing in the Philippines' peer-to-peer lending platform. These include:

a. Borrowers with bad credit and higher default risk

b. Not a liquid investment

c. Possible loss of investment during economic downturns

Singapore

Singapore's economy grew more than initially estimated in the second quarter. The Merlion Country's GDP grew 14.7% on an annual basis in the second quarter. The figure was higher than the initial estimate of 14.3%. This economic growth was also higher than the prediction of a Reuters poll that forecasted a 14.2% increase. In absolute terms, GDP remained 0.6% below pre-pandemic levels in Q2 2019. Singapore has an advanced trade-oriented market economy. Singapore's economy is one of the most open in the world, seventh lowest in corruption, most pro-business, with low taxes (14.2% of Gross Domestic Product) and has the world's third-highest GDP per capita.

The Singapore monetary authority also issued a P2P lending regulation in 2015. In contrast to Malaysia and Thailand, Singapore is taking a more cautious step. Singapore only allows individual investors to engage in P2P lending if they have obtained AI (Accredited Investors) status, with a minimum total asset of S$ 2 million.

The behaviour of societies in Singapore related to P2P lending makes an important yet time-sensitive and urgent purchase. The government rules have been already conducive, supported by the transactions of Fintech, which are more transparent. It is also supported that Singapore has a cash-intensive economy where a great deal of lending and borrowing is already done outside the established banking systems.

Thailand

Thailand is dubbed the Rice Barn of Southeast Asia, not without reason. This country is ambitious in agriculture. In addition, the tourism sector cannot be underestimated. Thailand is a country located in Southeast Asia. With tropical climate conditions and fertile soil, Thailand has successfully developed its agricultural sector. Their main agricultural products are rice and corn, logs, tapioca, fruits, and rubber for export. Indonesia is one of the recipients of rice from Thailand. By 2021, Thailand has ambitions to export six million tons of rice to Indonesia, China, Bangladesh and Iraq. The Thai government also allows individual investors to play in P2P lending with a maximum investment of THB 500,000.

P2P lending is expected to transform the lending business and reduce funding gaps in the Thai market. The Bank of Thailand (BOT) first announced their attention to regulate P2P lending in September 2018, and in January 2019, circulated a draft of the proposed regulations in order to seek opinions and comments from interested parties. Thai notification is 'Thailand's first legislation relating to P2P lending, and it provides a number of parameters within which P2P platform providers and P2P lenders must operate.

Vietnam

Vietnam's economy is in the position of the 47th largest in the world by nominal gross domestic product (GDP) and the 35th largest in the world when measured by the purchasing power balance (PPP). The country is also a member of APEC, ASEAN and the WTO. Since the mid-1980s, during the Doi Moi reform period, Vietnam has shifted from a centrally planned economy to a mixed economy that uses indicative planning through five-year plans. During that period, the economy experienced rapid growth. In the 21st century, Vietnam is in a period of being integrated into the global economy. Almost all, Vietnamese companies are small and medium enterprises (SMEs). Vietnam has become a leading agricultural exporter and an attractive destination for foreign investment in Southeast Asia. Currently, Vietnam's economy relies mainly on foreign direct investment to attract capital from abroad to support its economy.

P2P lending in Vietnam is a relatively new and growing field. It also remains unregulated. The state bank of Vietnam acknowledged that the space lacked regulation and warned banks and credit institutions of various dangers inherent in operating P2P lending platforms. However, it has not stopped Vietnamese businesses from developing P2P lending platforms. P2P lending in Vietnam may be subject to regulations governing three different sectors: e-commerce, credit rating and appraisal, and lending. In 2021, the government of Vietnam was likely to impose regulations in the near future. The government published a draft decree about basic requirements for a FinTech regulatory sandbox.

Australia

Australia is one of the strongest economies in the world, with economic growth for nearly two consecutive decades and unemployment falling to a generation low. As a result of nearly three decades of structural and policy reforms, the economy is now becoming more flexible, resilient and increasingly integrated with global markets. The strength of the Australian economy has been evident in recent years in its ability to withstand a number of internal and external events, including severe droughts, exploding housing developments and the Asian financial and economic crisis.

Since 1991, Australia's real economy has grown at an average rate of 3.3 percent per year. The value of Australia's GDP in 2007 was around $1 trillion. Unemployment has also fallen, from a high of almost 11 percent 15 years ago to below 5 percent in 2008—the lowest level since the 1970s. As a result of successive budget surpluses, Australia is now in a strong fiscal position. Between 2002–03 and 2006–07, Australia's budget surplus averaged between 1 percent and

1.6 percent of GDP. This surplus has been used primarily to pay off government debt. After peaking at 18.5 percent of GDP ($95.8 billion) in 1995–96, net government debt was paid off in 2005–06, and Australia is now a net creditor of approximately 2.7 percent of GDP ($28.1 billion).

P2P lending or market lending has a number of key risks which may impact investors and borrowers using an online platform; these include:

a) Fraud and cyber security risk

b) Risk that conflicts of interest of the marketplace lending provider are not adequately managed

c) Risk that investors and borrowers do not have sufficient understanding of the marketplace lending product.

China

According to the World Economic Forum, People's Republic of China, one of the RCEP members, currently holds the largest volume in the world for P2P lending, with the disbursement of funds reaching USD 40 billion at the end of 2014. This predicate is followed by the United States, with a volume of around USD 9 billion (Positive). Planets, 2015). The U.K. is ranked third by channelling volumes to just over USD 5 billion (Positive Planet, 2015). Indeed, this country was the birthplace of the world's first P2P lending platform, Zopa, in 2005. Meanwhile, the total disbursement volume that has been issued by Europe (minus the U.K.) is around USD 305 million (Crowdfund Insider, 2015). The volume of P2P lending in Asia, excluding China, is still below these figures, giving an extensive scope for the development of P2P lending in the largest continent in the world.

The economy of China is a developing market-oriented mixed economy that incorporates economic planning through industrial policies and strategic five-year plans. Dominated by state-owned enterprises (SOEs) and mixed-ownership enterprises, the economy also consists of a large domestic private sector and openness to foreign businesses in a system described as a socialist market economy. State-owned enterprises accounted for over 60% of China's market capitalisation in 2019 and generated 40% of China's GDP of US$15.66 trillion in 2020, with domestic and foreign private businesses and investment accounting for the remaining 60%. As of the end of 2019, the total assets of all China's SOEs, including those operating in the financial sector, reached US$78.08 trillion. Ninety-one of these SOEs belong to the 2020 Fortune Global 500 companies. China has the world's second-largest economy when measured by nominal GDP and the world's largest economy since 2014, measured by Purchasing Power Parity (PPP). It has been the second-largest by nominal GDP since 2010, with data relying on fluctuating market exchange rates. A forecast states that China will become the world's largest economy in nominal GDP by 2028. Historically, China was one of the world's foremost economic powers for most of the two millennia from the first until the 19th century.

China is also one of the countries with the highest fintech adoption rate in the world, based on Ernst & Young's Global Fintech Adoption Index. Fintech adoption in the bamboo curtain country reached 87%; this percentage rate is the same as in India. The adoption rate in China exceeds the global average for fintech adoption, which is only 64%. One of the most developed fintech services today is P2P Lending, an online financing platform that makes it easy for users to borrow money in nominal terms provided by each platform.

In China, an online P2P lending platform first appeared in 2006. In these years, the number of P2P platforms and the volume of transactions have been steadily increasing. According to statistics, in China, the number of online P2P platforms reached 2448 by the end of 2016, while the turnover reached 2,063 billion RMB, which is an increase of 110% compared with turnover in 2015. Online lending provides new financing channels for small, micro-enterprises and individual borrowers. With the rapid development of the online P2P lending market, more and more problems are encountered. China needs government support so that this industry can survive. The P2P Lending platform in China previously experienced a known moral hazard, where it was very easy for borrowers to falsify loan information.

Japan

From an economic point of view, Japan is one of the most developed countries in the world. GDP (gross domestic product, *i.e.*, the value of all goods and services produced in Japan in a year) is the third highest in the world, and Japanese brands such as Toyota, Sony, Fujifilm, and Panasonic are well known worldwide. The manufacturing industry is one of Japan's strengths, but the country is poor in natural resources. His general pattern is as follows: Japanese companies import raw materials, and then process and manufacture them as finished goods, which are sold domestically or exported. There has been a rapid increase in the number of outstanding loans in P2P lending in recent years in Japan. Under the current legal arrangement in Japan, investors assume the credit risk of P2P lending platforms and propose utilising schemes such as specific purpose companies and specific trust companies to strengthen investor protection. In Japan, funds provided by a silent partner (*i.e.*, investors) are considered to be the property of the business operator (*i.e.*, the P2P lending platform). Therefore, if a P2P lending platform fails, the investors would have only a general claim against the bankruptcy estate and would only be repaired pro rata with other general creditors.

To minimise bankruptcy risk of P2P lending platforms in Japan, the schemes of specific purpose companies and specific purpose trusts can be used to segregate 'investor's loans from the other assets of the P2P lending platform (Anshari *et al.*, 2019). This scheme can strengthen investor protection in the context of the failure of P2P lending platforms and could contribute to establishing confidence in the P2P lending market (Sugiantoro *et al.*, 2020).

New Zealand

New Zealand has rich fertile soil. The air quality is also relatively clean, and the air temperature is friendly. Due to this, agriculture, forestry, and animal husbandry in New Zealand are very successful and have even become one of the factors behind the high economic growth of New Zealand. The products obtained from the livestock, agriculture, and forestry sectors include dairy milk. The dairy cow's milk is processed into cheese and butter. Apart from milk, New Zealand is also a producer of meat, honey, and eggs. Sheep are also found in abundance, so there is a lot of wool production. Vegetables and fruits such as apples and kiwis also have a high selling value. For the forestry sector itself, the products that contribute significantly are derived from wood.

Apart from agriculture and livestock, New Zealand's economy also depends on the tourism sector. This is natural because, as we know, New Zealand is an archipelagic country, and the island nation is famous for its natural beauty. Many natural attractions can be enjoyed in New Zealand, as the atmosphere is relatively calm. New Zealand's tourism sector contributed 3.9 percent of the total GDP (Gross Domestic Product) in 2015. The New Zealand tourism sector also increases employment opportunities for residents of New Zealand. Many residents are recruited to work in the tourism sector. Even the number of tourists per year is almost the same as the population of New Zealand.

New Zealand has very few P2P lending platforms available. As the platforms get more experienced, their credit assessment likely improves, protecting investors from losing some or all of their investments. P2P lending can work well as a long-term investment. Starting in 2014, Harmoney company, New Zealand's first peer-to-peer lending firm, was a success in raising funds of $100 million. New Zealand's Financial markets Authority stated that P2P lending was designed to provide a new investment opportunity for New Zealanders.

South Korea

South Korea's economy is the twelfth largest economy in the world by gross domestic product. South Korea is a member of several international economic organisations, such as the G20, the Asia-Pacific Economic Cooperation, the World Trade Organization and the Organization for Economic Cooperation and Development. South Korea has passed a new law on P2P lending, which is expected to address deceptive practices and better protect consumers. P2P lending in South Korea has been unregulated despite seeing massive growth, which has created a range of problems, including fraud and loan delinquency. The outstanding P2P loans extended by 241 companies stood at almost $9.52b (KRW11.3t) as of August 25, compared with $7.33b (KRW8.7t) at the end of 2021.

There are some contradictions about how P2P lending in South Korea, whether it had a future since the legislation passed in August 2020 to curb malfeasance in the industry, had made it harder to operate legally. This legislation banned P2P lenders from lending money they borrowed from commercial banks, having paid-in capital of at least $440 million (KRW500 million), and registering with the Financial Services Commission (FSC) within a year.

CONCLUSION

In conclusion, P2P is indeed convenient in order to boost the economy among the RCEP member states. However, to build confidence for each member to practice P2P, the members needed to set up their own regulations to conduct this lending platform successfully. P2P has the potential to bring economic benefits to the members, which can lead to closer ties to one another. Also, the experience of South Korea, China and Singapore in practicing P2P can be seen as a good example where this can entice some members to follow their steps. Apart from financial inclusivity among the RCEP members and creating connections with the people, most members have different uses for the P2P lending platform. It can be concluded that four ASEAN countries, namely Singapore, Malaysia, Thailand and Indonesia, have somewhat developed their P2P Lending services. These are business-friendly countries; hence their P2P Lending services are highly regulated by their respective governments. Indonesia practices financial inclusion for almost any business to the extent that one P2P lending platform caters solely to women entrepreneurs. Compared to Singapore, the opportunities are limited to individual investors who wish to engage in P2P lending. Other countries such as Myanmar, Lao, Vietnam, and the Philippines are yet to fully practice P2P Lending services, and there are no P2P regulations from their governments.

CONSENT FOR PUBLICATION

Not applicable.

CONFLICT OF INTEREST

The author declares no conflict of interest, financial or otherwise.

ACKNOWLEDGEMENTS

Declared none.

REFERENCES

Ahad, A.D., Anshari, M., Razzaq, A. (2017). Domestication of smartphones among adolescents in Brunei Darussalam. *International Journal of Cyber Behavior, Psychology and Learning, 7*(4), 26-39. [http://dx.doi.org/10.4018/IJCBPL.2017100103]

Anshari, M. (2020). Workforce mapping of fourth industrial revolution: Optimization to identity. *J. Phys. Conf. Ser., 1477*(7), 072023. IOP Publishing. [http://dx.doi.org/10.1088/1742-6596/1477/7/072023]

Anshari, M., Alas, Y. (2015). Smartphones habits, necessities, and big data challenges. *Journal of High Technology Management Research, 26*(2), 177-185. [http://dx.doi.org/10.1016/j.hitech.2015.09.005]

Anshari, M., Almunawar, M.N., Masri, M., Hamdan, M., Fithriyah, M., Fitri, A. (2021). Digital wallet in supporting green fintech sustainability. *2021 Third International Sustainability and Resilience Conference: Climate Change., 352-357.* IEEE. [http://dx.doi.org/10.1109/IEEECONF53624.2021.9667957]

Anshari, M., Arine, M.A., Nurhidayah, N., Aziyah, H., Salleh, M.H.A. (2021). Factors influencing individual in adopting eWallet. *J. Financ. Serv. Mark., 26*(1), 10-23. [http://dx.doi.org/10.1057/s41264-020-00079-5]

Anshari, M., Almunawar, M.N., Masri, M., Hrdy, M. (2021). Financial Technology with AI-Enabled and Ethical Challenges. *Society, 58*(3), 189-195. [http://dx.doi.org/10.1007/s12115-021-00592-w]

Anshari, M., Almunawar, M.N., Masri, M. (2020). Financial Technology and Disruptive Innovation in Business. *International Journal of Asian Business and Information Management, 11*(4), 29-43. [http://dx.doi.org/10.4018/IJABIM.2020100103]

Anshari, M., Almunawar, M.N., Masri, M., Hamdan, M. (2019). Digital marketplace and FinTech to support agriculture sustainability. *Energy Procedia, 156*, 234-238. [http://dx.doi.org/10.1016/j.egypro.2018.11.134]

Anshari, M., Sumardi, W.H. (2020). Employing big data in business organisation and business ethics. *International Journal of Business Governance and Ethics, 14*(2), 181-205. [http://dx.doi.org/10.1504/IJBGE.2020.106349]

Arifin, F., Hariadi, M., Anshari, M. (2017). Extracting Value and Data Analytic from Social Networks: Big Data Approach. *Adv. Sci. Lett., 23*(6), 5286-5288. [http://dx.doi.org/10.1166/asl.2017.7360]

Atikah, I. (2020). Consumer Protection and Fintech Companies in Indonesia. *Innovations and Challenges of The Financial Services Authority, 9*(1), 132-153. [http://dx.doi.org/10.25216JHP.9.1.2020.132-153]

Aggarwal, V.K. (2016). *Mega-FTAs and The Trade-Security Nexus: The Trans-Pacific Partnership (TPP) and the Regional Comprehensive Economic Partnership.* RCEP.

Aung, H.W.Y. (2021). Marketing Strategy of Fintech Peer-to-Peer (P2P) Lending Platforms: A Solution to Increase Myanmar SMEs' Access to the External Finance. Ritsumeikan Asia Pacific University. https://ritsumei.repo.nii.ac.jp/?action=repository_action_common_download&item_id=15281&item_no=1&attribute_id=20&file_no=1

Australian Securities & Investment Commission. (2020). Marketplace Lending (Peer to Peer Lending) Products https://asic.gov.au/regulatory-resources/financial-services/marketplace-lending/marketplce-lending-peer-to-peer-lending-products/

Bachmann, Alexander (2011). *Online Peer-to-Peer Lending-A Literature Review. Journal of Internet Banking and Commerce, 16*(2), 1.

Australian Fintech. (2022). *Peer to Peer Products.*https://australianfintech.com.au/products-2/peer-to-peer/

Bank of Thailand. (2020). *List of P2P Lending Platform in Regulatory Sandbox.* https://www.bot.or.th/English/PaymentSystems/FinTech/Pages/P2PLendingSandbox.aspx

Banking and Finance. (2021). *South Korea Passes New Law on P2P Lending.*https://asianbankingandfinance.net/lending-credit/news/south-korea-passes-new-law-p2p-lending

Cheong, I., Tongzon, J. (2013). Comparing the Economic Impact of the Trans-Pacific Partnership and the Regional Comprehensive Economic Partnership. *Asian Econ. Pap., 12*(2), 144-164. [http://dx.doi.org/10.1162/ASEP_a_00218]

Gao, M., Yen, J., Liu, M. (2020). Determinants of Defaults on P2P Lending Platforms in China. *Int. Rev. Econ. Finance, 72*, 334-348. [http://dx.doi.org/10.1016/j.iref.2020.11.012]

Hamdan, M., Anshari, M. (2020). Paving the Way for the Development of FinTech Initiatives in ASEAN. *Financial technology and disruptive innovation in ASEAN.* IGI Global. [http://dx.doi.org/10.4018/978-1-5225-9183-2.ch004]

Hamdan, M., Chen, C.K., Anshari, M. (2020). Decision Aid in Budgeting Systems for Small & Medium Enterprises. *In 2020 International Conference on Decision Aid Sciences and Application (DASA).,* 253-257. IEEE. [http://dx.doi.org/10.1109/DASA51403.2020.9317018]

Harmoney. (2015). The Rise of Peer-to-Peer Lending. https://www.harmoney.co.nz/making-it-happen/rie-of-p2p-lending

Hoffmann, V., Rao, V., Surendra, V., Datta, U. (2020). Relief from Usury: Impact of a Self-Help Group Lending Program in Rural India. *J. Dev. Econ., 148*, 102567. [http://dx.doi.org/10.1016/j.deveco.2020.102567]

Kapronasia. (2021). *P2P Lenders in South Korea Clear Hurdle with Successful Registration.* .https://www.kapronasia.com/asia-banking-research-category/p2p-lenders-in-south-korea-clear- hurdle-wit--successful-registration.html

Khan, M.T.I., Xuan, Y.Y. (2021). *Drivers of Lending Decision in Peer to Peer Lending in Malaysia.* [http://dx.doi.org/10.1108/RBF-08-2020-0200/full/html]

Khmer Times. (2020). *Peer to Peer Lender Rai Capital Opens in Cambodia.* https://www.khmertimeskh.com/50786785/ peer-to-peer-p2p-lender-rai-capital-opens-in-cambodia/

Kraiwanit, T. (2021). Factors Affecting Understanding of P2P Lending in Thailand. *Pathumthani University Academic Journal.Factors Affecting Understanding of P2P Lending in Thailand.* https://so05.tci-thaijo.org/index.php/ptujournal/article/view/252741

Mulya, Dhiar Humara (2019). Pengaruh Ekspor Impor Konsumsi Dan Inflasi Terhadap Pertumbuhan Ekonomi Di 5 Negara Asean. *PhD Thesis.* Universitas Islam Indonesia.

Mulyani, M.A., Razzaq, A., Sumardi, W.H., Anshari, M. (2019). Smartphone Adoption in Mobile Learning Scenario. *In 2019 International Conference on Information Management and Technology (ICIMTech), 1*, 208-211. IEEE.
[http://dx.doi.org/10.1109/ICIMTech.2019.8843755]

Mulyani, M.A., Yusuf, S., Siregar, P., Nurihsan, J., Razzaq, A., Anshari, M. (2021). Fourth Industrial Revolution and Educational Challenges. *In 2021 International Conference on Information Management and Technology (ICIMTech), Vol. 1*, 245-249. IEEE.
[http://dx.doi.org/10.1109/ICIMTech53080.2021.9535057]

Myanmar Times. (2018). Myanmar Takes Small Steps towards Providing Greater Liquidity for SMEs.
https://www.mmtimes.com/news/myanmar-takes-small-steps-towards-providing-greater-liquidity-smes.html

Nemoto, N. (2019). *Optimal Regulation of P2P Lending for Small and Medium Sized.*
https://www.adb.org/publications/optimal-regulation-p2p-lending-small-and-medium-sized-enterprises
[http://dx.doi.org/10.2139/ssrn.3313999]

Noda, T. (2018). *P2P Lending Platforms in Philippines Rising.*https://fintechnews.sg/19702/lending/p2p-lending-in-philippines-rising/

Nguyen, L.T.P. (2021). *P2P lending Platforms in Malaysia: What Do We Know?.* https://f1000research.com/articles/10-1088

Oh, E.Y., Rosenkranz, P. (2020). *Determinants of Peer-to-Peer Lending Expansion: The Roles of Financial Development and Financial Literacy.* https://www.adb.org/sites/default/files/publication/575061/ewp-61--peer-peer-lending-expansion.pdf
[http://dx.doi.org/10.22617/WPS200107-2]

Pramasty, D.E., Rosintan, L. (2015). Determinasi Pertumbuhan Ekonomi Di Tujuh Negara ASEAN Periode Tahun 1996-2013. *Media Ekonomi, 23*(2), 107-120.
[http://dx.doi.org/10.25105/me.v23i2.3323]

Ravenhill, J. (2016). The Political Economy of an "Asian" Mega-FTA. *Asian Surv., 56*(6), 1077-1100.
[http://dx.doi.org/10.1525/as.2016.56.6.1077]

Razzaq, A., Samiha, Y.T., Anshari, M. (2018). Smartphone habits and behaviors in supporting students self-efficacy. *International Journal of Emerging Technologies in Learning (iJET), 13*(2), 94.
[http://dx.doi.org/10.3991/ijet.v13i02.7685]

Securities and Exchange Commission. (2020). *Enforcement and Investor Protection Department.*https://www.sec.gov.ph/wp-content/uploads/2020/09/2020Advisory_Philhelp.pdf

Sugiantoro, B., Anshari, M., Sudrajat, D. (2020). Developing Framework for Web Based e-Commerce: Secure-SDLC. *J. Phys. Conf. Ser., 1566*(1), 012020. IOP Publishing.
[http://dx.doi.org/10.1088/1742-6596/1566/1/012020]

Suryono, R.R., Purwandari, B., Budi, I. (2019). Peer-to-Peer Lending Problems and Potential Solutions: A Systematic Literature Review. *The Fifth Information Systems International Conference 2019.* Procedia Computer Science. 204-214.
[http://dx.doi.org/10.1016/j.procs.2019.11.116]

Suryono, R.R., Budi, I., Purwandari, B. (2021). Detection of fintech P2P lending issues in Indonesia. *Heliyon, 7*(4), e06782.
[http://dx.doi.org/10.1016/j.heliyon.2021.e06782] [PMID: 33981873]

Swasdee, A., Anshari, M., Hamdan, M. (2020). Artificial Intelligence as Decision Aid in Humanitarian Response. *2020 International Conference on Decision Aid Sciences and Application (DASA)* IEEE.
[http://dx.doi.org/10.1109/DASA51403.2020.9317111]

Thani, F.A., Anshari, M. (2020). Maximizing Smartcard for Public Usage. *International Journal of Asian Business and Information Management, 11*(2), 121-132.
[http://dx.doi.org/10.4018/IJABIM.2020040108]

Tracxn. (2021). *Fintech Startups in Myanmar.*https://tracxn.com/explore/FinTech-Startups-in-Myanmar

Tilleke and Gibbins. (2020). *Fintech Law in Southeast Asia.*https://www.tilleke.com/wp-content/uploads/2020/12/Tilleke-Regional-Guide-to-Fintech-Law.pdf

Yoon, L. (2021). *Total Amount of P2P Lending South Korea 2016-2020.* https://www.statista.com/statistics/1127789/south-korea-total-amount-of-p2p-lending/

Yunus, U. (2018). A Comparison Peer to Peer Lending Platforms in Singapore and Indonesia. [http://dx.doi.org/10.1088/1742-6596/1235/1/012008]

Zulkarnain, N., Anshari, M. (2016). Big data: Concept, applications, & challenges. *2016 International Conference on Information Management and Technology (ICIMTech).,* 307-310. IEEE. [http://dx.doi.org/10.1109/ICIMTech.2016.7930350]

Zulkarnain, N., Anshari, M., Almunawar, M.N. (2017). Big data and mobile learning in generating pervasive knowledge. *2017 International Conference on Information Management and Technology (ICIMTech),* 177-180. IEEE. [http://dx.doi.org/10.1109/ICIMTech.2017.8273533]

CHAPTER 8

Regional Comprehensive Economic Partnership (RCEP) and ASEAN Sustainable Development Goals

Blessing Gweshengwe[1,*]

[1] *Department of Rural and Urban Development, Great Zimbabwe University, Zimbabwe*

Abstract: An economic partnership can play a significant role in poverty reduction in the countries involved. The partnership's contribution to poverty alleviation is, however, a function of its scope and the nature of participating countries, which could be constrained by various factors. Considering this, the chapter addresses the question of whether the RCEP can contribute meaningfully to the achievement of the UN Sustainable Development Goal 1 within the ASEAN region. This aspect is yet to be subjected to scholarly examination. The chapter examines the potential of the RCEP to help ASEAN countries to eradicate poverty, the factors that could jeopardise this endeavour and the measures that could be taken to address these factors. Findings show that the RCEP could indeed contribute to the realisation of Sustainable Development Goal 1 in ASEAN countries since it has the potential to contribute to poverty eradication. This is because of the partnership's capacity to, among other aspects, drive economic growth, boost real convergence and optimise the poverty eradication potential of Micro, Small and Medium Enterprises in the ASEAN region. This contribution may, however, be jeopardised with the advent of adverse events like the COVID-19 pandemic, and because of political instability in some ASEAN countries. In order to mitigate the impact of both of these challenges, ASEAN countries could reinforce their social protection systems, intensify their commitment to the RCEP and address the needs of the losers in the RCEP.

Keywords: ASEAN, Economic Integration, Poverty Reduction, Regional Comprehensive Economic Partnership, SDG 1.

INTRODUCTION

The world is currently grappling with the scourge of poverty (Gweshengwe *et al.*, 2020a). In 2020, 1.7 billion people in 107 countries were found to be multi-dimensionally poor and global levels of extreme poverty rose, for the first time in over 20 years, due to the COVID-19 pandemic (UNDP & Oxford Poverty and

---

[*] **Corresponding author Blessing Gweshengwe:** Department of Rural and Urban Development, Great Zimbabwe University, Zimbabwe; E-mail: gweshengwe@yahoo.com

Mahani Hamdan, Muhammad Anshari and Norainie Ahmad (Eds.)

Human Development Initiative, 2020; World Bank, 2020). In the ASEAN region, the incidence of poverty is high in countries such as Myanmar, Lao People's Democratic Republic, the Philippines and Cambodia, and it is low in countries such as Brunei Darussalam, Singapore and Malaysia (Asian Development Bank, 2020; Gweshengwe, 2020; Gweshengwe *et al*., 2020a; UNDP & Oxford Poverty and Human Development Initiative, 2020; Sumarto & Moselle, 2015; World Bank, 2019). Poverty eradication is, therefore, the most significant priority of both developing and developed countries (Mansi *et al*., 2020). Accordingly, in 2015, the United Nations made the elimination of all forms of poverty throughout the world the primary goal (SDG 1) of the 2030 Global Agenda for Sustainable Development (Atkinson, 2019; United Nations, 2015).

ASEAN countries, like other member countries of the United Nations, are working towards achieving SDG1. The question that arises is: can the Regional Comprehensive Economic Partnership (RCEP) – an economic grouping of ASEAN countries, China, Japan, Korea, Australia and New Zealand ratified in November 2020 – help ASEAN countries to make significant strides towards attaining SDG1? Economic partnerships have enormous potential to contribute to poverty eradication, but their success depends on the scope of the partnership, the structure of the economies involved and the constraints faced by poor people, among other factors (Ayuk & Kabore, 2013; Gasiorek *et al*., 2016; Martuscelli, & Gasiorek, 2018; Sala-i-Martin, 2007; Southern Africa Trust, 2011). Thus, an economic grouping can positively affect poverty reduction efforts in some of the countries involved and negatively affect others. The East Africa Community, for example, had a positive impact on poverty alleviation in Rwanda, Tanzania and Uganda but did not really have a meaningful impact on poverty reduction in Burundi (Gasiorek *et al*., 2016). In the example of *Bienvenidos al Mercado Común del Sur* (MERCOSUR), poverty reduction indices were positive for Uruguay but negative for Paraguay (Borraz *et al*., 2012).

It is, therefore, crucial to ascertain whether the RCEP could contribute to the achievement of SDG1 within the ASEAN region. To this end, the current chapter examines the poverty eradication potential of the RCEP in ASEAN countries and the challenges that could impede the partnership's potential for poverty eradication in these countries. The chapter also proffers recommendations on how ASEAN countries can maximise the poverty eradication potential associated with the RCEP. The findings of this chapter could be of use in shaping ASEAN countries' efforts toward attaining SDG1. The potential of the RCEP to contribute to poverty eradication in ASEAN and other countries involved in the partnership is yet to be subjected to scholarly examination. The findings of this chapter are, therefore, also expected to trigger scholarly debates on economic partnerships and poverty eradication, especially in the ASEAN context.

METHODOLOGY

This chapter contains secondary data drawn from different sources, which were purposively selected based on the aim of the study. Data about the scope and nature of the RCEP and participating countries was drawn from RCEP leaders' statements. The chapter also contains government reports and publications from development and research institutions for data on economic integration and socio-economic development in ASEAN and other countries used as examples in the chapter. Lastly, data on the economic growth trend in ASEAN countries (Fig. **1**) was extracted from the World Bank.

Poverty Eradication Potential of The RCEP

The RCEP has the potential to contribute to poverty eradication within the ASEAN region by spurring economic growth, boosting real convergence, capitalising on the region's firm commitment towards redistributive policies, enabling the sharing of policy experiences and optimising the poverty eradication potential of Micro, Small and Medium Enterprises. These poverty eradication opportunities are explained in detail hereunder.

Economic Growth Opportunity and Poverty Eradication

The RCEP has a significant capacity to drive economic growth within the ASEAN region. As the world's largest economic grouping, it had a combined GDP of USD 26.2 trillion (nearly 30% of the Global GDP) and accounted for about 28% of global trade in 2019 (RCEP Leaders Statement, 2020). Its scope covers trade liberalisation investment and competition promotion, economic and technical cooperation and dispute settlements (RCEP Leaders Statement, 2012), which are engines of economic growth (Ayuk & Kabore, 2013; Bui *et al*., 2016; Lee & Vivarelli, 2006; Moyo, 2018; Sala-i-Martin, 2007). Trade liberalisation, for example, fuels economic growth in countries like China, Singapore, Hong Kong, Malaysia and Indonesia (Amiti & Konings, 2007; Moyo, 2018; Sala-i-Martin, 2007). Conversely, trade restrictions tend to stifle economic growth, as was the case in South Sudan (Varela *et al*., 2016). The ASEAN countries are ready to seize the opportunity for economic growth. They have conditions for and have implemented economic policies that are conducive to economic growth, as evidenced by the sustained economic growth that they have experienced in past years (Asian Development Bank, 2021; KPMG International Cooperative, 2015; Maude, 2021; Vu, 2020).

Economic growth is a key instrument for poverty eradication (Moyo, 2018; Rao, 1998; Son & Kakwani, 2004). It accounts for the substantial reduction in global poverty that has been recorded in the past years (Barro & Sala-i- Martin, 2004;

Moyo, 2018; Srinivasan, 2009). It is worth noting that the economic growth rate required for substantial poverty reduction in a country is not even that high (Son & Kakwani, 2004; Sala-i-Martin, 2007). China and Nepal, for example, required a pro-poor growth rate of 0.95 and 1.10, respectively, to realise a significant reduction in poverty under World Bank's previous USD 1 a day poverty line (Son & Kakwani, 2004). However, a significant reduction in poverty through economic growth depends mainly on a country's initial levels of economic development and income inequality (Fosu, 2010a; Nallari & Griffith, 2011; Son & Kakwani, 2004).

A combination of a high initial level of economic development and a low initial level of income inequality results in substantial poverty reduction (Adams, 2004; Fosu, 2010a, b; Son & Kakwani, 2004). ASEAN countries, including the poorest ones, meet this requirement. In the past decade, and before the outbreak of the Covid-19 pandemic, the Gross Domestic Product (GDP) of all ASEAN countries but Brunei Darussalam was trending upwards (Fig. **1**). Despite the nosediving of its GDP between 2012 and 2016 and its sluggish improvement thereafter, Brunei Darussalam has a high GDP per capita and is the second highest-income country in the ASEAN region (Gweshengwe, 2021; OECD/ERIA, 2018; World Bank, 2021a). In the same decade and before the pandemic, Indonesia (not included in Fig. (**1**). experienced a phenomenal increase in GDP (World Bank, 2021b).

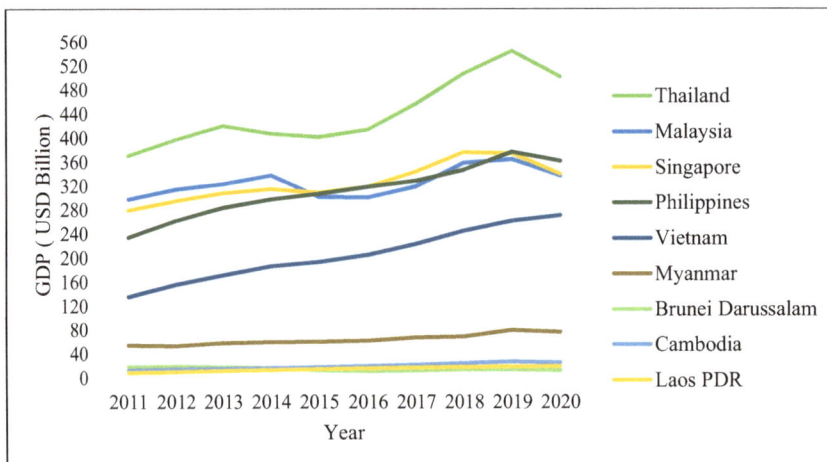

Fig. (1). GDP trends between 2011 and 2020. Source: World Bank (2021a, b, c, d, e, f, g, h, j, k).

The Gini Indexes of ASEAN countries are far below 1 or 100%. A Gini Index is a measure of income inequality, whose value ranges from 0 or 0% (perfect inequality) to 1 or 100% (perfect inequality) (Fuso, 2010b). The Gini Indexes of all ASEAN countries, save for the Philippines and Brunei Darussalam, hover around 0.3 or 30% (Department of Statistics Malaysia, 2019; General Statistics Office of Vietnam, 2021; Hansen & Gjonbalaj, 2019; Ho, 2020; Lim, 2020; United Nations ESCAP, 2018; Warr *et al.*, 2015). In 2015, the Philippines had a Gini Index of 0.44 or 44% (Rivera, 2020). Although the Gini Index of Brunei Darussalam is not available, the country has a very high Human Development Index (0.838, 2020 estimates): this implies that Brunei has a high level of human development, which could means fewer inequalities in terms of access to the opportunities required for a better life (Gweshengwe *et al.*, 2020b; United Nations Development Programme, 2005;2020).

The GDP trends and Gini Indexes highlighted above reveal that ASEAN countries have levels of economic development and income inequality that are ideal for significant poverty reduction. Thus, the countries can translate RCEP-driven economic growth into substantial poverty reduction. In fact, both rich and poor ASEAN countries have realised a significant reduction in poverty in past years, which is largely attributable to economic growth (World Bank, 2019; Warr, 2006; Warr *et al.*, 2015).

Real Convergence and Poverty Eradication

Real convergence means the 'catching' or 'levelling' up of the standard of living of poor countries to that of rich countries, and this implies a reduction in poverty (Ayuk & Kabore, 2013; Chassem, 2013; del Hoyo *et al.*, 2017; Wetta & Yerbanga, 2013). It is anchored on economic growth but fuelled by economic integration, which necessitates the flow of capital from capital-rich to capital-poor countries in response to the removal of trade barriers, mobility of production factors, knowledge and technology exchange, structural transformation and the harmonisation of regulations (Aurel, 2009; Ayuk & Kabore, 2013; Balcerowicz & Fischer, 2006; Gammadigbe, 2021; Glodowska & Pera, 2019; Ingianni & Zdarek, 2009; Parente & Prescott, 2006; Wetta & Yerbanga, 2013). The RCEP has eliminated barriers in the aspects highlighted above. Thus, it is now possible for capital to flow easily from capital-rich countries, such as Australia, New Zealand, Japan and China in the RCEP to the ASEAN region, and especially to capital-poor countries, such as Laos PDR, Cambodia and the Philippines. This will allow ASEAN countries to level up their living standards, eradicating poverty in the process.

Redistributive Policy Commitment and Poverty Eradication

The ASEAN region is highly committed to redistributive policies, particularly those associated with social protection, and this could catalyse the RCEP's poverty eradication potential within the region. In 2013, the region adopted the ASEAN declaration on strengthening social protection, and in 2015, it developed a regional framework and action plan for social protection initiatives (The ASEAN, 2020). Both rich and poor ASEAN countries place great importance on social protection. By way of example, Brunei Darussalam, Singapore, Malaysia, Indonesia, Cambodia, Laos PDR and Myanmar, have sound social insurance, assistance and transfer policies and legal instruments that ensure that the disadvantaged and vulnerable people (the poor, old-aged, disabled and unemployed, single mothers, orphans *etc.*) have access to basic needs such as housing, education, health and food and to employment and entrepreneurial opportunities (Beng, 2012; Fraser, 2011; Gweshengwe & Hassan, 2019; Hansen & Gjonbalaj, 2019; Hassan, 2017; Government of Myanmar, 2014; Laos PDR Department of Planning and Cooperation, 2020; The ASEAN, 2020; World Bank, 2007; Zin, 2012). This commitment to social protection can enhance the RCEP's contribution to poverty eradication within the ASEAN region in two ways.

(i) Enhancing the ability of ASEAN countries to translate the RCEP-induced economic growth into meaningful gains in terms of poverty reduction. It is now widely accepted that economic growth, albeit vital for substantial poverty reduction, is not, in and of itself, sufficient (Mansi *et al.*, 2020; Moyo, 2018; Mulok, 2012). It needs to be complemented with redistributive policies, especially those in the form of social protection (Arjona *et al.*, 2003; Carneiro & Sirtaine, 2017; Esarey *et al.*, 2012; Government of Liberia, 2013). In the Dominican Republic, for example, the 1992-2000 average economic growth rate of 6.7% per year did not translate into substantial poverty reduction due, among other factors, to failure to commit sufficient public resources to social protection (Carneiro & Sirtaine, 2017). Thus, significant investment in social protection by ASEAN countries offers favourable conditions for RCEP-driven economic growth to result in significant poverty reduction in the region.

(ii) Helping poor and disadvantaged people in ASEAN countries to overcome barriers to accessing the benefits associated with the RCEP. In addition to economic growth benefits, economic partnerships are also associated with a reduction in prices of goods and services, increased migration, knowledge and technology exchange and improvement in social capital, among other benefits (Anukoonwattaka & Heal, 2014; Chen, 2000; Gasiorek *et al.*, 2016; Southern Africa Trust, 2011). Poor and disadvantaged people's access to these benefits are constrained by poor human capital, weak purchasing power and lack of communication and entrepreneurial skills, among other factors (Gasiorek *et al.*, 2016). The success of economic groupings in poverty eradication also depends on the ability of the poor to overcome the constraints highlighted above (Gasiorek *et al.*, 2016). Social protection initiatives in the ASEAN countries will therefore help poor and disadvantaged people to access benefits associated with RCEP.

Sharing Policy Experiences and Poverty Eradication

The RCEP comprises countries with outstanding economic and redistributive policy experiences relating to policy design, implementation, challenges and reforms. Australia, for example, due to its sound economic and social policies, has a high standard of living, and in 2020, its living standards rose significantly despite the Covid-19 pandemic (Karp, 2021; OECD, 2017a). New Zealand, a pioneer welfare state, managed to successfully reform its welfare policies in response to fiscal and other challenges, giving rise to a sustained high standard of living in the country (Boston, 1993; Jensen *et al.*, 2003; OECD, 2017b; 2021). China implemented exceptional economic and redistributive policies that resulted in poverty reduction, which was unparalleled both in scale and intensity (Goodman, 2021, Moyo, 2018; UNDP China & IPRCC, 2011; The State Council Information Office, 2021). The country lifted more than 500 million people out of poverty, achieved the Millennium Development Goal (MDG) 1 of halving extreme poverty within the set deadline and is considered to be on track towards attaining SDG 1 (UNDP China & IPRCC, 2011; The State Council Information Office, 2021). The standard of living of most countries within the ASEAN region is improving (Booth, 2019), and they have invaluable policy experiences to share. Brunei Darussalam, for instance, has the most generous and resilient welfare systems in the ASEAN region, which made it possible for the country to achieve a high standard of living, realising MDG 1 before the 2015 deadline, and to be on course towards achieving SDG 1 (Booth, 2019; Gweshengwe & Hassan, 2019; Gweshengwe *et al.*, 2020b; Inoguchi & Fujii, 2013). Vietnam also has an outstanding policy reform success story. In 1986, Vietnam launched the *Doi Moi* "renovation" reforms, which resulted in remarkable economic growth and a reduction in poverty (Binh, 2008; Green, 2008; Hieu & Koo, 2007). Vietnam, which is among the fastest-growing economies in the world, had an average growth rate of 7.5% between 1993 and 2002 (Hieu & Koo, 2007); and as shown in Figure 1, economic growth in this country is still exceptional in spite of the global pandemic. The country achieved MDG1 10 years before the set deadline, reducing poverty from 58.1% in 1993 to only 19.5% in 2004 (Binh, 2008). Such policy experiences are significant to ASEAN countries in their poverty eradication efforts, as these countries could draw invaluable policy insights that would enable them to realise substantial poverty reduction, especially in the wake of the Covid-19 pandemic.

THE RCEP, MICRO, SMALL AND MEDIUM ENTERPRISES AND POVERTY REDUCTION

The RCEP also has the capacity to optimise the poverty eradication potential of Micro, Small and Medium Enterprises (MSMEs) within the ASEAN region. ASEAN countries have a vibrant MSME sector, which accounts for 80 to 99% of all enterprises and 60 to 80% of total employment, and contributes significantly to poverty eradication (Asian Development Bank, 2020b; Abdullah, 2015; Lee *et al.*, 2019; Nursini, 2020; Yoshino & Taghizadeh-Hesary, 2016). Governments in all ASEAN countries realise the significance of the MSME sector to the economy and poverty reduction and have therefore enacted policies to support the growth of the sector in their respective countries (Asian Development Bank, 2020b). Trade liberalisation, investment and competition promotion, and economic and technical cooperation – which are at the heart of the RCEP – are key to the growth of MSMEs in ASEAN countries. These integration initiatives will benefit MSMEs in different ways, which include the exchange of entrepreneurial knowledge and skills as well as access to technology, foreign markets and investment funds. This will bolster the role of MSMEs in poverty eradication within the ASEAN region.

Challenges

The Covid-19 pandemic could constrain the potential of RCEP to contribute meaningfully to poverty eradication within the ASEAN region. The pandemic has already disrupted economic and social progress in the region in an unprecedented way (ASEAN Policy Brief, 2020; Asian Development Bank, 2020; 2021; Chong *et al.*, 2021). In 2020, for example, the pandemic decelerated economic growth in ASEAN countries: by 9.6% in the Philippines, 6.1% in Thailand, 5.6% in Malaysia and 5.4% in Singapore (Asian Development Bank, 2021). It mainly affected tourism, restaurants, construction, supply chain, retail and the operations of Micro, Small and Medium-sized Enterprises (MSMEs) and weakened consumer and business confidence (ASEAN Policy Brief, 2020; Asian Development Bank, 2021). The pandemic has also pushed a substantial number of people into poverty and worsened the levels of deprivation of those who were already poor before its outbreak (Asian Development Bank, 2021; Dutta *et al.*, 2020; OECD Economy Surveys, 2020). Covid-19 could be endemic, considering the tendency of the virus to mutate and the surge in new cases in 2021 (Asian Development Bank, 2021; Phillips, 2021). The ability of RCEP to drive economic growth and enhance real convergence in ASEAN countries could be jeopardised. Due to a sudden increase in the numbers of people facing poverty and illness as a result of Covid-19, social protection systems are overwhelmed, and the RCEP's poverty eradication potential in ASEAN countries cannot be effectively catalysed.

Some ASEAN countries are experiencing political instability, which could also adversely affect the RCEP's potential to contribute to poverty eradication in the region. Political instability, which refers to the propensity of governments to collapse (Abott, 2021; Malik & Mansur, 2017), derails GDP growth, reduces private investments and fuels inflation (Aisen & Veiga, 2006; 2010; Alesina & Perotti, 1996; Alesina *et al.*, 1996; Jong-a-Pin, 2009). The political instability in Zimbabwe in 2007-2008, for example, caused a substantial reduction in GDP growth, a halt in investment, and hyperinflation, which peaked at 89 sextillions per cent in November 2008 (Fournier & Whittall, 2009; Ward 2015). In the ASEAN region, the ongoing political turmoil in Myanmar is decelerating economic growth, reversing gains in poverty reduction and compounding the socio-economic impacts of the Covid-19 pandemic (Asian Development Bank, 2021; Bjarnegard, 2020; Marston, 2017; UNDP Asia and Pacific, 2021). The trade volume in ports, on which Myanmar's economy is based, fell between 55 and 64% immediately after the outbreak of the political crisis (UNDP Asia and Pacific, 2021). The political turmoil also contributed to the fall of economic growth in the country, from 6.8% in 2019 to 3.3% in 2020 (Asian Development Bank, 2021). Myanmar's poverty rate, which fell significantly from 48.2% in 2005 to 24.8% in 2017, could therefore be substantially reversed by 2022 if the political instability continues (UNDP Asia and Pacific, 2021). Thailand and Malaysia have recently had their share of the political crisis, which is already constraining economic growth (Henke, 2018; Mariadas *et al.*, 2020). Political protests throughout 2020 into early 2021 in Thailand have undermined investment and derailed GDP growth (Abbott, 2021; Foon, 2020). Malaysia experienced power transitions twice between 2018 and 2020, and this growing political uncertainty is already hurting the economy (Malik & Mansur, 2017; Mariadas *et al.*, 2020; Teo, 2021). Thus, such political instability in these countries could stymie the countries from benefiting from the poverty eradication opportunities associated with the RCEP.

Recommendations

The RCEP has a significant potential to contribute to the eradication of poverty in ASEAN countries, but that could be jeopardised by the constraints highlighted above. For countries to capitalise on the RCEP's poverty eradication potential, they need to bolster their social protection systems, intensify their commitment to the RCEP pact, identify the losers in the RCEP and address their needs. Social protection initiatives, such as social assistance and insurance and labour market interventions, help poor and vulnerable people to cope with and recover from shocks (Browne, 2015; Devereux & Sabates-Wheeler, 2004). Such initiatives, therefore, play a significant role in mitigating the effects of the Covid-19 crisis, such as sickness, death (especially of a breadwinner) and loss of employment and entrepreneurial opportunities (International Labour Organization & Asian Development Bank, 2020; Kind, 2020). ASEAN countries have various social protection initiatives, but given the unprecedented impact of the Covid-19 pandemic, these need to be bolstered, making them more responsive and resilient in the face of the adverse effects of the pandemic (ASEAN Policy Brief, 2020; Kind, 2020). The focus should be on improving the comprehensiveness, coverage and adequacy of these social protection initiatives. As Kind (2020) recommends, this could be achieved by designing social protection programmes to effectively manage the large-scale shocks, building novel programmes on the existing social protection infrastructure, and identifying the new poor and vulnerable people. Social protection is key to inclusive growth required for the ASEAN countries to emerge from the Covid-19 crisis and should therefore be integrated into the recovery plans of these countries (ASEAN Policy Brief, 2020; Asian Development Bank, 2021). As part of their economic recovery, ASEAN countries need to up and re-skill vulnerable workers in both formal and informal sectors and to support the resilience of MSMEs (Asian Development Bank, 2021; OECD Economic Surveys, 2020). Social protection initiatives, especially those that focus on the labour market and MSME development, also become significant in this situation.

ASEAN countries could also intensify their commitment to the RCEP pact in order to alleviate the effects of the Covid-19 pandemic and political instability. Since the Covid-19 crisis has transcended borders, regional or collective efforts are integral to the crisis containment efforts and to safeguarding socio-economic stability and livelihoods (ASEAN Policy Briefs, 2020). Given its membership, the RCEP offers ASEAN countries the opportunity to address the impacts of the Covid-19 pandemic through regional or collective efforts. The scope of the RCEP also includes dispute settlement, and the partnership could therefore be a tool for rebuilding political stability in countries like Myanmar.

It is inevitable that some will lose out in the RCEP since, according to Ciuriak (2010), the distribution of benefits and costs of economic integration is usually unequal at sector, society and household levels. In Mexico, for example, farmers, local manufacturers and wage-earners in the manufacturing sector were some of the losers of the North American Free Trade Agreement (NAFTA), which necessitated the removal of tariffs on several products (Ciruak, 2010; Uchitelle, 2007). Another example is that of the Canada-United States Free Trade Agreement, which contributed to the massive loss of jobs in the manufacturing sector in Canada in the 1990s (Ciruak, 2010). Those who lose out in contexts of economic integration are usually the poor and vulnerable groups like peasant farmers and unskilled workers, as was the case in Mexico (Ciruak, 2010), local MSMEs, women and the youth. It is, therefore, significant to identify the losers in the RCEP and address their specific needs. Since these are usually poor and vulnerable members of society, identifying them and addressing their challenges ensures that no one in the ASEAN region is left behind in accessing economic growth and the other benefits associated with the RCEP. This is essential, given that under the 2030 Agenda for Sustainable Development, poverty eradication is anchored on the 'leave no one behind' development principle (Gweshengwe *et al.*, 2020).

CONCLUSION

Like other countries in the world, ASEAN countries are also aspiring to achieve SDG1, which calls for an end to poverty in the world by 2030. Economic partnerships can contribute significantly to poverty reduction depending, among other factors, on the scope of the partnership and the nature of the countries involved. Against this background, the chapter addressed the question: Can the RCEP enable the ASEAN region to make significant strides towards attaining SDG1? The chapter does that by examining the potential of the RCEP to contribute to poverty eradication in ASEAN countries, the challenges that could impede the partnership's contribution to poverty eradication in these countries and how the challenges could be addressed.

The RCEP has the potential to eradicate poverty in ASEAN countries since it can drive economic growth, boost real convergence and optimise the poverty eradication potential of MSMEs in the ASEAN region. It also offers ASEAN countries the opportunity to draw invaluable policy insights on poverty eradication from countries in the grouping which have achieved remarkable results in poverty eradication. These insights will be essential to the poverty eradication efforts of ASEAN countries. The ASEAN region is very much committed to redistributive policies, which could enhance RCEP poverty reduction efforts within the region. The RCEP could therefore contribute to the realisation of SDG1 within the ASEAN region. This potential contribution is, however, at stake due to the Covid-19 pandemic and, in some ASEAN countries, political instability. These challenges could be managed if ASEAN countries strengthen their social protection systems, redouble their commitment to the RCEP pact and identify losers in the RCEP and address their needs.

CONSENT FOR PUBLICATION

Not applicable.

CONFLICT OF INTEREST

The author declares no conflict of interest, financial or otherwise.

ACKNOWLEDGEMENTS

Declared none.

REFERENCES

Abbott, M. (2021). https://thediplomat.com/2021/03/how-are-thailands-youth-protests-impacting-freign-investment/

Abdullah, R. (2015). *Poverty and Microfinance in Brunei Darussalam..* Banda Seri Begawan: Sultan Sharif Ali Islamic University.

Adams, R. H. (2004). Economic Growth, Inequality and Poverty: Estimating the Growth Elasticity of Poverty. *World Development, 32*(12), 1989.

Aisen, A., Veiga, F.J. (2006). Does political instability lead to higher inflation? A panel data analysis. *J. Money Credit Bank., 38*(5), 1379-1389.
[http://dx.doi.org/10.1353/mcb.2006.0064]

Aisen, A., Veiga, F.J. (2020). *How does political instability affect economic growth?.* https://www.imf.org/external/pubs/ft/wp/2011/wp1112.pdf

Alesina, A., Perotti, R. (1996). Income distribution, political instability, and investment. *Eur. Econ. Rev., 40*(6), 1203-1228.
[http://dx.doi.org/10.1016/0014-2921(95)00030-5]

Alesina, A., Ozler, S., Roubini, N., Swagel, P. (1996). Political instability and economic growth. *J. Econ. Growth, 1*(2), 189-211. https://www.jstor.org/stable/40215915
[http://dx.doi.org/10.1007/BF00138862]

Amiti, M., Konings, J. (2007). Trade liberalisation, intermediate inputs, and productivity: evidence from Indonesia. *Am. Econ. Rev., 97*(5), 1611-1638.
[http://dx.doi.org/10.1257/aer.97.5.1611]

Anukoonwattaka, W., Heal, A. (2014). *Regional integration and labour mobility: Linking trade, migration and development.* https://www.unescap.org/sites/default/files/publications/STESCAP2688_No81.pdf

Arjona, R., Ladaique, M., Pearson, M. (2003). Growth, inequality and social protection. *Can. Public Policy, 29*, S119. https://www.jstor.org/stable/3552279
[http://dx.doi.org/10.2307/3552279]

ASEAN Policy Brief. (2020). *Economic impact of COVID-19 outbreak on ASEAN.* ASEAN Secretariat. Jakarta: https://asean.org/storage/2020/04/ASEAN-Policy-Brief-April-2020_FINAL. pdf

Asian Development Bank. (2020a). Basic statistics 2020. Mandaluyong: Statistics and Data Innovation Unit. https://www.adb.org/sites/default/files/publication/ 601126/basicstatistics-2020.pdf

Asian Development Bank. (2020b). Asia small and medium-sized enterprise monitor 2020: Volume I – country and regional reviews. Mandaluyong: Asian Development Bank. https://www.adb.org/sites/default/files/publication/646146/asia-sme-monitor-2020-volume-1.pdf

Asian Development Bank. (2021). Asian development outlook 2021: Financing a green and inclusive recovery. Mandaluyong: Asian Development Bank.

Atkinson, A.B. (2019). *Measuring poverty around the world..* New Jersey: Princeton University Press.

Aurel, I. (2009). Real convergence and integration (Working Papers, No. 090102). *Bucharest: Romanian Academy, National Institute for Economic Research.*

Ayuk, E.T., Kabore, S.T. (2013). Introduction: Why integrate? In: Ayuk, E.T., Kabore´, S.T., (Eds.), *Wealth through integration: Regional integration and poverty-reduction strategies in West Africa.* (pp. 1-18). Ottawa: Springer.

[http://dx.doi.org/10.1007/978-1-4614-4415-2]

Balcerowicz, L., Fischer, S. (2006). Introduction and Summary. In: Balcerowicz, L., Fischer, S., (Eds.), *Living standards and the wealth of nations successes and failures in real convergence.* (pp. 3-16). Cambridge: The MIT Press.

Beng, C.S. (2012). Employment-based Social Protection in Singapore Issues and Prospects. *ASEAN Econ. Bull., 29*(3), 218-229.
[http://dx.doi.org/10.1355/ae29-3d]

Binh, L.Q. (2008). *What has made Viet Nam a poverty reduction success story?.* https://oxfamilibrary. openrepository.com/bitstream/handle/10546/112471/fp2p-cs-what-has-made-vietnam-poverty-re-uction-success-story-140608-en.pdf?sequence=1&isAllowed=y

Bjarnegård, E. (2020). Introduction: Development challenges in Myanmar: Political development and politics of development intertwined. *Eur. J. Dev. Res., 32*(2), 255-273.
[http://dx.doi.org/10.1057/s41287-020-00263-2]

Booth, A. (2019). *Living standards in Southeast Asia changes over the long Twentieth Century, 1900-2015..* Amsterdam: Amsterdam University Press.

Borraz, F., Rossi, M., Ferres, D. (2012). Distributive effects of regional trade agreements on the "Small Trading Partners": Mercosur and the Case of Uruguay and Paraguay. *J. Dev. Stud., 48*(12), 1828-1843.
[http://dx.doi.org/10.1080/00220388.2012.682984]

Boston, J. (1993). Reshaping Social Policy in New Zealand. *Fisc. Stud., 14*(3), 64-85. https://www.jstor.org/stable/24437313
[http://dx.doi.org/10.1111/j.1475-5890.1993.tb00487.x]

Browne, E. (2015). *Social protection: Topic guide.* Birmingham: GSDRC, University of Birmingham.

Carneiro, F., Sirtaine, S. (2017). Overview. In: Carneiro, F., Sirtaine, S., (Eds.), *When growth is not enough: Explaining the rigidity of poverty in the Dominican Republic.* (pp. 1-14). Washington, DC: World Bank Publications.
[http://dx.doi.org/10.1596/978-1-4648-1036-7_ov]

Chassem, N.P. (2013). Has there been real and structural convergence in WAEMU countries? In: Ayuk, E.T., Kabore´, S.T., (Eds.), *Wealth through integration: Regional integration and poverty-reduction strategies in West Africa.* (pp. 69-90). Ottawa: Springer.

Chen, X. (2000). Both Glue and lubricant: Transnational ethnic social capital as a source of Asia-Pacific sub-regionalism. *Policy Sci., 33*(3/4), 269-287.
[http://dx.doi.org/10.1023/A:1004882907559]

Chong, T.T.L., Li, X., Yip, C. (2021). The impact of COVID-19 on ASEAN. *Econ. Polit. Stud., 9*(2), 166-185.
[http://dx.doi.org/10.1080/20954816.2020.1839166]

Ciuriak, D. (2010). Winners and losers in international economic integration: The distributional effects of the NAFTA. In ASEAN Studies Center (Ed). *ASEAN-Canada Forum 2008 (pp.158-194). Singapore: Institute of Southeast Asian Studies.*

del Hoyo, J.L.D., Heinz, D.F.F., Muzikarova, S. (2017). https://www.ecb.europa.eu/pub/pdf/scpops/ecb. op203.en.pdf

Department of Statistics Malaysia. (2020). Household income and basic amenities survey report 2019. Putrajaya: Department of Statistics Malaysia. https://www.singstat.gov.sg/-/media/files/publications/households/pp-s26.pdf

Department of Statistics Singapore. (2021). *Key Household Income Trends, 2020.* https://www.singstat.gov.sg/-/media/ files/news/ press080022021a.pdf

Devereux, S., Sabates-Wheeler, R. (2004). Transformative social protection (IDS Working Paper 232). *Brighton: Institute of Development Studies.*

Dutta, P., Khanna, D., Nixon, N. (2020). https://thediplomat.com/2020/12/the-new-poor-asean-tackles- the-challenge-of-rising-inequalities/

Esarey, J., Salmon, T., Barrilleaux, C. (2012). Social insurance and income redistribution in a laboratory experiment. *Polit. Res. Q., 65*(3), 685-698. https://www.jstor.org/stable/41635264 [http://dx.doi.org/10.1177/1065912911411096]

Foon, H.W. (2020). *Political instability to hit Thai economy.*https://www.thestar.com.my/business/business-news/2020/09/19/political-instability-to-hit-thai-economy

Fosu, A.K. (2010). The effect of income distribution on the ability of growth to reduce poverty: Evidence from rural and urban African economies. *Am. J. Econ. Sociol., 69*(3), 1034-1053. [http://dx.doi.org/10.1111/j.1536-7150.2010.00736.x]

Fosu, A.K. (2010). *Growth, inequality and poverty reduction in developing countries: recent global evidence..* Paris: OECD Development Centre.

Fournier, C., Whittall, J. (2009). https://odihpn.org/wp-content/uploads/2009/07/humanitarianexchange043.pdf

Fraser, E.M. (2011). *Helpdesk Research Report: Social Protection Systems in Singapore.* Birmingham: Governance and Social Development Resource Centre.http://gsdrc.org/docs/open/hdq766.pdf

Gammadigbe, M., Byiers, B., Byiers, B. (2021). *Is Regional Trade Integration a Growth and Convergence Engine in Africa? (IMF Working Paper 21/19). Washington DC: International Monetary Fund.* [http://dx.doi.org/10.5089/9781513567716.001]

Gammadigbe, V., Gammadigbe, V., Gammadigbe, V. (2016). https://ecdpm.org/wp-content/uploads/DP20--Regional-Integration-Poverty-East-African-Community-November-2016.pdf

General Statistic Office of Vietnam. (2021). https://www.gso.gov.vn/en/data-and-statistics/2021/06/t-e-trend-of-inequality-in-income- distribution-in-vietnam-2016-2020-period/

Głodowska, A., Pera, B. (2019). On the relationship between economic integration, business environment and real convergence: The experience of the CEE Countries. *Economies, 7*(2), 54. [http://dx.doi.org/10.3390/economies7020054]

Goodman, J. (2021). *Has China lifted 100 million people out of poverty?.* https://www.bbc.com/news/56213271

Government of Liberia. (2013). *National social protection policy and strategy.* Monrovia: Government of Liberia.

Government of Myanmar. (2014). *Myanmar National Social Protection Strategic Plan.* https://www.social-protection.org/gimi/gess/RessourcePDF.action?ressource.ressourceId=50377#:~:text=Myanmar%20social%20protection%20includes%20policies,manage%20and%20cope%20with%20shocks

Green, D. (2008). *Poverty to power: how active citizens and effective states can change the world.* Oxford: Oxfam International.

Gweshengwe, B., Hassan, N.H. (2019). https://fass.ubd.edu.bn/SEA/vol19/SEA-v19-Gweshengwe-Noor Hasharina.pdf

Gweshengwe, B. (2020). Seasonal poverty in Zimbabwe and Cambodia: A comparative analysis of the developing world. *Cambodia Journal of Basic and Applied Research, 2*(1), 49-71. http://www.rupp.edu.kh/CJBAR/files/Vol-2-Issue-1/5-BLESSING-2020.pdf

Gweshengwe, B. (2021). Poverty and Microfinance in Brunei Darussalam by Rose Abdullah. *International Journal of Community and Social Development, 3*(2), 181-184. [http://dx.doi.org/10.1177/25166026211015486]

Gweshengwe, B., Hassan, N.H., Ali Maricar, H.M. (2020). Perceptions of the language and meaning of poverty in Brunei Darussalam. *J. Asian Afr. Stud., 55*(7), 929-946.

[http://dx.doi.org/10.1177/0021909619900218]

Gweshengwe, B., Hassan, N.H., Ali Maricar, H.M. (2020). Understanding Quality of Life in Brunei Darussalam. *Cogent Soc. Sci.,   6*(1), 1838705.
[http://dx.doi.org/10.1080/23311886.2020.1838705]

Hansen, N.H., Gjonbalaj, A. (2019). Advancing Inclusive Growth in Cambodia. *(IMF WP/19/187).* International Monetary Fund.Tokyo:
[http://dx.doi.org/10.5089/9781513510552.001]

Hassan, N.H., Gjonbalaj, A. (2017). Everyday finance and consumption in Brunei Darussalam.

Henke, J. (2018). *Political instability in Thailand. Which effects does it have on the economy of the country?.* Aachen: RWTH Aachen University.

Hieu, L.T., Koo, S. (2007). The Recent Economic Performance and Poverty Reduction in Vietnam. *J. Int. Area Stud., 14*(2), 17-35.https://www.jstor.org/stable/43107154

Ho, G. (2020). Singapore sees rising incomes, falling inequality. *Singapore: The Straits Times.*https://www.straitstimes.com/singapore/politics/singapore-sees-rising-incomes-falling-inequality

Ingianni, A., Žd'árek, V. (2009). Real convergence in the new member states: Myth or reality? *J. Econ. Integr.,   24*(2), 294-320.https://www.jstor.org/stable/23000882
[http://dx.doi.org/10.11130/jei.2009.24.2.294]

Inoguchi, T., Fujii, S. (2013). *The Quality of Life in Asia 1: A comparison of Quality of Life in Asia.* Dordrecht: Springer.
[http://dx.doi.org/10.1007/978-90-481-9072-0]

International Labour Organization & Asian Development Bank. (2020). Tackling the COVID-19 youth employment crisis in Asia and the Pacific. Mandaluyong: Asian Development Bank. (2020).

International Monetary Fund. (2021). *Vietnam country report No. 21/42..* Washington, DC: International Monetary Fund.

Jensen, J., Krishnan, V., Spittal, M., Sathiyandra, S. (2003). New Zealand living standards: their measurement and variation, with an application to policy. *Soc. Policy J. N. Z.,   20*, 72-97.https://www.msd.govt.nz/documents/about-msd-and-our-work/publicat-ons-resources/journals-and-magazines/social-policy-journal/spj20/20-pages72-97.pdf

Jong-A-Pin, R. (2009). On the measurement of political instability and its impact on economic growth. *Eur. J. Polit. Econ., 25*(1), 15-29.
[http://dx.doi.org/10.1016/j.ejpoleco.2008.09.010]

Karp, P. (2021). Australia's living standards have risen and economy is 'roaring back', Deloitte says. *The Guardian.*https://www.theguardian.com/business/2021/apr/12/australias-living-standards-have-rise--and-economy-is-roaring-back-deloitte-says

Kind, M. (2020). *COVID-19 and a primer on shock-responsive social protection systems (Policy Brief No.82).* New York: United Nations DESA.

KPMG International Cooperative. (2015). *ASEAN: Poised for accelerated economic growth.* Singapore: KPMG International Cooperative.

Laos PDR Department of Planning and Cooperation. (2020). *National Social Protection Strategy Vision 2030 Goal 2025.* Vientiane: Ministry of Labour and Social Welfare . https://www.ilo.org/wcmsp5/groups/public/---asia/---ro-bangkok/documents/publication/wcms_757945.pdf

Lee, C., Narjoko, D., Oum, S. (2019). Introduction. In: Lee, C., Narkojo, D., Oum, S., (Eds.), *SMEs and Economic Integration in Southeast Asia.* (pp. 1-8). Singapore: ISEAS-Yusof Ishak Institute.
[http://dx.doi.org/10.1355/9789814818797-004]

Lim, I. (2020). Income inequality in Malaysia widened even while median household income rose to RM5,873 in 2019, according to latest statistics *Petaling Jaya: Malay Mail.* .https://www.malaymail.com/

news/malaysia/2020/07/10/income-inequality-in-malaysia-widened-even-while-median-househo-d-income-ro/1883232

Malik, N.A., Mansur, M. (2017). Impact of political instability on foreign direct investment and economic growth: Evidence from Malaysia. *Munich Personal RePEc Archive,* 1-19. https://mpra.ub.uni-muenchen.de/79418/1/MPRA_paper_79418.pdf

Mansi, E., Hysa, E., Panait, M., Voica, M.C. (2020). Poverty –A challenge for economic development? Evidences from Western Balkan countries and the European Union. *Sustainability (Basel), 12*(18), 7754. [http://dx.doi.org/10.3390/su12187754]

Mariadas, P.A., Murthy, U., Subramaniam, M., Abdullah, H. (2020). Political Instability, Property Investment, and Economic Growth: Are They Inter-Related? An Empirical Study in Malaysia. *Int. J. Manag., 11*(8), 1419-1429.https://ssrn.com/abstract=3699872

Marston, H. (2017). Domestic instability is holding back Myanmar's economic growth and regional vision. *World Politics Review.*https://www.worldpoliticsreview.com/articles/21474/domestic-instability-is-hold-ng-back-myanmar-s-economic-growth-and-regional-vision

Martuscelli, A., Gasiorek, M. (2018). Regional integration and poverty: a review of the transmission channels and the evidence. *J. Econ. Surv., 00*(0), 1-27. [http://dx.doi.org/10.1111/joes.12283]

Maude, R. (2021). *Southeast Asia's Economic Outlook: New variants threaten recovery.* New York, NY: Asia Society Policy Institute.https://southeastasiacovid.asiasociety.org/southeast-asias-economic-outl-ok-new-variants-threaten-recovery/

Min, C.H. (2021). Household incomes fall in 2020 due to COVID-19 impact, but rose in past 5 years. Singapore: Channel News Asia https://www.channelnewsasia.com/news/singapore/singapore-household-incomes-fall-in-2020-due-to-covid-19-impact-14137260#:~:text=Singapore's%20Gini%20coefficient%20was%200.452,transfers%2C%20a%20record%20low%20then

Moyo, D. (2018). *Edge of Chaos: Why democracy is failing to deliver economic growth – and how to fix it..* London: Little, Brown Book Group.

Mulok, D., Kogid, M., Asid, R., Lily, J. (2012). Is economic growth sufficient for poverty alleviation? Empirical evidence from Malaysia. *Cuad. Econ., 35*(97), 26-32. [http://dx.doi.org/10.1016/S0210-0266(12)70020-1]

Nallari, R., Griffith, B. (2011). *Understanding growth and poverty: Theory, policy, and empirics.* Washington, DC: World Bank. [http://dx.doi.org/10.1596/978-0-8213-6953-1]

Nursini, N. (2020). Micro, small, and medium enterprises (MSMEs) and poverty reduction: empirical evidence from Indonesia. *Dev. Stud. Res., 7*(1), 153-166. [http://dx.doi.org/10.1080/21665095.2020.1823238]

Economic Surveys, O.E.C.D. (2020). *Thailand: Economic assessment..* Paris: OECD. https://www.oecd.org/economy/surveys/Economic-assessment-thailand-overview-2020.pdf

OECD. (2017a). *OECD Economic Surveys: Australia OECD Economic Surveys: Australia 2017.* Paris: OECD Publishing.

OECD. (2017b). *OECD Economic Surveys: New Zealand OECD Economic Surveys: New Zealand 2017.* Paris: OECD Publishing.

OECD. (2021). *Economic policy reforms 2021: Going for growth.* Paris: OECD.https://www.oecd.org/economy/growth/New-Zealand-country-note-going-for-growth-2021.pdf

OECD/ERIA. (2018). *SME Policy Index: ASEAN 2018: Boosting competitiveness and inclusive growth.* Paris: OECD Publishing, Jakarta: ERIA.

Parente, S.L., Prescott, E.C. (2006). What a country must do to catch up to the industrial leaders. In: Balcerowicz, L., Fischer, S., (Eds.), *Living standards and the wealth of nations successes and failures in real convergence.* (pp. 17-40). Cambridge: The MIT Press.

Park, A., Wang, S. (2001). China's poverty statistics. *China Econ. Rev., 12*(4), 384-398. [http://dx.doi.org/10.1016/S1043-951X(01)00066-9]

Phillips, N. (2021). The Coronavirus will become endemic. *Nature, 590*, 382-384. [http://dx.doi.org/10.1038/d41586-021-00396-2] [PMID: 33594289]

Phua, R. (2021). Singapore economy shrinks a record 5.8% in a pandemic-hit 2020 Singapore: Channel News Asia. https://www.channelnewsasia.com/news/singapore/gdp-singapore-economy-2020-q4-contract-covid-19-13888300?cid=h3_referral_inarticlelinks_24082018_cna

Rao, V.V.B. (1998). East Asian Economies: Growth within an international context. *Econ. Polit. Wkly., 33*(6), 291-296.

Leaders Statement, R.C.E.P. (2012). *Joint declaration on the launch of negotiations for the Regional Comprehensive Economic Partnership.*https://rcepsec.org/wp-content/uploads/2019/10/56-RCEP_Joi-t-Leaders-Statement_8-September-2016.pdf

Leaders Statement, R.C.E.P. (2020). https://rcepsec.org/wp-content/uploads/2020/11/RCEP-Summit-4-J-int-Leaders-Statement-Min-Dec-on-India-2.pdf

Rivera, J.P.R. (2020). Estimating Gini Coefficient and FGT Indices in the Philippines Using the Family Income and Expenditure Survey. *J. Poverty, 24*(7), 568-590. [http://dx.doi.org/10.1080/10875549.2020.1737300]

Singapore Ministry of Finance. (2015). *Income growth, inequality and mobility trends in Singapore. Ministry of Finance 2015 Occasional Paper.* Singapore: Ministry of Finance.https://www.mof.gov.sg/docs/default-source/default-document-library/news-and-publications/featured-reports/income-growth-distribu-ion-and-mobility-trends-in-singapore.pdf

Son, H.H., Kakwani, N. (2004). *Economic growth and poverty reduction: Initial conditions matter..* Brasilia: International Poverty Centre.

Sukaesih, M. (2019). *Reducing regional inequality.* Jakarta: The Jakarta Post..https://www.thejakartapost.com/news/2019/09/11/reducing-regional-inequality.html

Sumarto, S., Moselle, S. (2015). *Addressing Poverty and Vulnerability in ASEAN: An Analysis of Measures and Implications Going Forward.*

Teoh, S. (2020). Uncertainty in politics, policymaking sours Malaysia's credit rating. *The Straits Times.*https://www.straitstimes.com/asia/se-asia/uncertainty-in-politics-policymaking-sours-mal-ysias-credit-rating

The ASEAN. (2020). *Social Protection for all in ASEAN.* Jarkta: The ASEAN.https://asean.org/storage/2020/07/The_ASEAN_Issue_03_July_2020.pdf

The State Council Information Office of the People's Republic of China. (2021). *Poverty alleviation: China's experience and contribution.*http://www.xinhuanet.com/english/download/2021-4-6/FullText.pdf

The World Bank. (2007). *Brunei Pension Report.* Bandar Seri Begawan: Centre for Strategic and Policy Studies.

Uchitelle, L. (2007). *NAFTA should have stopped illegal immigration, right?*The New York Times.https://www.nytimes.com/ 2007/02/18/weekinreview/18uchitelle.html

UNDP Asia and Pacific. (2021). *Covid-19, coup detat and poverty: Compounding negative shocks and their impact on human development in Myanmar.* Asia and Pacific: UNDP.https://www.asia-pacific.undp.org/content/rbap/en/home/library/democratic_governance/covid-19-co-p-d-etat-and-poverty-impact-on-myanmar.html

UNDP & Oxford Poverty and Human Development Initiative. (2020). *Charting pathways out of multidimensional poverty: Achieving the SDGs.* Oxford: Oxford Poverty and Human Development Initiative.

United Nations Development Programme. (2005). *Human Development Report 2005: International Co-*

operation at a Crossroads - Aid, Trade and Security in an Unequal World.. New York, NY: United Nations Development Programme.

United Nations Development Programme. (2020). *Human development report 2020: The next frontier, human development and the Anthropocene.* New York, NY: United Nations Development Programme.

United Nations ESCAP. (2018). *Inequality of opportunity in Asia and the Pacific: Myanmar country brief.* Bangkok: United Nations ESCAP . https://www.unescap.org/sites/default/d8files/2018.11.21%20Myanmar%20Country%20Brief.pdf

Varela, G., Cali, M., Pape, U., Rojas, E. (2016). *Market Integration and poverty: Evidence from South Sudan.* Washington DC: World Bank Group.http://documents.worldbank.org/curated/en/910361467990995887/Market-integration-and-poverty-evidence-from-South-Sudan [http://dx.doi.org/10.1596/1813-9450-7564]

Vu, K. (2020). *ASEAN economic prospects amid emerging turbulence: Development challenges and implications for reform.*. Washington, DC: The Brookings Institution.https://www.brookings.edu/wp-content/uploads/2020/07/FP_20200710_asean_economic_prospects_vu.pdf

Ward, G.F. (2015). *Political instability in Zimbabwe.*. New York NY: Council on Foreign Relations.https://cdn.cfr.org/sites/default/files/pdf/2015/03/CPA_ContingencyPlanningMemo_23.pdf

Warr, P. (2006). Poverty and Growth in Southeast Asia. *ASEAN Econ. Bull., 23*(3), 279-302. [http://dx.doi.org/10.1355/AE23-3A]

Warr, P., Rasphone, S., Menon, J. (2015). *Two decades of rising Inequality and declining poverty in the Lao People's Democratic Republic (ADB Economics WPS 461).*. Asian Development Bank.Mandaluyong:

Wetta, C., Yerbanga, A. (2013). Real convergence in the WAEMU Area: A Bayesian Analysis. In: Ayuk, E.T., Kabore´, S.T., (Eds.), *Wealth through integration: Regional integration and poverty-reduction strategies in West Africa.* (pp. 111-130). Ottawa: Springer.

World Bank. (2020). *COVID-19 to Add as Many as 150 Million Extreme Poor by 2021.* Washington D.C: World Bank. https://www.worldbank.org/en/news/press-release/ 2020/10/07/covid-19-to-add-as-mny-as-150-million-extreme-poor-by-2021

World Bank. (2019). *Malaysia. Poverty & Equity Brief, East Asia and Pacific: World Bank.* https://databank.worldbank.org/data/download/poverty/33EF03BB-9722-4AE2-A-C7-AA2972D68AFE/Archives-2019/Global_POVEQ_MYS.pdf

World Bank. (2021a). *GDP (current US$) Brunei Darussalam.* Washington DC: World Bank. https://data .worldbank.org/indicator/NY.GDP.MKTP.CD?locations=BN

World Bank. (2021b). *GDP (current US$)-Indonesia.* Washington DC: World Bank. https://data.worldbank. org/indicator/ NY.GDP.MKTP.CD?locations=ID

World Bank. (2021c). *GDP (current US$)-Singapore .* Washington DC: World Bank.https://data.worldbank. org/indicator/NY.GDP.MKTP.CD?locations=SG

World Bank. (2021). *GDP (current US$)-Malaysia.* Washington DC.World Bank. https://data.worldbank. org/indicator/ NY.GDP.MKTP.CD?locations=MY

World Bank. (2021). *GDP (current US$)-Lao PDR.*. Washington DC: World Bank. https://data.worldbank. org/indicator/NY.GDP.MKTP.CD?locations=LA

World Bank. (2021). *GDP (current US$)-Myanmar.* Washington DC: World Bank. https://data.worldbank. org/indicator/NY.GDP.MKTP.CD?locations=MM

World Bank. (2021). *GDP (current US$)-Philippines.* Washington DC: World Bank. https://data.worldbank. org/indicator/NY.GDP.MKTP.CD?locations=PH

World Bank. (2021h). *GDP (current US$)-Thailand.* Washington DC: World Bank. https://data.worldbank. org/indicator/NY.GDP.MKTP.CD ?locations=TH

World Bank. (2021j). *GDP (current US$)-Cambodia.* Washington DC: World Bank. https://data.worldbank

.org/indicator/NY.GDP.MKTP.CD?locations=KH

World Bank. (2021). *GDP (current US$)-Vietnam* . Washington DC: World Bank. https://data.worldbank.org/indicator/NY.GDP.MKTP.CD?locations=VN

Yoshino, N., Taghizadeh-Hesary, F. (2016). Optimal credit guarantee ratio for Asia. In: Vandenberg, P., Chantapacdepong, P., Yoshino, N., (Eds.), *SMEs in developing Asia: New approaches to overcoming market failures.* (pp. 179-208). Tokyo: Asian Development Bank Institute.

Zin, R.M. (2012). Malaysia: Towards a Social Protection System in an Advanced Equitable Society. *ASEAN Econ. Bull., 29*(3), 197-217.
[http://dx.doi.org/10.1355/ae29-3c]

CHAPTER 9

Regional Trade Deal with China for a New Digital Economy

Abdur Razzaq[1,*]

[1] *Universitas Islam Negeri Raden Fatah Palembang, Indonesia*

Abstract: The Regional Comprehensive Economic Partnership (RCEP) will be one of the most important free trade agreements in the history of the Asia-Pacific region and the world. Its objective is to improve trade ties across the Asian-Pacific region's economies. In the midst of the COVID-19 pandemic that has spread over the world, it has emerged as a topic that can have an influence on business. As China is one of the RCEP members that possesses a strong economic background, the country is innovating in the way it trades by taking advantage of the digital economy; even during the pandemic. It is apparent that China's economy benefits from this strategy to some extent. This study is an exploratory research using secondary data to investigate whether or not the RCEP will pose as a new economic platform in the Asia-Pacific region. The findings show that China's economy recovers partly due to the implementation of this digital system, becoming the world's first to do so. Throughout the outbreak of COVID-19, the country has demonstrated that it is inventive and capable of supporting its economy and speeding its development. The RCEP agreement will have a greater impact on China and on the participating members.

Keywords: Asia-Pacific, China, Digital Economy, Regional Comprehensive Economic Partnership (RCEP).

INTRODUCTION

The Regional Comprehensive Economic Partnership (RCEP) is a free trade agreement between countries in the Asia-Pacific region (FTA). According to Seth (2020), the RCEP would form the world's largest trading bloc and will be a key milestone for China as it competes with the United States for regional leadership and economic domination. It was envisioned that the Regional Comprehensive Economic Partnership would be a means of strengthening trading links among Asia-Pacific countries while also encouraging commerce and economic growth in

---

[*] **Corresponding author Abdur Razzaq:** Universitas Islam Negeri Raden Fatah Palembang, Indonesia;
E-mail: abdurrazzaq_uin@radenfatah.ac.id

Mahani Hamdan, Muhammad Anshari and Norainie Ahmad (Eds.)

the area. The RCEP is significant primarily for economic reasons (Trada, 2018). As a cornerstone for the multilateral trading framework, the agreement can consolidate regulations and streamline market activity across Asia-Pacific's several competing free trade agreements. The worldwide implications of the RCEP, on the other hand, are crucial since it has the ability to build a new framework.

The Regional Comprehensive Economic Partnership (RCEP) represents a commitment to go forward in the direction of greater regional integration. By building on the existing market structure, trade patterns, and potential investment, the agreement may be able to assist in improving intra-regional trade while also encouraging investment ties and strengthening further regional cooperation. This is possible because of the current global economic and political instability. As a result, trade, foreign direct investment (FDI), and value chain integration will all experience significant economic effects of the Regional Comprehensive Economic Partnership (RCEP), which will have implications both within and outside the community in the country itself, as well as posing new challenges to existing supply chain systems (Low & Anshari, 2013). It is necessary to consider the political and economic aspects of the decision and environmental aspects.

In addition to being a worldwide concern, the Covid-19 epidemic has far-reaching effects on many aspects of society and economic life, some of which are irreversible. The impact of the pandemic has produced a separate global recession, the deepest in more than eight decades (Fu, Zhang, & Wang, 2020, as cited in World Bank, 2020). In China, after the outbreak of Covid-19, the disease significantly impacted the country's economy by limiting worldwide economic development, consumption and investment (Anshari *et al*, 2021b). This has had a negative impact on China's foreign trade and cross-border capital flows on both the supply and demand sides of the economy. Studies are being undertaken to determine China's impact on trade and FDI (Foreign Direct Investment), with FDI playing a part in aiding the Regional Comprehensive Economic Partnership (RCEP), as indicated by Fu, Zhang, and Wang (2020). They revealed that China's exports and imports, as well as foreign direct investment (FDI) in the country, all experienced significant declines in the first quarter of 2020 (Duan, Zhu & Lai, 2020). China's exchange and foreign direct investment (FDI) measures have improved significantly since the second quarter when many nations' restrictive policies were repealed. These metrics are currently increasing at a positive rate in the third quarter. As a result, it appears that the pandemic has only a limited impact on trade and that foreign direct investment (FDI) is only temporary. To facilitate China's trade and outward FDI in the post-pandemic period, they recommend a variety of countermeasures related to risk reduction, creativity, opening up, e-commerce, and logistics system growth.

China responded to the pandemic by making certain modifications to its economic structures, with a particular emphasis on the role of digital technology as a response. The Chinese economy was the first to recover from the pandemic, and its V-shaped recovery provides cause for optimism for the rest of the world's post-pandemic recovery as a result of the virus (Fu, Zhang & Wang, 2020). Conventional ways of working and conducting business have been transformed as a result of the stringent restrictions, which have spurred change and growth in a variety of industries, particularly through the application of digital technologies. According to a survey, the pandemic hastened worldwide digitisation at the corporate and business levels, as well as at the individual level (Fu, Zhang, and Wang, as cited in McKinsey & Company, 2020).

The pandemic operates as an accelerator for the Chinese digital economy in general, with a specific emphasis on the banking industry (Ba and Bai, 2020). These authors agree that the use of digital technologies to assist with equitable finance and supply chain management has aided firms in restoring development as quickly as possible, which has proven critical to the economy's swift recovery. Moreover, Covid-19 has accelerated economic transitions by strengthening domestic industry chains and raising the rate of growth in innovative activities (Swasdee *et al*, 2020). This chapter examines the Regional Comprehensive Economic Partnership (RCEP) from the perspective of China, as well as the foundations of its digital economy.

LITERATURE REVIEW

The Regional Comprehensive Economic Partnership (RCEP) is a free-trade agreement between ASEAN member states and the remaining five regional countries (Australia, China, Japan, South Korea and New Zealand). When all participating nations join, it is estimated that the RCEP will contribute 30% to the global economy and unite 30% of the world's people (Peter & Michael, 2020). The RCEP collaborated with the Comprehensive and Progressive Agreement for Trans-Pacific Partnership (CPTPP) to enhance northern and Southeast Asia by efficiently connecting them and improving their technological, manufacturing, agricultural, and natural resource capacities (Peter & Michael, 2020). China is unquestionably the beneficiary of these deals and would stand to benefit the most. When the RCEP is in action, China's economy will undoubtedly benefit. According to Robert Ward's IISS blog post, the RCEP would increase Asia's interdependence, resulting in Asia becoming closer to China, where their supply chain is in great demand. As a result, they are able to attract foreign investors and business people to engage in the economy.

Digital Economy

A vast number of business leaders and innovators, consultants, and journalists have already recognised the potential for the digital economy to be a thriving industry (Li *et al*, 2020). Channel News Asia reported that according to the World Economic Forum and the Group of Twenty, the digital economy encompasses a "wide range of economic activities that use digitized information and knowledge as key factors of production, modern information networks as an important activity space, as well as information and communications technology to drive productivity growth," according to the World Economic Forum and the Group of Twenty (Kit, 2020, para. 10). According to Fourcade and Klutz (2020), the digital economy, which is characterised by the new invention of technologies such as mobile internet, cloud computing, big data analytics, and artificial intelligence (AI), has significantly increased following the United States financial crisis around 2007 to 2008, whereas traditional economic development was declining at the time. In addition to developing rapidly in Western countries, the digital economy is also advancing rapidly in Asian countries, and this development encourages the integration of digital technology and traditional economic activities (Ali, Hoque & Alam, 2018). It has been observed that the digital economy "would penetrate all elements of society, including interpersonal interactions, the economic environment, and political decision-making" (Gopal, Ramesh, and Whinston (2003, p. 2).

According to (Fig. **1**) on DESI (The Digital Economy and Society Index) scores, the lowest scores as of 2018 show that few of the countries lacked vital infrastructure for wider financial inclusion as a method of encouraging e-commerce on digital platforms. There were five countries with DESI scores that were less than 30 points, which includes Bangladesh, Pakistan, Vietnam, Indonesia and India. The scores of the other countries ranged between 50 and 60. Because these collaborations can aid in the provision of cross-border payments and family remittance services, it is necessary to investigate further some of the challenges surrounding platform collaborations (Anshari *et al*, 2020). One success story highlighted in this study is that of Tranglo Pte. Ltd. (Singapore), which has partnered with Chinese FinTech payment provider Alipay to achieve great success (Singapore, 2021). Some more technological applications that can help to strengthen the digital economy include merging messaging apps with platform service capabilities and other similar initiatives. This feature can assist with digital purchasing *via* mobile cash services, which can take advantage of low-cost digital messaging support to make purchases online. Consumers can gain a better understanding of the items and services that they are interested in purchasing with the assistance of digital messaging support (Anshari & Lim, 2017). Another app example comes from KT Corp, which was just named the winner of the 2019

Global Mobile Award (Korea Telecom). The purpose of this apps' development is to merge artificial intelligence-based and voice-certified mobile services in order to enable mobile payments for digital platforms (Corp., 2021; Mulyani *et al*, 2019). These advancements contribute to the creation of new opportunities for research innovations involving new technology and services in novel corporate and societal situations (Anshari *et al*, 2021a).

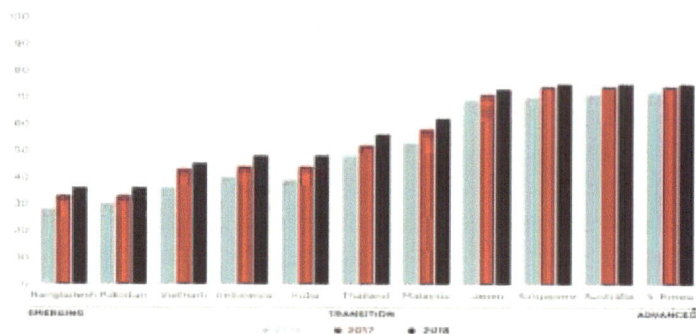

Fig. (1). Platform Readiness (Source: GSMA Intelligence, 2019).

China and Digital Economy

For the past few years, China has made dramatic changes in its global economy and society, transforming the country into an industrial reality and the most promising and rapidly growing emerging nation. China has risen to the level of industrialized countries such as the United States, Canada, Western Europe, Australia, New Zealand, and Japan (Liberto, 2021).

China holds the leading position in the digital economy, mostly as a result of its economic growth, which has been considerably aided by technological advancements and its ability to adapt to new technologies (Zhang & Chen, 2019). China is rapidly advancing to become the world's leading eCommerce market. It has surpassed the United States in terms of online B2C sales turnover, with €566 billion in revenue (Tang *et al*, 2021). Their presence in online firms such as Alibaba, the primary Chinese e-commerce platform, is transforming the retailing industry in particular, as Chinese consumers become more accustomed to shopping online as a result of their involvement in these businesses (Winter, 2016). In light of the stagnation of the western countries, these (Fig. **2**) indicate that China is currently the most attractive market in the world, and any company from anywhere in the world, including those from the United States, that wishes to expand their operations in China will see this as the most important investment opportunity.

Forbes magazine said in 2010 that all-American corporations such as Apple, Ford Motor, Nike, HJ Heinz, and the Gap are expanding in mainland China. According to the U.S.-China Business Council, American companies made $3.6 billion in foreign direct investment in China last year, representing a significant increase from the $2.9 billion invested in the same year in 2008. Starbucks and Coca Cola both continue to see China as their most important growth market—while Coke rival Pepsi has seen its profits in China decline in part because the company has committed $1 billion over the next four years to build 14 new beverage production plants, a move that will almost double its production capacity in the country, according to Pacific Epoch, a China-focused equities and macroeconomics research firm based in Shanghai. Starbucks and Coca Cola both continue to see China as their most important growth market.

According to market research conducted by Nielsen (2016), E-Commerce in China has proven to be the most effective channel for starting an online business due to its involvement in a higher penetration of the total retail market (13 percent) and an impressive average growth rate, which has approximated around 50 percent plus over the years, among other factors. Also likely to purchase foreign goods are Chinese consumers who shop for items on the international market.

Chinese online buyers are also more likely to purchase products from other countries. According to a study conducted by Paypal, an American company that provides online payment services, more than a quarter of online shoppers in China purchase foreign goods *via* the internet, primarily from the United States and the United Kingdom, but also from closer countries such as Japan and Hong Kong (Paypal, 2014). Furthermore, according to a recent poll done in China by Nielsen, 38 percent of customers in Tier 1 cities and 27 percent of customers in Tier 2 cities rely on cross-border internet purchases (Nielsen, 2016).

The Impact of Covid-19 and Post-pandemic Recovery

A significant 6.8 percent decline in China's economy was recorded during the first quarter of 2020, according to the National Bureau of Statistics of China (2020). Subsequently, during the second quarter of 2020, it began to rise to 3.2% gradually, and it maintained its upward trajectory until it reached 4.9 percent in the third quarter of 2020. China became the first country to see a significant economic rebound, and the country's recovery provided encouragement for the rest of the world to experience a similar recovery. Because of China's intrusive quarantine regulations, the country has been obliged to abandon its conventional ways of doing business and make full use of digital technologies. According to Mckinsey & Company (2020), the pandemic expanded the use of digital technology at the organizational and industrial levels around the world, as "consumers have shifted drastically toward online channels" as a result of the epidemic (para. 3). In addition, they claimed in their study that, compared to before the pandemic, 80 percent of their respondents indicated that they preferred using digital channels for client contacts.

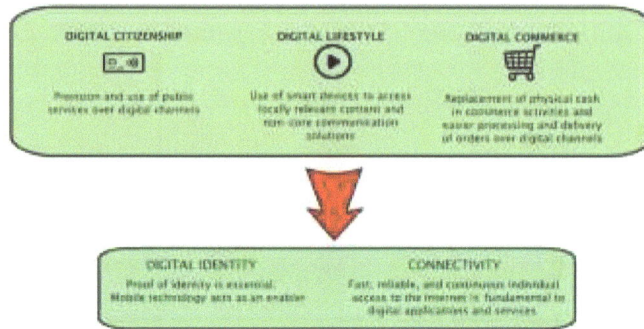

Fig. (2). Key Components of a Digital Society (Source: GSMA Intelligence, 2019).

During the pandemic, Jiang (2020) observes a significant increase in digital technology, which he believes opens the door to many new prospects for "new consuming patterns" because it is more extensively used as the lockdown encourages more food and beverage delivery services as well as e-commerce. Despite the fact that this pandemic is a situation that "will shape the ongoing competition and collaboration between major political and economic powers in the world," Fu, Zhang, and Wang (2020) asserted that this pandemic is a situation that "will shape the ongoing competition and collaboration between major political and economic powers in the world." The writers, on the other hand, argue that the RCEP appears to be in rivalry with the CAI (Comprehensive Agreement on Investment), which was negotiated between the EU and China following China's difficulties with the United States. Economic cooperation and bilateral investment between the EU and China would reach "historic heights in the post-pandemic age," according to Fu, Zhang, and Wang (2020) after the EU–China CAI was signed. It was their opinion that CAI could be viewed as more significant for global economic recovery than the Regional Comprehensive Economic Partnership (RCEP), which aims to lower tariffs and reduce non-tariff barriers, and they stated that "further elimination of investment and trade barriers between China and Europe should lead to steady recovery and growth of the global economy in a previously unseen narrative."

Wang (2014) believes that potential and problems of global e-business exist in the areas of China that have been noted as having bonded import zones established. Several cities in China, including Shanghai, Hangzhou, and Ningbo, as well as Zhengzhou (Guangdong) and Chongqing (Guangdong), have been designated as "bonded import districts" for the purpose of concentrating on international trade following the establishment of a successful e-commerce pilot program. As part of the Regional Comprehensive Economic Partnership (RCEP), China will be able to expand its international e-business operations as a result of the agreement. Competitive advantage has been provided to the six cities mentioned above as a result of the establishment of bonded warehouses in certain areas. In China, it is anticipated that the number of cross-border internet shops will increase as a result of the implementation of the Regional Comprehensive Economic Partnership (RCEP). To put it another way, the Regional Comprehensive Economic Partnership (RCEP) will encourage multinational e-commerce businesses to make use of the agreement in order to maximise profits.

In order to be successful, the Regional Comprehensive Economic Partnership (RCEP) and the digital economy must be centred on what the region's community wants and requires. The participating RCEP member countries are also able to harmonize and familiarize themselves with one another's cultures and values as a result of the program's worldwide commercial platform, which is helpful to all countries engaging in the program (Alas & Anshari, 2021). Organizations that engage in e-commerce should prioritize resource management as their top priority in the long run. This covers resources that are bonded and those that are not bonded, as well as logistical and offline support resources.

Methodology

As an exploratory research study, this study made use of secondary data to determine whether or not the Regional Comprehensive Economic Partnership (RCEP) will function as a new economic platform in the Asia-Pacific area. All of the information is based only on qualitative data in order to aid in the research process.

DISCUSSION

The Regional Comprehensive Economic Partnership (RCEP) can attract around 30 percent of the world economy, which will aid in developing and strengthening their technology and natural resources, including China. As a result, it has a positive impact on their economic situation. China, being the country with the largest population and the most developed supply chain, made it possible for international investors to invest in their company. The literature asserts that due to the RCEP, China was able to establish itself as a country that many investors desired to invest in. Because of the presence of Covid-19, however, there has been a slowdown in the increase of economic production. This virus has the potential to cause death, necessitating the need for social isolation and the shutting down of enterprises. As a result, it had a negative impact on economic production (Ahad *et al*, 2017).

Nonetheless, digital economics, such as the online market, contributed to the growth of economies by increasing their revenue. This also aided in preventing intimate contact with other people, which is necessary in order to keep the virus from spreading. Although the digital economy has assisted China in boosting its economies, it has also presented a number of challenges, including the fact that the economic impact of Covid-19 has been unevenly distributed across countries, as well as the disparity between policy responses and the size of the most affected areas in different countries as a result of the virus. This chapter determines how the digital economy contributed to the success of China's economy during the influenza epidemic.

Business leaders have also embraced the digital economy. With the exception of internal activities, the digital economy refers to the economy that is done through the internet, such as through the use of information technology (IT) (Anshari *et al*, 2019a). Not only does it apply to business, government, and charity organizations, but it also applies to transactions between organizations or individuals who function as both purchasers and consumers. This statement was made by Cohen *et al* (2001), who noted that information technology (IT) served as a tool for the creation of new organizational forms as well as for the organization of existing organizational forms (Anshari & Almunawar, 2021).

Gopal and colleagues (2003) also stated that the digital economy would contribute to the improvement of the economy. The rise of the internet economy accelerated even further, particularly when the pandemic began to spread. This serves as a wake-up call for organisations that have been resisting digital transformation, as it forces them to make trade-offs with their employees' health, resulting in a dramatic drop in demand. Small and medium-sized businesses (SMEs) are scrambling to shift their operations and workforces into virtual environments (Almunawar & Anshari, 2021; Sugiantoro *et al*, 2020; Hamdan *et al*, 2020).

Businesses that had not only developed but also implemented digital strategies before the pandemic, on the other hand, are now in a better position to overcome their less nimble competitors in terms of profitability. Nevertheless, this is not to downplay the difficulties they are currently experiencing as a result of COVID-19, which they face regardless of their current level of digital maturity. Going digital is not a panacea for the problems that businesses are experiencing in today-

's environment. They do, however, have many more resources at their disposal, allowing them to not only survive the storm but also to emerge from it stronger.

The use of information technology, the Internet, and/or applications have been used as methods to boost the digital economy. It can be improved by partnering with messaging apps that offer a variety of platform services, making it easier to make online purchases using a mobile phone that is also less expensive. Furthermore, all firms may begin developing websites or mobile applications that would assist them in regaining their lost clients and earnings. It was done in order to maintain a certain level of distance from customers, avoiding actual touch through methods such as online payment and delivery (Ahad & Anshari, 2017).

Furthermore, China's economy is steadily rebounding, and the country has created a positive image of itself among other countries that are attempting to revive the world economy. Because of China's stringent regulations, all enterprises were compelled to adopt digital technology. The resulting opportunities were a result of this (Jiang, 2020). Furthermore, Fu and colleagues (2020) argued that CAI, as opposed to the Regional Comprehensive Economic Partnership (RCEP), may aid in the recovery of the global economy by removing obstacles between China and Europe, resulting in a more balanced recovery and growth for the global economy.

Generally speaking, the use of the digital economy increased steadily throughout the pandemic. As reported by the National Bureau of Statistics of China in the first quarter of 2020, China's GDP experienced a significant decline (2020). It was due to a lack of familiarity with and knowledge of the digital economy, as opposed to the traditional economy, that this occurred. Not only that, but the pandemic also resulted in the temporary closure of the whole country's internal infrastructure, including all buildings, retail malls, restaurants, and schools (Anshari, 2020). In terms of the external environment, they reduced the barriers between countries by restricting the entry of foreigners and the exit of people from the country. There would be a lack of food supplies in the country, thus, this would include food supplies as well (Razzaq *et al*, 2018). The Regional Comprehensive Economic Partnership (RCEP) is also recognized for making products and services from each country available throughout the region. It is estimated that the pandemic will cause a significant economic decline around the world, particularly in China, which was the first country to be impacted by Covid-19.

Although the economy experienced a significant downturn, all firms began to look for ways to recoup the losses they had suffered, particularly in terms of consumers and earnings lost (Razzaq *et al*, 2018; Anshari *et al*, 2019b). This was the point at which firms began to turn to the digital economy in an attempt to recoup some of their losses. This might be achieved by developing websites and apps that offer services like delivery in order to lessen physical contact between people while simultaneously fostering social distancing. This may also aid in reducing the number of people who are infected by the virus in the future (Ahad *et al*, 2017). The digital economy has other advantages as well, including the ability to provide more information and choices to consumers as well as the ability to know the specifics of a product before purchasing it, as well as being more flexible in terms of allowing people to work from home and assisting the country's economic development Privacy difficulties, hacking, and interference with traditional economies were all brought on by the digital economy, which contributed to a high rate of unemployment and the possibility of future financial hardship (Mulyani *et al*, 2021).

This could be improved when laws, technology, and data protection all need to be updated, for example, by creating a law for digital technology and services that is applicable to all countries in order to keep up with digital technology by standardizing the law, renewing the copyright regulations that allow consumers to access the content while also being protected, and updating the copyright regulations. Essentially, by enhancing the laws and regulations governing the digital economy, it was able to contribute to the expansion of the global economy during the pandemic period.

CONCLUSION

The Regional Comprehensive Economic Partnership (RCEP) will support China in growing its economy. The grouping is expected to expand the global economy by 30 percent, which is a significant step forward for the country. Even throughout the pandemic, China has successfully regained control of its economy and even thrive due to digitisation, increasing its economic growth and ease of doing business. This cutting-edge technology enables China to take on the role of a global supply network for the benefit of other countries. Since then, the digital economy has enabled China to generate revenue from its digital businesses without having to deal directly with buyers or dealers.

CONSENT FOR PUBLICATION

Not applicable.

CONFLICT OF INTEREST

The author declares no conflict of interest, financial or otherwise.

ACKNOWLEDGEMENTS

Declared none.

REFERENCES

Ali, M.A., Hoque, M.R., Alam, K. (2018). An empirical investigation of the relationship between e-government development and the digital economy: the case of Asian countries. *Journal of Knowledge Management, 22*(5), 1176-1200.
[http://dx.doi.org/10.1108/JKM-10-2017-0477]

Ahad, A.D., Anshari, M., Razzaq, A. (2017). Domestication of smartphones among adolescents in Brunei darussalam. *International Journal of Cyber Behavior, Psychology and Learning, 7*(4), 26-39.
[http://dx.doi.org/10.4018/IJCBPL.2017100103]

Ahad, A.D., Anshari, M. (2017). Smartphone habits among youth: Uses and gratification theory. *International Journal of Cyber Behavior, Psychology and Learning, 7*(1), 65-75.
[http://dx.doi.org/10.4018/IJCBPL.2017010105]

Alas, Y., Anshari, M. (2021). Initiating Brunei Cross-Border Tourism (BCBT) as a Gateway to Borneo. *International Journal of Asian Business and Information Management, 12*(3), 15-25.
[http://dx.doi.org/10.4018/IJABIM.20210701.oa2]

Almunawar, M.N., Anshari, M. (2021). Digital enabler and value integration: revealing the expansion engine of digital marketplace. *Technol. Anal. Strateg. Manage.,* 1-11.

Anshari, M., Almunawar, M.N., Masri, M. (2020). Financial Technology and Disruptive Innovation in Business. *International Journal of Asian Business and Information Management, 11*(4), 29-43.
[http://dx.doi.org/10.4018/IJABIM.2020100103]

Anshari, M., Almunawar, M. N. (2021). Financial Technology and Disruptive Innovation in Business: Concept and Application. *International Journal of Asian Business and Information Management (IJABIM), 11*(4), 29-43.

Anshari, M., Arine, M.A., Nurhidayah, N., Aziyah, H., Salleh, M.H.A. (2021). Factors influencing individual in adopting eWallet. *J. Financ. Serv. Mark., 26*(1), 10-23.
[http://dx.doi.org/10.1057/s41264-020-00079-5]

Anshari, M., Almunawar, M.N., Younis, M.Z., Kisa, A. (2021). Modeling Users' Empowerment in E-Health Systems. *Sustainability (Basel), 13*(23), 12993.
[http://dx.doi.org/10.3390/su132312993]

Anshari, M., Almunawar, M.N., Masri, M., Hamdan, M. (2019). Digital marketplace and FinTech to support agriculture sustainability. *Energy Procedia, 156*, 234-238.
[http://dx.doi.org/10.1016/j.egypro.2018.11.134]

Anshari, M., Almunawar, M.N., Lim, S.A., Al-Mudimigh, A. (2019). Customer relationship management and big data enabled: Personalization & customization of services. *Applied Computing and Informatics, 15*(2), 94-101.
[http://dx.doi.org/10.1016/j.aci.2018.05.004]

Anshari, M., Lim, S.A. (2017). E-government with big data enabled through smartphone for public services: Possibilities and challenges. *Int. J. Public Adm., 40*(13), 1143-1158.
[http://dx.doi.org/10.1080/01900692.2016.1242619]

Ba, S., Bai, H. (2020). Covid-19 pandemic as an accelerator of economic transition and financial innovation in China. *J. Chin. Econ. Bus. Stud., 18*(4), 341-348.
[http://dx.doi.org/10.1080/14765284.2020.1855394]

Cohen, S. S., Delong, J. B., Weber, S., Zysman, J. (2001). Tracking a transformation: e-commerce and the terms of competition in industries, BRIE-IGCC economy project task force.

Corp., K. (2021). KT Corp. Debuts New 5G Services at MWC 2019. Retrieved 25 February 2021, from https://www.prnewswire.com/news-releases/kt-corp-debuts-new-5g-services-at-mwc-2019-300804026.html

Das, S.B. (2013). *RCEP and TPP: Comparisons and Concerns.*. Institute of Southeast Asian Studies.

Fourcade, M., Kluttz, D.N. (2020). A Maussian bargain: Accumulation by gift in the digital economy. *Big Data Soc., 7*, 1. [http://dx.doi.org/10.1177/2053951719897092]

Fu, X., Zhang, J., Wang, L. (2020). Introduction to the special section: the impact of Covid-19 and post-pandemic recovery: China and the world economy. *J. Chin. Econ. Bus. Stud.,* 1-9. [http://dx.doi.org/10.1080/14765284.2020.1712645]

Gopal, R.D., Ramesh, R., Whinston, A.B. (2003). Microproducts in a Digital Economy: Trading Small, Gaining Large. *Int. J. Electron. Commerce, 8*(2), 9-30. [http://dx.doi.org/10.1080/10864415.2003.11044292]

Intelligence, G.S.M.A. (2019). DESI and Platform Readiness. *Asia,* 2016-2018.https://ec.europa.eu/commission/presscorner/detail/en/qanda_20_1022

Hamdan, M., Chen, C.K., Anshari, M. (2020). Decision Aid in Budgeting Systems for Small & Medium Enterprises. *2020 International Conference on Decision Aid Sciences and Application (DASA)* IEEE. [http://dx.doi.org/10.1109/DASA51403.2020.9317018]

Jiang, X. (2020). Digital economy in the post-pandemic era. *J. Chin. Econ. Bus. Stud., 18*(4), 333-339. [http://dx.doi.org/10.1080/14765284.2020.1855066]

Kit, T. (2020). The rise of the digital economy: What is it and why it matters for Singapore Retrieved 20 February 2021 https://www.channelnewsasia.com/news/business/what-is-digital-economy-why-it-m-tters-mobile-app-12240630

Low, K.C.P., Anshari, M. (2013). Incorporating social customer relationship management in negotiation. *Int. J. Electron. Cust. Relatsh. Manag., 7*(3/4), 239-252. [http://dx.doi.org/10.1504/IJECRM.2013.060700]

Li, K., Kim, D.J., Lang, K.R., Kauffman, R.J., Naldi, M. (2020). How should we understand the digital economy in Asia? Critical assessment and research agenda. *Electron. Commerce Res. Appl., 44*, 101004. [http://dx.doi.org/10.1016/j.elerap.2020.101004] [PMID: 32922241]

Liberto, D. (2021). *Advanced Economies*. Investopedia. Retrieved 16 Jan 2022 from https://www.investopedia.com/terms/a/advanced-economies.asp

McKinsey & Company. (2020). *How Covid-19 Has Pushed Companies over the Technology Tipping Point and Transformed Business Forever.* Retrieved 13 March 2021, from https://www.mckinsey.com/business-functions/strategy-and-corporate-finance/our-insights/how-covid-19-has-pushed-compani-s-over-the-technology-tipping-point-and-transformed-business-forever

Mulyani, M.A., Razzaq, A., Sumardi, W.H., Anshari, M. (2019). Smartphone Adoption in Mobile Learning Scenario. *2019 International Conference on Information Management and Technology (ICIMTech)* IEEE. [http://dx.doi.org/10.1109/ICIMTech.2019.8843755]

Mulyani, M.A., Yusuf, S., Siregar, P., Nurihsan, J., Razzaq, A., Anshari, M. (2021). Fourth Industrial Revolution and Educational Challenges. *2021 International Conference on Information Management and Technology (ICIMTech)* IEEE. [http://dx.doi.org/10.1109/ICIMTech53080.2021.9535057]

National Bureau of Statistics of China. (2020). Economic Growth of the First Three Quarters Shifted from Negative to Positive. Retrieved 13 March 2021, from http://www.stats.gov.cn/english/PressRelease/202010/t20201019_1794616.html#:~:text=The%20economic%20growth%20of%20the,people's%20livelihood%20were%20well%20guaranteed

Nielsen. (2016). China Maintains Robust E-commerce Growth Retrieved 16 Jan 2022 from https://www.nielsen.com/cn/en/insights/article/2016/china-maintains-robust-e-commerce-growth/

Paypyal. (2015). PayPal 3rd Annual Global Report Retrieved 16 Jan 2022 from https://newsroom.paypal-corp.com/2016-11-15-PayPal-3rd-Annual-Global-Report-Shows-Asia-Pacific-as-Leaders--n-Mobile-Cross-Border-Shopping

Panda, J.P. (2014). Factoring the RCEP and the TPP: China, India and the Politics of Regional Integration. *Strategic Analysis, 38*(1), 49-67.
[http://dx.doi.org/10.1080/09700161.2014.863462]

Plummer, M.A.P.P.A. (2020). *RCEP: A new trade agreement that will shape global economics and politics..* Brookings.https://www.brookings.edu/blog/order-from-chaos/2020/11/16/rcep-a-new-trade-agreeme-t-that-will-shape-global-economics-and-politics/

Razzaq, A., Samiha, Y.T., Anshari, M. (2018). Smartphone habits and behaviors in supporting students self-efficacy. *International Journal of Emerging Technologies in Learning (iJET), 13*(2), 94.
[http://dx.doi.org/10.3991/ijet.v13i02.7685]

Robert, W. (2020). *RCEP trade deal: a geopolitical win for China.* IISS. https://www.iiss.org/blogs/analysis/2020/11/rcep-trade-deal

Singapore, F. (2021). Tranglo First in Asia to Launch Global Remittance Partnership with Alipay - Fintech Singapore Retrieved 25 February 2021, from https://fintechnews.sg/35871/remittance/tranglo-first-in-asi--to-launch-global-remittance-partnership-with-alipay/

Seth, S. (2020). Regional Comprehensive Economic Partnership (RCEP), Investopedia Retrieved from: https://www.investopedia.com/terms/r/regional-comprehensive-economic-partnership-rcep.asp

Sugiantoro, B., Anshari, M., Sudrajat, D. (2020). Developing Framework for Web Based e-Commerce: Secure-SDLC. *J. Phys. Conf. Ser., 1566*(1), 012020.
[http://dx.doi.org/10.1088/1742-6596/1566/1/012020]

Swasdee, A., Anshari, M., Hamdan, M. (2020). Artificial Intelligence as Decision Aid in Humanitarian Response. *2020 International Conference on Decision Aid Sciences and Application (DASA)* IEEE.
[http://dx.doi.org/10.1109/DASA51403.2020.9317111]

Tang, H.C., Tan, Y. (2021). *What is driving China's e-commerce growth?.* Retrieved 16 Jan 2022 from https://www.eastasiaforum.org/2021/10/13/what-is-driving-chinas-e-commerce-growth/

Thangavelu, S. M., Urata, S., Narjoko, D. A. (2021). Impacts of the Regional Comprehensive Economic Partnership on ASEAN and ASEAN Least Developed Countries in the Post-pandemic Recovery.

Terada, T. (2018). *RCEP Negotiations and the Implications for the United States..* The National Bureau of Asian Research.

Wang, J. (2014). Opportunities and challenges of international e-commerce in the pilot areas of China. *International Journal of Marketing Studies, 6*(6), 141.
[http://dx.doi.org/10.5539/ijms.v6n6p141]

Zhang, M.L., Chen, M.S. (2019). *China's digital economy: Opportunities and risks..* International Monetary Fund.

CHAPTER 10

Empowering The Underprivileged Community through Social Innovation and Entrepreneurship

Fahmi Ibrahim[1,*] and **Dayangku Rodzi Pengiran Haji Rahman**[1]

[1] School of Business, Universiti Teknologi Brunei (UTB), Brunei Darussalam

Abstract: There is increasing awareness of being socially responsible and the need to address social problems involving various key stakeholders in the public and private sectors, the corporate world and businesses, as well as the community. With social issues experienced globally, such as introducing diversity in society and eradicating poverty, it is imperative to use social innovation to improve or replace the way things are currently done. The purpose of this paper is to analyse the impact of social innovation on entrepreneurship as a way of providing stable income to underprivileged and unemployed segments and youth. It discusses key elements that support the development of entrepreneurship to ensure sustainability and growth, to ensure the underprivileged segment and youth will continue to earn income, thus reducing reliance on welfare assistance support. The research was conducted based on interviews and observation methods. Two significant projects were investigated that employed the social innovation model, how they were applied, and the implications to the society that participated in these projects. These include the processes, the role of individuals and the collective action of key strategic stakeholders in managing and structuring the programmes. We conclude with the importance of entrepreneurship in driving economic growth and empowering the targeted segment, such as the underprivileged, through entrepreneurship to provide employment and sustainable income. Recommendations include: managing social issues, uncover the importance of social inclusivity, introducing social innovation to develop individuals and drive economic growth, involvement of all parties from the public and private sectors, as well as non-profit and non-government organisations to expand the initiatives to include those who are entitled to receive the support.

Keywords: Social Innovation, Social Entrepreneurship, Underprivileged Community.

INTRODUCTION

There is increasing awareness of being socially responsible and the need to address social problems involving various key stakeholders in the public and

* **Corresponding author Fahmi Ibrahim**: School of Business, Universiti Teknologi Brunei (UTB), Brunei Darussalam; E-mail: fahmi.ibrahim@utb.edu.bn

Mahani Hamdan, Muhammad Anshari and Norainie Ahmad (Eds.)

private sectors, as well as the corporate and businesses and the community included (Cunha, Benneworth and Oliveria, 2019). Rising social issues experienced globally, such as diversity in society and eradicating poverty, has made it imperative to use social innovation to improve or replace the way things are currently done (Lettice and Parekh, 2010). Social innovation has the ability to attend to the main social problems faced by humanity in a more efficient way (Portales, 2019). Social issue is impacting society worldwide, including Brunei. A drop in the oil and gas business in 2013 impacted Brunei and resulted in a downward spiral in economic activities, an increase in unemployment, and the community seeking welfare assistance from relevant government agencies. Compared to ASEAN countries, Brunei has the highest youth unemployment rate at 28.4 percent in the region (The Scoop, 2019). The ASEAN Post reported that GDP per capita in Brunei has dropped significantly over the past five years or so (Ariffin, 2018).

The concept of social innovation emerges as part of the search to find new ways of coordinating and mobilising local problems. This has also been a result of rapid positioning and effort on the part of many organisations, companies, and institutions to generate this type of innovation. There is no agreed definition of the concept; however, all approaches mentioned the interest of creating social change by addressing a specific need or specific problem. Likewise, social innovation is a new area in the context of Brunei, but today is key in advancing ideas, technology, and process forward to remain competitive, earn a sustainable income and grow the economy. The promise of social change by social innovation leads to the position of the concept within the agenda of governments, companies, non-profit organisations, and academia, who, through various initiatives, promote their development from a practical perspective. As a consequence of this impulse, the generation of initiatives of all sectors of society to encourage the creation of a greater number of social innovations, especially in contexts characterised by exclusion, marginalisation, and poverty. This is significant for Brunei's economic diversification strategy, as developing a diversification strategy is foremost crucial towards promoting high economic growth and developing high-quality employment that can be appropriately distributed among the people in Brunei (Bhaskaran, 2010).

The purpose of this study is to examine the impact of social innovation on society by looking into the entrepreneurship initiative that has been implemented by Bank Islam Brunei Darussalam (BIBD) through its Corporate Social Responsibility (CSR) initiative under the Empowerment Initiative for Social Safety Net, that is BIBDSeed programme, as a case study. The study investigates the determining factors that instill empowerment and sustainable business ventures that address issues of unemployment and poverty, providing greater impact to broader segments of society such as youth and women. The study also analysed how social innovation and entrepreneurship lead to the creation of employment for different target segments and further contribute towards generating sustainable income and supporting the improvement of the socio-economy of the country.

INTRODUCTION

Brunei experienced a challenging period due to economic adversity from a drop in the oil and gas price in 2013. Consequently, its economic activity slowed down, and this triggered the public and private sectors and other institutions to take cautious and prudent measures in spending, including holding off on the recruitment process (Cheong *et al.*, 2016). Because of this, the situation further aggravated the unemployment (approximately 9% unemployment rate) situation due to limited job availability. In his report, Bhaskaran (2010) highlighted that despite many notable and appropriate suggestions to take advantage of some of the strengths of Brunei, the country has not been successful in making substantial development toward diversification. He added that economic diversification is not progressing as expected due to the country's continuous reliance on the oil and gas industry.

The social issue of unemployment has significant implications on human existence, especially on the well-being of the community (Jakimovski, 2010), and an extensive period of unemployment cause major challenge in development initiatives and its detrimental effect is the loss of earnings. Inadequate educational attainment can also lead to a lack of employment opportunities, and long-term unemployment contributes to the inability to earn a steady income. Additionally, relatively low income or single income earner for a family means their inability to sustain the basic standard of living. This is a condition in which people lack the minimum amount of income needed in order to maintain the average standard of living in the society where they live.

Based on UN Millennium Development Goals (MDG) Report in 2011 stated that 5.04 percent of Brunei's population falls below the poverty line. This was further supported by statistics released in 2012 by the Department of Community Development (JAPEM), Ministry of Culture Youth and Sports and the Brunei Islamic Religious Council (MUIB), Ministry of Religious Affairs, reporting that up to 20,790 individuals live below the poverty line (www.thepovertyline.net/brunei, 2015). As reported by Kakar (2017), Brunei does not have enough information to support the claim made in regard to poverty status and threshold. The poverty line in Brunei is set in accordance to the standards and policy under Majlis Ugama Islam Brunei (MUIB) and Jabatan Pembangunan Masyarakat (JAPEM), which is based on the net income after the deduction of monthly expenses such as rent, utilities and financing. Brunei Darussalam continues to provide welfare assistance to (registered) underprivileged communities struggling to make ends meet through (monetary) welfare assistance offered by JAPEM and MUIB, as well as non-government organisations. The statistics show that the number of registrants seeking welfare assistance from the government is increasing up to 19,913 persons in 2019 (Borneo Bulletin, 2019; Media Permata, 2019). This is an indication of the status of the well-being of the community in the country who are registered as underprivileged.

Based on the salience of the socio-economic situation mentioned above, this study aims to discuss the application and implementation of social innovation initiatives, particularly in entrepreneurship, to empower the underprivileged society, individuals who are unemployed and living in a state of poverty., The unemployment rate in Brunei reached 9.3 percent in 2017, equivalent to 19,200 people and reduced to 6.8% in 2019 (Haris and Bandial, 2021). Although with the decline of the unemployment rate, this remains a concern with insufficient work opportunities in the market, resulting from slow economic growth, despite oil and gas prices experiencing a modest increase in recent years. The number of welfare assistance recipients also increased by 13% in 2018 and increased to 7000 people in 2020, unprecedentedly due to Covid-19 (Abu Bakar, 2020). This demonstrates the government agencies' measures in provisioning higher budgets to provide financial support for targeted segments of society. However, prolonged welfare assistance can result in over-dependence making recipients idle and lacking the drive to work for a living. Because welfare reduces work effort and promotes illegitimacy and poverty-prone single-parent families, it actually may cause an overall decrease in family incomes (Bane and Ellwood, 1986). Welfare is extremely efficient at replacing self-sufficiency with dependence but relatively ineffective in raising incomes and eliminating poverty. Therefore, there is a need to examine the root cause and identify appropriate solutions at the earliest stage. This includes the creation of employment through social innovation and entrepreneurship. In today's fast and dynamic environment, social change by deploying innovative entrepreneurship is crucial because it is considered one of the key conditions for successful entrepreneurship, and it brings about transformational and financial sustainability to society and the economy (Carvalho, 2016).

Social Innovation and Entrepreneurship

Schumpeter and Hochgerner (2011) highlighted that the fundamental concept of innovation was originally developed in the first half of the twentieth century in terms of the execution and propagation the new ideas, which are still being recognised today. Other researchers have asserted that innovation and entrepreneurship concepts are believed to be the most unique economic contribution developed by Schumpeter. In fact, his philosophies of innovation and entrepreneurship continued to be relevant and are the motivating factor behind current economic development (Richter, 2019). Social innovation has a variety of connotations, but generally, it involves creating fresh ideas and new products that can help to fulfill a social requirement or address social concerns. It also relates to developing innovative operations and services driven by individuals and organisations whose key objective is to support society in need (Mulgan, 2007).

Innovation provides an opportunity for new development and improvement and positively impacts the economy. There are various forms of innovation that include new and superior quality goods; enhancements in the production process; expansions in a new market; wider options for the supply of raw materials and resources; organisational transformations and change in management structure; development of improved business models and services, and creative marketing approaches (Lisetchi and Brancu, 2014). During the past decades, there have been considerable advancements in the development of technology in related innovation concepts. Previously, innovation strategies tended to concentrate on supporting business and technological innovations and refrained from developing comparable strategies to understand and support social innovation (Mulgan, 2007; Phillips, 2011). Today, a comprehensive application of the social innovation process must be employed to ensure the initiatives remain sustainable. Social innovations can stem from collective campaigns when companies work together with NGOs, local communities and government agencies to tackle societal issues.

Today, social innovation is becoming more crucial due to its ability to support economic growth, which can be utilised to provide solutions to various challenges faced by stakeholders such as:

i) For individuals - access and opportunities to participate and contribute to the economy, using social innovation as a strategic tool that involves highly creative and collaborative efforts.

ii) For organisations – take advantage of economic gains; the ability to achieve sustainable competitive benefits; strengthen supply chains; talent retention, as well as access to emerging markets or expand their consumer segments.

iii) For community – assist in enhancing the standard of living of society through social innovation initiative of entrepreneurship.

Another source of social innovation is a social invention, and Conger (1974, p. 163) described the social invention as a new policy, institution or process that transformed the way individuals interact with one another, either independently or jointly. Inevitably, it is through concerted and integrated efforts that social innovation can create a means of identifying alternative solutions with the purpose of providing society with options to resolve problems.

Innovation is a significant ingredient of entrepreneurship, and this impels the drafting of the proposal and the development of an indicator for innovative entrepreneurship; therefore, it is important the progress and success of entrepreneurship are measured (Low and Isserman, 2012). Measuring entrepreneurship progression and growth is not easy, either due to the lack of key relevant data or information or because the area of coverage or number of entrepreneurship is huge (Low & Isserman, 2012). Sustainable entrepreneurship can empower society to be more responsible in managing and supporting their daily lives. In addition, innovative entrepreneurship can contribute to stimulating the overall business sector growth and economic prosperity in a country (Rajendra, 2017).

Entrepreneurship and innovation are interconnected and can be a reflection of a country's economic growth and strength when executed effectively (Tidd and Bessant, 2015). The combination of innovation and technology can be exploited to drive business beyond local shores and help in overcoming social challenges, and facilitate businesses to secure new opportunities (Thomas, 2019). Social innovation means being more strategic, more ambitious and more collaborative in searching for opportunities that can be provided to the low-income community so that they too can participate and contribute to the global economy (Audretsch *et al.*, 2006). It is also directed towards overcoming various social concerns and socio-economic challenges (Schachter *et al.*, 2012), hence promoting the quality of life in the community, with the public and private sectors' participation and through collective engagement deploying measures and utilising technology to effectively tackle risks and social issues.

The existence and sustainability of entrepreneurship can be triggered through the implementation of innovation and creativity. Sustainable entrepreneurship can empower society to be more responsible in managing and supporting their daily lives. In addition, innovative entrepreneurship can contribute to stimulating the overall business sector growth and economic prosperity in a country (Rajendra, 2017). Therefore, it is important for businesses to appreciate that to thrive, it requires being able to emphasise creating originality in products and services, integrating innovation; and adopting strategic business practices. It is equally key to note that innovation does not emerge within a day as it requires investing time and great efforts to come up with something that is truly innovative in order to make a difference. The ultimate test of an entrepreneur's success is based on whether a product or service can provide value to the lives of the customers (Rajendra, 2017).

Entrepreneurship and innovation are interconnected and can be a reflection of a country's economic growth and strength when executed effectively. A highly innovative product and service can help businesses to enter new markets outside the current market environment because with technological advancement, the global becomes more connected. The combination of innovation and technology can be exploited to drive business beyond local shores, help overcome social challenges, and facilitate businesses to secure new opportunities (Thomas, 2019). The public sector continues to be crucial and needs to be amplified further through the development of relevant schemes and programmes that support the growth of entrepreneurs as key drivers of a nation's economic success and prosperity.

Empowering the Underprivileged Society

Akpan (2015) acknowledged the importance of empowerment of individuals or communities who earns a minimum salary. Empowerment is best understood as a series of tasks that will transpire in breaking poverty patterns and initiating activities that encourage wealth development and reinforce productivity. It is defined as the idea of empowering the poor by providing them with substantial information and knowledge, financial means, and resources, as well as showing them the steps and processes to enable them to become independent. It is further emphasised the significance of empowerment – as offering underprivileged citizens access to productive resources that will enable them to boost their income, thus making goods and services accessible to them; and to engage them with the process of growth and understanding the conditions affecting them – which will ensure that the empowerment efforts will become successful and sustainable. Knowledge of entrepreneurship has become fundamental in modern economic strategy in order to stimulate employment. The consequence of entrepreneurship education is an environment surrounding an energetic generation of entrepreneurs who are able to establish employment for themselves and as well as for others (Khan and Almoharby, 2007). The cross-sector collaboration created through a strategic partnership between the private, public, and relevant industries, is key and can contribute to participative processes and people's empowerment (Carvalho, 2016). Entrepreneurship can address problems such as shortages of food and water, decline in environmental pollution and significantly enhance sustainability through innovative and accessible techniques (Zahra and Wright, 2016). A strong entrepreneurial activity contributes toward wealth generation for business owners, employees as well as the local economy.

Entrepreneurship Empowerment Programme in Brunei

Amongst the many initiatives is the BIBDSEED Programme, a BIBD Entrepreneurship Empowerment Programme developed by the local financial institution, Bank Islam Brunei Darussalam (BIBD), under its Corporate Social Responsibility (BIBD CSR) Initiative. BIBD CSR consists of three main pillars (as shown below), and the BIBDSEED Programme falls under Entrepreneurship.

Education	Entrepreneurship	Community
Nurturing Future Leaders through Education & Financial literacy.	Powering the Nation's Diversification through SME, Technology, & Innovation.	Help bring about the changes required to preserve our way of life in evolving merit & social development in Brunei.

The Entrepreneurship Empowerment Programme was developed with the aim of supporting the development, growth and strength of local micro, small and medium enterprises. This is accomplished through the development of customised entrepreneurship programmes and conducted in collaboration with key stakeholders in the public and private sectors. BIBDSEED was established in late 2018, is the product of this programme and is specifically designed to provide training towards empowering underprivileged women and single mothers with relevant knowledge and skills in entrepreneurship. It is the first known comprehensive entrepreneurship empowerment programme developed in the country. BIBDSEED vision is to transform the lives of underprivileged and single women to become successful entrepreneurs who are able to survive and compete in local and international markets. It aims to provide business opportunities through a capacity-building platform and to build strong and self-reliant entrepreneurship (*Muslimpreneurs*).

The creation of BIBDSEED aims to:

• To develop human capital capabilities in the way of thinking and behaving, emulating successful *Muslimpreneurs* (entrepreneurs).

• To improve productivity and service through innovation and automation in line with current entrepreneurial practices.

• To transform lives through optimal business skills, knowledge and training and able to adapt into the business ecosystem.

The collaborative support and involvement of key strategic partners such as the Ministry of Religious Affairs and Ministry of Culture, Youth and Sports, corporates, government-linked companies and higher educational institutions were key in the effective implementation of the programme. The programme was developed due to findings that the majority of recipients of welfare benefits provided by the government are women, and most of them are either from an underprivileged background, do not have a steady job or earn minimal income, which is not sufficient for saving or set aside as investment.

The fifteen-month programme consists of five phases is aimed towards:

• Imparting relevant entrepreneurial knowledge and skills.

• Strengthening the participant's business acumen and capabilities.

• Facilitate in setting up and business management, opening a business account and developing unique products/ services.

Several workshops are conducted throughout the five phases covering the different learnings that include developing a business plan; financial planning and basic accounting; food preparation and ingredients preparation; product development; packaging; pricing; branding and marketing; proper usage of the social media. By the end of each phase, there is an assessment to review the women's performance and their understanding of the learning. This is key to the effectiveness and success of the BIBD Entrepreneurship Empowerment Programme. By the end of the BIBDSeed programme, BIBD hopes to equip the women with real business knowledge, traits and skills (to run and manage their businesses ethically and efficiently); transform them (in the way of behaving and thinking; be a focus and resilient) and to become successful entrepreneurs to economically sustain themselves and pull them out of poverty. BIBDSeed seeks to increase the number of un-bankable communities to be bankable so that they can be part of the society that can contribute to the economic dynamic and growth of the country.

Methodology

This research was conducted by using the case study method with a qualitative interview approach. Social-related issues were addressed in interviews, as it is feasible to identify the root-cause of the issues; propose appropriate solutions to the problem; enhance collaborative efforts by encouraging and pulling together key stakeholders; and align the execution of solutions (Downs, 2007). Qualitative research usually draws information from fieldwork, where the researcher dedicates time to be engaged (participate) within the environment of research, such as a programme, organisation, or society, where changes can be monitored. In addition, the researcher would also benefit by observing first-hand activities and interactions of participants in the programme. This is recommended by Patton (2005), where the researcher may participate in activities and interact with the participants in order to observe the participant's emotions. In view of gaining data on entrepreneurship experience through the programme with their source of income, a list of open-ended semi-structured questionnaires was prepared for a face-to-face interview with the BIBDSeed Programme participants. The aim is to draw information on their experience of the programme; aspect of the programme that benefits them, applying and sutilising learnt skills and knowledge, and understanding the status of their business. A total of nine (9) BIBDSeed participants were interviewed, along with training development and motivational consultants, policymaker and former economists from The Brunei Economic Development Board, and relevant government stakeholders related to community and youth development.

Nevertheless, this study has its limitations because most data information is gathered from discussions with key stakeholders in the public sector, consultants, and industry experts without the support of relevant documentation such as reports or statistics. Despite many entrepreneurial initiatives that have been implemented and support provided to new business startups in recent years, however, these efforts are all relatively new in the country. At the moment, there is no literature or formal report to support and justify the success of entrepreneurship in empowering the targeted segments, importantly in examining how it can be sustained over long period of time.

Findings and Analysis

Findings are divided into a number of categories as follows;

Fragmented Entrepreneurial Support

With the prevailing situation, and in response to urgent calls by the Monarch, the country's senior leaders took swift action towards diversification efforts. Several initiatives were expeditiously executed by public and private sectors and other stakeholders to spur economic growth and transform local Micro, Small and Medium Enterprises and entrepreneurial activities in Brunei. The Ministry of Culture, Youth and Sports (MCYS) put in place different programmes targeting specific segments such as the underprivileged and community in need, youth, and special abilities individuals. In 2012, MCYS created the Poverty Issue Special Committee, primarily tasked to examine the poverty situation in the country, hence the development of an Action Plan for Eradicating Poverty. Unfortunately, there is insufficient information reporting on the effectiveness of this initiative.

In 2016, the former Minister of Energy and Industry at the Prime Minister's Office and Chairman of DARE (Darussalam Enterprise) announced the formation of the Manpower Planning Council, which aimed to track, handle and create policy measures for manpower planning to lower unemployment rate. The Ministry (now known as the Ministry of Energy, Manpower, and Industry) also opened the Capacity Development Center (PPK) in 2017 with the objective to provide (up-skilling) training to prepare job-ready trainees. In the same year, it introduced the I-ready Apprenticeship Programme with the objective of providing job placement in public and private sectors for unemployed graduates, with the ultimate aim of securing permanent employment in the respective organisation.

The Ministry of Education also played its part in promoting entrepreneurship efforts through educational awareness and established the National Entrepreneurship Agenda (NEA) that aims towards developing and encouraging high-growth entrepreneurs, promoting employment opportunity and improving the country's economic growth. A product of NEA is the Entrepreneurship Village at Universiti Brunei Darussalam which provides outreach programmes such as the community incubation programme that can be accessed by potential entrepreneurs and business startups.

There is no shortage of support and a multitude of initiatives established and implemented by various sectors to create jobs; empower the underprivileged and community in need through entrepreneurship to generate income; reduce poverty and reduce reliance on welfare assistance. Despite collaborative efforts between public and private sectors, GLCs, associations and NGOs, from observations and engagements, there is still a sense of working in silo, protective of own initiatives, and reluctance to accept or provide assistance. Such acts will only impede the progress and development of programmes, ineffective management of spending and resources; as a result, inability to achieve positive outcomes at the national level.

Unavailability of Customize Entrepreneurship Programme

There are different entrepreneurship programmes introduced and developed in the market by different parties that aim to provide alternative solutions to different social problems. These programmes are unique but have the same goals and desires:

• To equip targeted segments with basic knowledge and skills that would enable participants to secure and create jobs and earn consistent income.

• To impart empowerment capabilities and to entice individuals towards entrepreneurship.

• To deliver the desired benefits for the participants and meet the expectations of the programme's developers.

According to BIBDSeed participants who attended other stakeholder's entrepreneurship programmes, the courses provided basic information about business, and there was no follow-up to check the application of knowledge and skill of the participants. The participants appreciate for the opportunity to attend the BIBDSeed programme, which provides comprehensive content and modules, knowledge sharing and skill development, which are crucial for becoming new entrepreneurs.

From the responses and views of a local expert, the programmes and initiatives in Brunei are designed to eradicate poverty and sustainable development. However, there is a lack of integrated strategy and systematic approach at the national level, to align and refine programmes from various stakeholders. These efforts are managed and implemented in isolation by respective organisations and their strategic partners. Due to the lack of alignment and concerted efforts resulted in many mismatched programmes and the inability to achieve intended objectives at the national level.

Findings from interviews also supported the view that these entrepreneurial and self-development programmes are not comprehensive enough and do not cover the overall business development ecosystem. Further findings also revealed that some programmes are developed by non-industrial experts, hence do not contain significant components that support basic of business needs; methods for formation of ideas; product research and development and testing; market testing and so on. Today, there are still many newly established entrepreneurs who are not equipped with basic knowledge of setting up a business nor have the relevant information and training that are useful in developing and sustaining their businesses.

Absence of Centralised Entrepreneurship Framework

Entrepreneurship policy and framework is a crucial condition that would make or break entrepreneurs. Proper guidelines and references for business development should be made available and easy to access in order to grow and strengthen business activities in Brunei. With a lot of hype in Brunei to stimulate economic growth through entrepreneurial activities, some stakeholders overlooked to ensure the proper formulation of business strategy and framework for entrepreneurial programmes. Many business startups are established without first meeting basic requirements such as a business license and opening a business/corporate bank account. In the long run, potential challenges will arise if businesses plan to expand their business, such as:

• The need for a business license to indicate legitimacy to operate as a business entity in the market.

• To warrant the safety and (financial) health of the business for financing and investment.

• To protect entrepreneurs and their businesses from any potential legal implications.

The absence of policy and framework implies that entrepreneurship establishments are not aligned with the local regulations and law set by local authorities, and international standards. In recent years, business registration has been made easier to encourage prudent business activities and financial institutions conducted campaigns on the importance of corporate accounts. Despite these efforts, many business startups are still unaware or ignore this requirement, hence many businesses in the country still operate without proper legal documents. In the long run, the unavailability of relevant policy as a guiding framework will impede local MSMEs opportunity for growth and expansion, both locally and internationally, due to non-compliance to global standards (Gonzalez, 2014).

Ineffective Distribution Of Fund

Amongst the key conditions in ensuring the continued survival of business startups and entrepreneurship is access to financial support. In Brunei, financial support and funding have long been provided by the relevant government agencies, private sectors and government-linked companies (GLCs). Below are some examples:

Public Sectors

During Legislative Council Meeting, the Ministry of Culture, Youth and Sports is awarded an approved budget for the distribution of monthly welfare assistance and provisions of training and development programmes for targeted segments. The Ministry of Religious Affairs through MUIB is the custodian of the Dana Zakat fund for identified Asnaf (the poor and underprivileged, community in need and Muallaf. The Dana is distributed towards supporting various programmes under Asnaf Zakat Empowerment Programme (PROPAZ), such as the Az-Zira'ah Agripreneur Programme, which was implemented in collaboration with Agriculture Research Centre (BARC) to provide technical training, business matching, as well as mentorship, to the participants (Bakar, R. 2018).

Government Linked Companies (GLC)

Darussalam Enterprise introduced a co-matching grants scheme aims toward driving economic growth through fostering entrepreneurial growth and to boost Brunei's GDP contribution.

Corporate Sectors

Shell LiveWIRE (Brunei), Brunei Shell Petroleum (BSP) allocates an annual budget for funding scheme and awarded as financial grant to successful "LiveWIRE Brunei Business Awards" recipients as modal for their businesses. One such scheme is the Agrobiz Padi Agroprenuer Programme that aims to provide technical skills and capabilities in rice production for economic independence.

Financial Institution Sectors

Bank Islam Brunei Darussalam (BIBD) established a Micro, Small and Medium Enterprises Account (BIBD MSME) in 2018. As part of the Bank's initiatives to grow local MSMEs and strengthen the country's economy, this microfinance product aims to provide access to financial support for new MSMEs with a minimal deposit to open a business account and provide an attractive financing limit. This financing facility allows entrepreneurs to get financing to grow their business.

By combing the above financial capabilities of various sectors, there is a sufficient budget to support selected and potential business establishment and development. However, funds that are managed by public sectors may not be easily accessed or properly distributed; as such unable to effectively reach the targeted and qualified segments. In addition, lack of planning may also hinder proper management and efficient and effective utilisation of budget; rigid internal process, level bureaucracy and red tapes may contribute to difficulty in accessing these funds.

DISCUSSION

The challenging socio-economic experience by Brunei set the tone for immediate action in overcoming the rising social concerns and compelled the speedy development of several new initiatives that complement existing and established programmes that several organisations have introduced. However, initiatives may be developed prematurely, and programmes that already existed over the years may not have shown fruition. The support of various stakeholders is acknowledged and commendable for their drive to help the underprivileged and community in need, involving unemployed youth in the diversification activities that aim to improve and stabilise the country's economy. Based on the findings and analysis, discussions are structured in the following sub-section;

Developing Collaborative Efforts

A concerted and centralised entrepreneurial support from key stakeholders is crucial to ensure the alignment of strategies and plans, efforts and activities, and implementation of programmes to achieve the desired outcome at the national level. This will also ensure greater and more noticeable benefits for the programme and for the participants in ensuring the sustainability of business and entrepreneurial activities in the country. In today's environment, collaborative efforts between the public and private sectors and other strategic partners are inevitable to progress the current slow economy. The involvement of industry can be seen in:

• Share expertise that can strengthen current entrepreneurial activities, to overcome any deficiencies in existing stagnant or slow-moving programmes.

• Facilitate in development of more strategic partnerships.

• Formulate solutions and recommendations for entrepreneurship development and growth in the country.

Standardisation of Entrepreneurship Programme

Many programmes that are available in the country are differentiated in content but have similar end goals. The majority of entrepreneurial programmes available are leaning towards:

• Providing relevant skills for unemployed individuals so they would be able to secure jobs.

• Providing training to the underprivileged community to attain relevant knowledge to empower them in entrepreneurship.

• Developing capacity building platform for potential or current entrepreneurs is the key factor in providing a better opportunity for employability and strengthening their entrepreneurial skills.

Developing standardised entrepreneurial programmes and content can eliminate duplication, ensure alignment, and develop proper strategic plans and roadmaps. The programme should also be customised to meet the requirements of different segments of the community to ensure effectiveness in delivering the programme and ensure a positive return on investments for the investor (organisations). In doing so, it will ensure a more structured, clear, and manageable programme that includes proper content and a timeline that address specific target, monitoring and assessment process. The involvement and collaborative support of the public sector continue to be crucial and need to further be amplified through the development of relevant schemes and programmes in order to elevate entrepreneurial initiatives - as key drivers of a nation's economic success and prosperity.

When developing key modules for the entrepreneurship programmes, this should involve the industry expert to ensure that the subjects and modules which are incorporated are relevant to business and in keeping with current trends and practices, as well as to share real business and industry know-how and experience. Identifying a collaborative key strategic partner is crucial to ensuring the well-coordinated, effective, and successful implementation of initiatives (Ayob, *et al.*, 2016). A blend of expertise from the public and private sectors is important to impart experience and expertise in terms of local policy and governance and real industry experience.

Development of Centralised Entrepreneurship Framework

The creation of policies for entrepreneurship programmes and ecosystem are important for developing entrepreneurial talent, governing entrepreneurial activities, and monitoring and assessing entrepreneurship activities and overall operations (Mason and Brown, 2014). For a business to remain sustainable, it is important to put in place relevant frameworks and policies to encourage entrepreneurial growth both within the business and the relevant public sector that is responsible for enhancing entrepreneurship development (Low & Isserman, 2015). Entrepreneurial activity is an integral feature in the development and growth of a country's economy. In Brunei, it has existed for many years and is becoming more dynamic recently due to the sluggish economic situation. In view of this, it is timely for Brunei to have its own centralised entrepreneurship policy and framework, as this will further encourage strong entrepreneurship growth and expansion for the country.

With reference to Malaysia (Nasir & Subari, 2017), it developed an entrepreneurship policy, the national entrepreneurship framework that provides guidance to key stakeholders in paving the way to implement best practices to intensify entrepreneurship activities. A similar effort can be emulated by Brunei by having in place a policy and framework to ensure that appropriate support is extended to entrepreneurs and micro, small and medium enterprises to flourish and facilitate in driving the country's economic strategy, importantly, the creation of an integrated ecosystem of entrepreneurship. In addition, this policy would be able to provide proper and clear guidelines for fostering a healthy but competitive business environment that would promote dynamic economic activity in the country.

Systematic Distribution of Funds

It has been reported that a large amount of funds is allocated by different stakeholders for developments and entrepreneurial programmes; although access to the fund may not be easy, however, may be attained through several efforts:

• Planning and developing plan and timeline - It is important to ensure proper planning, allocation, and utilisation of the budget for different projects for different target segments.

• Well-designed, customised Programme and Content – this would ensure the proper development of comprehensive programmes, with proper management, monitoring, assessment mechanism, and extended support to the participants. Significantly, the programme must be designed and customised to best suit and meet the basic and ongoing needs of empowerment and entrepreneurship efforts for the participants.

• Allocation of the budget – this is crucial in ensuring the proper running and sustainability of the programme and the participants' continuous efforts. There should be clear and proper planning, allocation of budget and monitoring of budget utilisation.

By initiating the above and investing in relevant programmes, the fund can be efficiently utilised, and a positive impact can be seen on the participants.

CONCLUSION AND RECOMMENDATION

Although the term social innovation is not broadly used, in recent years, various innovative-related initiatives have been implemented in Brunei. Based on research on social innovation, such as entrepreneurship has been associated with helping to solve social issues such as unemployment and poverty. Brunei continues to be dependent on oil exports, and the fall in oil prices in 2013 greatly affected its economic growth, which compelled the government to accelerate the implementation of entrepreneurial and agribusiness initiatives as diversification efforts to improve the country's economy, importantly to mitigate the issues of unemployment and poverty. As a result, in the last few years, there has been a growing number of entrepreneurship and agribusinesses undertaken by different segments of society with the support of government agencies and its related stakeholders - as a vehicle to empower targeted segments through the creation of jobs (and to improve quality of life) by generating steady and sustainable income for its people. However, it is far too early to conclude that these initiatives have effectively enabled the target segment to earn a sustainable income without creating a proper policy framework governing, monitoring and measuring the development of business ventures and how to take it forward.

As mentioned earlier, there are limitations to this paper, but there are a lot of opportunities to expand on the topic, such as to explore in-depth the root cause of current social issues, particularly unemployment and poverty. These are key issues that are frequently highlighted at various levels in the public sector as well as by concerned parties in Brunei. It is suggested that further research be directed towards examining the impacts of women's participation in entrepreneurship to verify women's ability and drive to overcome life challenges and as a key economic backbone in the country. Many case studies exemplify the importance and capabilities of entrepreneurship in countries around the world, therefore, it would be interesting to conduct research based on a case study on entrepreneurship and empowerment in the Brunei context. Further study needs to be conducted to analyse the requirement of a proper system and process as a continuous process for assessing and monitoring entrepreneurship activities in Brunei. This is specifically vital in ensuring sustainable income and supporting continuous entrepreneurship growth.

CONSENT FOR PUBLICATION

Not applicable.

CONFLICT OF INTEREST

The author declares no conflict of interest, financial or otherwise.

ACKNOWLEDGEMENTS

Declared none.

REFERENCES

Ariffin, E. (2018). *Brunei needs to move away from dependency on oil*.https://theaseanpost.com/article/brunei-needs-move-away-dependency-oil

Asean.org. (2017). *ASEAN Statistical Report on Millennium Development Goals 2017*.[online] Available at https://asean.org/storage/2012/05/ASEAN_MDG_2017.pdf

Audretsch, D., Keilbach, M., Lehmann, E. (2006). *Entrepreneurship and economic growth.* Oxford: Oxford University Press.
[http://dx.doi.org/10.1093/acprof:oso/9780195183511.001.0001]

Ayob, N., Teasdale, S., Fagan, K. (2016). How Social Innovation 'Came to Be': Tracing the Evolution of a Contested Concept. *J. Soc. Policy, 45*(4), 635-653.
[http://dx.doi.org/10.1017/S004727941600009X]

Bakar, R. (2018). *HM says to tackle poverty, management of zakat funds must improve.* The Scoop. [online] The Scoop. Available at https://thescoop.co/2018/06/02/hm-tackle-poverty-zkat-management-must-improve/

Bakar, R. *Pilot farming programme to help zakat recipients break out of poverty cycle.* The Scoop. [online] The Scoop. Available at 2018https://thescoop.co/2018/10/31/pilot-farming-programme-to-help--akat-recipients-break-out-of-poverty-cycle/

Bakar, R. (2019). *Sultan calls for remedies to unemployment, sluggish economy.* The Scoop. [online] The Scoop. Available at https://thescoop.co/2019/03/07/sultan-calls-for-remedies-for-unemployment-sl-ggish-economy/

Bhaskaran, M. (2010). Available at http://www.csps.org.bn/wp-content/uploads/ 2018/07/CSPS-Journa--Volume-I-07July2010.pdf

Bane, M.J., Ellwood, D.T. (1986). Slipping into and out of Poverty: The Dynamics of Spells. *J. Hum. Resour., 21*(1), 1-23.
[http://dx.doi.org/10.2307/145955]

Bessant, J., Tidd, J. (2018). *Innovation and entrepreneurship.*. Chichester, England: John Wiley & Sons.

Borneo Bulletin. (2018). Crucial for Brunei to achieve rapid economic diversification. Available at https://borneobulletin.com.bn/crucial-for-brunei-to-achieve-rapid-economic-diversification

Brabeck-Letmathe, P. *Why social innovation matters to business.* [online] Social Innovation. Available at http://reports.weforum.org/social-innovation/why-social-innovation-matters-to-business/?doing_wp_cron=15 59214811.4633378982543945312500

Bricefoundation.org. (n.d.). *Our Concept of Empowering the Poor.* [online] Available at https://www.brice foundation.org/empower-the-poor

Carvalho, J.M.S. (2016). *Social Innovation and Entrepreneurship The Case of Porto Region.* [online] Available at https://pdfs.semanticscholar.org/74e8/003835e782bbf8505ccf31a5f5f44dec6776.pdf

Cheong, D., Milojević, I., Rajak, R. (2016). Trends and Emerging Issues: Implications For Brunei Darussalam *CSPS Strategy and Policy Journal, 6*, 1-23. [online] Available at: http://www.csps.org.bn/ wp-content/uploads/2017/11/Volume6_Abstract.pdf

Cunha, J., Benneworth, P., Oliveira, P. (2015). Social Entrepreneurship and Social Innovation: A Conceptual Distinction. In: Carmo Farinha, L.M., Ferreira, J.J.M., Lawton Smith, H., Bagchi-Sen, S., (Eds.), *Handbook of Research on Global Competitive Advantage through Innovation and Entrepreneurship.* IGI Global.
[http://dx.doi.org/10.4018/978-1-4666-8348-8.ch033]

Downs, T.J. (2007). A systematic integrated approach for crafting poverty reduction and sustainable development projects. *Nat. Resour. Forum, 31*(1), 35-50.
[http://dx.doi.org/10.1111/j.1477-8947.2007.00129.x]

Edwards-Schachter, M.E., Matti, C.E., Alcántara, E. (2012). Fostering Quality of Life through Social Innovation: A Living Lab Methodology Study Case. *Rev. Policy Res., 29*(6), 672-692.
[http://dx.doi.org/10.1111/j.1541-1338.2012.00588.x]

Akpan, G.E. (2015). Empowering Women and Youth in Micro- And Small-Scale Enterprises (MSSEs) For Wealth Creation. *International Journal of Asian Social Science, 5*(2), 52-63.
[http://dx.doi.org/10.18488/journal.1/2015.5.2/1.2.52.63]

Gonzalez, A. (2014). Helping Small Business To Be an Engine of Growth and Employment [Blog] World Bank Blogs. Available at http://blogs.worldbank.org/trade/helping-small-business-be-engine-growth-and-employment

Haris, N., Bandial, A. (2021). Unemployment rate drops to 4.2% The Scoop, March 17. Available at https://thescoop.co/2021/03/17/unemployment-rate-drops-to-4-2/

Hitt, M., Ireland, R., Sirmon, D., Trahms, C. (2012). Strategic Entrepreneurship: Creating Value for Individuals, Organizations, and Society. *SSRN.*https://papers.ssrn.com/sol3/papers.cfm?abstract_id=1994491 online
[http://dx.doi.org/10.2139/ssrn.1994491]

Insight Report . (2017). *The Global Risks Report 2017* World Economic Forum, The Global Competitiveness and Risks Team.

Jakimovski, J. (2010). [online] Vps.ns.ac.rs. Available at: ns.ac.rshttp://www.vps.ns.ac.rs/SB/2010/1.7.pdf

Hochgerner. Josef. (2011). The Analysis of Social Innovations as Social Practice Available at http://socialinnovation2011.archiv.zsi.at/wp-content/uploads/2011/04/The-Analysis-of-Social-Innovations-as-Social-Practice.pdf

Kakar, A. (2017). *The Hidden Face Of Poverty In Brunei.* [Online] The Borgen Project. Available at https://borgenproject.org/tag/poverty-in-brunei/

Khan, G., Almoharby, D. (2007). Towards Enhancing Entrepreneurship Development In Oman *Journal of Enterprising Culture,   15*(04), 371-392. [online] Available at: https://www.worldscientific.com/doi/abs/10.1142/S0218495807000198
[http://dx.doi.org/10.1142/S0218495807000198]

Lettice, F., Parekh, M. (2010). The social innovation process: themes, challenges and implications for practice. *Int. J. Technol. Manag., 51*(1), 139-158.
[http://dx.doi.org/10.1504/IJTM.2010.033133]

Lisetchi, M., Brancu, L. (2014). The Entrepreneurship Concept as a Subject of Social Innovation. *Procedia Soc. Behav. Sci., 124*, 87-92.
[http://dx.doi.org/10.1016/j.sbspro.2014.02.463]

Low, S., Isserman, A. (2013). Where Are the Innovative Entrepreneurs? Identifying Innovative Industries and Measuring Innovative Entrepreneurship. *International Regional Science Review, 38*(2), 171-201. [online] Available at 10.1177/0160017613484926

Mason, C., Brown, R. (2014). *Entrepreneurial Ecosystems And Growth Oriented Entrepreneurship.* OECD LEED Programme.

Mulgan, G., Simon, T., Rushanara, A., Ben, S. (2007). *Social Innovation, What It Is, Why It Matters, and How it Can Be Accelerated..* The Young Foundation.

Nasir, N.R., Subari, M. (2017). *A Review of Social Innovation Initiatives in Malaysia, 3*, 1. https://www.researchgate.net/publication/318361307

Patton, M. (2005). Qualitative Research *Encyclopedia of Statistics in Behavioral Science.* [online] Available at https://onlinelibrary.wiley.com/doi/abs/10.1002/0470013192.bsa514

Portales, L. (2019). *Social Innovation and Social Entrepreneurship: Fundamentals.* Palgrave-Macmillan, Switzerland: Concepts and Tools.
[http://dx.doi.org/10.1007/978-3-030-13456-3]

Rajendra, A. (2017). *Why Innovation Is Increasingly Becoming Critical to Entrepreneurship.* [online] Entrepreneur. Available at: https://www.entrepreneur.com/article/296912

Richter, H. (2015). *Innovation and Entrepreneurship - The Austrian Economist Joseph A..* Schumpeter. [online] Austria. Available at: https://www.austria.org/austrianinformation/2015/3/27/innovation-an--entrepreneurship-the-austrian-economist-joseph-a-schumpeter

The Poverty Line. (2015). *Brunei — The Poverty Line.* [online] Available at http://www.thepovertyline.net/brunei

The Scoop. (2019). *HM: Brunei must hinge its growth strategy on ASEAN.* The Scoop. [online] Available at https://thescoop.co/2019/01/01/hm-this-new-year-seize-opportunities-and-do-not-be-lazy/

Thomas, R. (2019). *Developing innovation, entrepreneurship and technology for global competitiveness.* http://www.jamaicaobserver.com/the-agenda/developing-innovation-entrepreneurship-and_technology_for_global_competitiveness_148303?profile=1096

Zahra, S.A., Wright, M. (2016). Understanding the Social Role of Entrepreneurship. *J. Manage. Stud., 53*(4), 610-629.
[http://dx.doi.org/10.1111/joms.12149]

SUBJECT INDEX

www.ingramcontent.com/pod-product-compliance
Lightning Source LLC
Chambersburg PA
CBHW061135030426
42334CB00003B/43